CAPTIVATING SUBJECTS

Writing Confinement, Citizenship, and Nationhood in the Nineteenth Century

Edited by Jason Haslam and Julia M. Wright

Ever since Michel Foucault's highly regarded work on prisons and confinement in the 1970s, critical examination of the forerunners to the prison – slavery, serfdom, and colonial confinements – has been rare. However, these institutions inform and participate in many of the same ideologies that the prison enforces.

Captivating Subjects is a collection of essays that fills several crucial gaps in the critical analysis of the relations between Western state-sanctioned confinement, identity, nation, and literature. Editors Jason Haslam and Julia M. Wright have brought together an esteemed group of international scholars to explore nineteenth-century writings by prisoners, slaves, and other captives, tracing some of the continuities among the varieties of captivity and their crucial relationship to post-Enlightenment subjectivities.

This volume is the first sustained examination of the ways in which diverse types of confinement intersect with Western ideologies of subjectivity, investigating the modern nation-state's reliance on captivity as a means of consolidating notions of individual and national sovereignty. It details the specific historical and cultural practices of confinement and their relations to each other and to punishment through a range of national contexts.

JASON HASLAM is an assistant professor of English at Dalhousie University.

JULIA M. WRIGHT is a Canada Research Chair in European Studies at Dalhousie University.

CAPTIVATING SUBJECTS

Writing Confinement, Citizenship, and Nationhood in the Nineteenth Century

Edited by Jason Haslam and Julia M. Wright

UNIVERSITY OF TORONTO PRESS
Toronto Buffalo London

© University of Toronto Press 2005
Toronto Buffalo London
utorontopress.com

Reprinted in paperback 2020

ISBN 978-0-8020-8958-7 (cloth)   ISBN 978-1-4875-2614-6 (paper)

Library and Archives Canada Cataloguing in Publication

Title: Captivating subjects : writing confinement, citizenship, and
  nationhood in the nineteenth century / edited by Jason Haslam
  and Julia M. Wright.
Names: Haslam, Jason, 1971– editor. | Wright, Julia M., editor.
Description: Paperback reprint. Originally published: 2005. | Includes
  bibliographical references and index.
Identifiers: Canadiana 20200209914 | ISBN 9781487526146 (paper)
Subjects: LCSH: Imprisonment – Western countries – History – 19th
  century – Sources. | LCSH: Imprisonment – Social aspects – Western
  countries – Sources. | LCSH: Prisoners' writings – History and criticism.
Classification: LCC HV8706 .C36 2020 | DDC 365/.9181209034 – dc23

This book has been published with the help of a grant from the Federation for the Humanities and Social Sciences, through the Awards to Scholarly Publications Program, using funds provided by the Social Sciences and Humanities Research Council of Canada.

University of Toronto Press acknowledges the financial assistance to its publishing program of the Canada Council for the Arts and the Ontario Arts Council, an agency of the Government of Ontario.

Contents

ACKNOWLEDGMENTS vii

Introduction 3
Jason Haslam and Julia M. Wright

The Subject of Captivity

1 Being Jane Warton: Lady Constance Lytton and the Disruption of Privilege 25
Jason Haslam

2 Form and Authority in Russian Serf Narratives 57
John MacKay

3 I, Hereby, Vow to Read *The Interesting Narrative* 86
Tess Chakkalakal

Captivating Discourses: Class and Nation

4 'From the Slums *to* the Slums': The Delimitation of Social Identity in Late Victorian Prison Narratives 113
Frank Lauterbach

5 'Stone Walls Do (Not) a Prison Make': Rhetorical Strategies and Sentimentalism in the Representation of the Victorian Prison Experience   144
Monika Fludernik

6 'National Feeling' and the Colonial Prison: Teeling's *Personal Narrative*   175
Julia M. Wright

Captivating Otherness

7 A Nation in Chains: Barbary Captives and American Identity   201
Jennifer Costello Brezina

8 A Prison Officer and a Gentleman: The Prison Inspector as Imperialist Hero in the Writings of Major Arthur Griffiths (1838–1908)   220
Christine Marlin

Bibliography   241

Contributors   263

Index   265

Acknowledgments

A number of grant organizations have helped to make this book and our own contributions to it possible, and we would like to begin by thanking them and all those who supported our applications for their generosity: the Social Sciences and Humanities Research Council of Canada (Haslam, Wright); the Northeast MLA Summer Fellowships Program (Haslam); and the Canada Research Chairs Program (Wright). We would also like to thank Holly Crumpton for her research assistance in the final stages of the project. Our thank are also due to Jill McConkey and others at the University of Toronto Press, as well as the anonymous readers of the volume, for their invaluable guidance during the process of turning this manuscript into a book.

We are grateful to our contributors for their commitment to this project and the various libraries that have assisted us with access to rare books and other essential resources: Wilfrid Laurier University library, the TriUniversity Group of Libraries, the British Library, and Dalhousie Library. We would also like to thank the audiences who commented on conference versions of the chapters: an early version of chapter 6 was presented at '1798 and Its Implications,' the first joint conference of the North American Society for the Study of Romanticism and the British Association for Romantic Studies, St Mary's University College (Strawberry Hill, England, 10 July 1998); a shorter version of chapter 1 was presented at 'Crime and Punishment,' the annual conference of the Victorian Studies Association of Western Canada (Winnipeg, Canada,

28 September 2002). We have also been fortunate in benefiting, in myriad ways, from advice and support from many colleagues, among them Dennis Denisoff, Joel Faflak, Glenn Hendler, M. Morgan Holmes, Tilottama Rajan, Elizabeth Sauer, and, of course, each other.

CAPTIVATING SUBJECTS

Introduction

Jason Haslam and Julia M. Wright

> At the risk of continuing a chain of appropriative allegories, I would like to [suggest that] captivity stories potentially address cultural experiences not typically accounted for in cultural mythology. ... [C]ritical accounts of the captivity narratives reveal the critics' own investments in creating the genres they purport only to name.
> Christopher Castiglia, *Bound and Determined: Captivity, Culture-Crossing, and White Womanhood from Mary Rowlandson to Patty Hearst*

> 'I just became a citizen again.'
> Danny Ocean, on being released from prison, in *Ocean's Eleven* (2002)

Over the past decade, there has been a surge in critical examinations of the relations between identity, nation, literature, and Western state-sanctioned confinement. Michel Foucault's *Discipline and Punish: The Birth of the Prison* has, of course, contributed to this surge in examinations of confinement in Western culture, but its influence has tended to limit such studies to the specific practices of institutionalized imprisonment as it has developed from the eighteenth century through to the present day. Discussions of the ways in which the methods employed by the nascent prison were influenced by and congruent with its precursors, especially as seen in the Atlantic slave industry, are relatively rare. Certainly, as early as H. Bruce Franklin's very important and influential *The Victim as Criminal and Artist: Literature from the American Prison* (first published in 1978), critics have recognized the relationship between the

American prison, specifically, and slavery. Franklin also points out that other socioeconomic institutions and relations are equally important. He argues that the writings and conditions of 'slaves, peons, and prisoners' are intrinsically related, and that 'Personal narratives of the lives of criminals – both fictional and actual – made their appearance along with colonialism and large-scale mercantile capitalism in the sixteenth century. Ever since, they have been developing as an integral part of the culture of capitalist society. In fact, the principal literary form of the capitalist epoch, the novel, originated as extended prose narratives of the lives of criminals.'[1]

This volume proceeds from this generative attention to the interrelations between various forms of captivity, but focuses less on material practices and print culture than on the ideological formations that inform and are in turn complicated by the figure of the captive in Western discourse. The essays collected here address the ontological implications of captivity in relation to narratives concerning slavery, serfdom, colonial expansion and maintenance, and the beginnings of the modern prison. Contributors thus delve into the heart of contemporary debates surrounding identity, politics, history, and writing, shedding new light on the ways in which captivity has aided the formation of both the modern nation state and its concomitant subjectivities. The volume as a whole, then, aims to add to recent calls to recognize the social and cultural centrality – and exemplarity – of captives, rather than see them only as silenced and marginal figures.[2] In particular, a number of the essays here investigate the modern nation state's reliance on captivity as a means of consolidating notions of individual and national sovereignty – both of which meet in the definition of the 'citizen' – as well as protecting economic and imperial interests.

As Franklin argues, prison and other confinement writings 'cannot be lumped in some timeless category ... as though prisoners of all times and places constituted a society.'[3] This important point not only demands a historical and regional specificity but also tacitly solicits an attention to the pressures and assumptions which inform this temptation to see prisoners and other captives as belonging to a society apart. In addressing Europe and the United States during the long nineteenth century (1789–1914), we focus on the West in the early stages of nationalism and related debates over citizenship, and also on an era during which many of the precursors of the prison were still institutionally enforced, allowing us to attend to a wide (though by no means comprehensive) range of disciplinary and confining practices.[4] Specifically focusing on first-person narratives by both the victims and perpetrators of these confining activities, however, this volume can trace in particular those practices' crucial relationships to post-Enlightenment subjectivities, especially since the nineteenth century was a period during which various constraining practices figured prominently in the sociopolitical and legal mechanisms of the Western world. The multifarious varieties of state-sanctioned confinement intersect with the mutually determining Western ideologies of subjectivity, such as the nominally universal Enlightenment individual and the solidifying deterministic group identities of nation, class, gender, and race (among others). Further, the Western nation emerges from this collection as an apparatus which must simultaneously guarantee the freedom of its citizens and the secure containment and/or exclusion of non-citizens. This double guarantee reveals the interdependence of the two: ideologically, terms of confinement arise from and reinforce notions of subjectivity which define the proper citizen; practically, the political and economic rights of the citizen rely on the use of penal servitude and slave labour. The captive thus does not belong to a society apart, loosed of historical and regional specificity, but is constituted by and, in crucial ways, constitutive of the modern Western nation.

Interrelations: Forms of Captivity and Western Nations

In the American context, the history of the Atlantic slave trade has had a strong impact on the structure and practices of imprisonment. Recent critics, including Angela Y. Davis and Joy James, have fleshed out the historical connection and the similarities of praxis between the two 'peculiar institutions' of slavery and the modern prison, simultaneously noting the silence surrounding this issue in the major discussions of the latter structure. Davis writes,

> Joy James's assertion that 'Foucault's elision of racial bias in historical lynching and contemporary policing predicts his silence on the racialization of prisons' points to the need to move beyond a strictly Foucauldian genealogy in examining histories of punishment. ... Even if the forms of punishment inherent in and associated with slavery had been entirely revoked with the abolition of slavery, the persistent second-class citizenship status to which former slaves were relegated would have had an implicit impact on punishment practices. However, an explicit linkage between slavery and punishment was written into the constitution precisely at the moment of the abolition of slavery. In fact, there was no reference to imprisonment in the US Constitution until the passage of the Thirteenth

Amendment declared chattel slavery unconstitutional: 'Neither slavery nor involuntary servitude, except as a punishment for crime whereof the party shall have been duly convicted, shall exist within the United States, or any place subject to their jurisdiction.'[5]

Davis goes on to argue that this explicit legal transference of slavery to the prison led to the transformation of 'the character of punishment into a means of managing former slaves as opposed to addressing problems of serious crime.'[6] Thus, a revisiting of the 'birth of the prison,' moving beyond Foucault's focus, leads to a radical revisioning of the purpose of captivity, allowing Davis, James, Franklin, Adam J. Hirsch, and others to address the historical processes lying behind the severe and glaring racial inequities of the American prison system, as part of an effort to address those inequities.[7]

Such radical revisionings have shed light on the ways in which the prison system serves motives other than those that it publicizes. To take a recent example, one of Davis's latest works argues that the use of convict labour, when connected to the black presence in post-bellum American prisons, the convict-lease system, and the integration of 'the punishment associated with slavery ... into the prison system,' leads to a radical conflict between 'the theory of punishment associated with the new U.S. penitentiaries and with the Benthamian concept of the panopticon' and 'the forms of punishment meted out to newly freed black people.'[8] Building on this, however, Jason Haslam has also recently argued elsewhere that such a conflict between theory and practice, combined with the 'punishment associated with slavery,' was present in the US, and other, prison systems before emancipation: 'Despite the justifying rhetoric of prison proponents, the earlier prisons did in fact systemically engage in physical punishments which were explicitly related to prisoners' productivity and labour rather than rehabilitation.'[9] Therefore, while emerging penitentiary systems used silence as a means of theoretically enabling a personal, internal reformation (thus *supposedly* shifting the emphasis of punishment away from the body, in Foucault's genealogy), Haslam points out that

> The actual practice of the prisons belies not only the effectiveness of this rule of silence, but also the general notions of human subjectivity that enable it. While the spectacle and practices of corporal punishment did, indeed, diminish in the nineteenth century, violent physical punishment did not disappear but was reorganized and shifted in emphasis. Rather

than using pain as a direct punishment for crime, the [nineteenth-century prison system] used it in part as a means of enforcing a second order of law – the prison rules, including those of silence and labour.[10]

Moving from the new analyses of the impact of slavery on prison punishment, then, all of these 'post-Foucauldian' punishment histories lead to new understanding of the carceral system, and therefore potentially to new genealogies of subjectivity, within the history not only of captivity but also of the modern nation state that is reliant upon it. The several revisitings of the history of captivity by the essays collected here similarly provide new insights into racial, class, gender, and colonial inequities.

The connection between the prison and the slave trade can be, and occasionally has been, expanded beyond the borders of America. Like the slave trade, the formation of the prison was an international effort, as evidenced by, to take only two of countless examples, Gustave de Beaumont and Alexis de Tocqueville's influential *On the Penitentiary System in the United States and Its Application in France* (1833), and 'the first international gathering of those interested in or specializing in penology ... held at Frankfort on the Main' in 1846 at which, as Orlando F. Lewis notes, the 'world's attention was being co-operatively directed to the problems of prisons.'[11] Frank Lauterbach's contribution to this volume also notes that this international focus was largely driven by an interest in the new American penitentiaries. Echoing Lauterbach's statement, Haslam has noted that if most critics (contemporary and otherwise) argue that 'American penological practices were defined during this period by the competing, but in many ways similar, Auburn and Philadelphia systems,' then these systems were also disseminated across the West.[12] Furthermore, if the practices of slavery influenced those of the American prison, then this influence, and – importantly – the related conflict between prison theory and practice, detailed above by Davis and Haslam, were likewise vastly extended through the international 'cooperation' in the prison project. Moreover, critics of prisoners' writings have noted the ways in which the prison is connected to a wide range of mechanisms of social control. Ioan Davies, for example, has examined the long history of Western carceral practices and the writings produced from within this history.[13] Franklin also discusses the connections between prison, peonage, and the working class[14] – a connection made most clear in the widespread nineteenth-century practice of indentured servitude. Barbara Harlow has addressed Third World and women's prison writing from a nationalist and postcolonial perspective, analysing the ways in which nations use the prison in an attempt to silence rebellion and bolster the strength of the ruling class.[15] In fact, the Thirteenth Amendment to the US Constitution can be cited here again, since it points to the wider colonial expansion which our volume also addresses. In addition to justifying the continuation of slavery as imprisonment, the Amendment also provides a loophole for the use of slavery by American colonial expansionists, allowing people in 'any place subject to US jurisdiction' to be under threat of penal servitude.

Penal servitude in general was also significant in British carceral practice in the eighteenth and nineteenth centuries. For instance, Britain's transportation of criminals – including people ranging from petty thieves through to political radicals – to nascent colonies (primarily in Australia) tellingly marks the reliance of the imperial project on captive bodies in a suggestive parallel to early America's reliance on slave labour to consolidate economic and territorial power. The British Empire was founded upon not only the captivity of indigenous peoples in colonized territories, but also the abjection – in a nearly literal variation on Julia Kristeva's sense of 'thrown off'[16] – of British subjects deemed unworthy of citizenship yet still seen as being serviceable within the imperial project as unpaid labourers. Scottish radical Thomas Muir, for instance, was charged with circulating seditious materials – including copies of writings by American radical Thomas Paine – and sentenced to transportation to Australia, where he was allowed to buy a farm and so participate in colonization: 'He laboured, with his own hands, to improve and cultivate the land he had purchased, and which, till then, was in a state of native wildness.'[17] Trial records from the period reveal dozens of cases in which Irish men were sentenced to transportation for a wide variety of crimes, from breaking curfews and stealing a handkerchief to sedition and treason; they were often accompanied by their families as 'free settlers,' with the costs of passage paid by the state.[18] The regular commutation of death sentences to transportation for life reveals that transportation has little to do with saving the state the costs of domestic incarceration; to put it baldly, the expense of sending a convict on a voyage of many months was much higher than a length of rope and a yardarm. But transportation in the British Empire, like the slave trade in North America, made possible the rapid settlement (and agricultural productivity) of new colonial spaces – hence the incentive to subsidize the transportation of convicts' families as well.

While it would be spurious, at the least, to suggest that a slave in the

United States was treated in the same way as a political prisoner in Australia or a gentleman convict in Britain, our concern in this volume is less with the material practices of captivity than with the assumptions on which those practices rest and the arguments through which they are contested – though certainly those varied material practices are addressed and critiqued by the captive authors and our contributors, in part as a means of highlighting the ideological framework through which they function. Claims about the power of the state, national authority, the formation of the proper citizen, class position, and subjectivity in general participate in a fairly coherent set of Western ideologies. These claims, moreover, were widely circulated through print culture and other forums for discursive exchange, such as the 1846 Frankfurt conference, and through continuities in the formation of governments and other institutions. They were also circulated through the forced migration of slaves, prisoners, and captives, and through the movement of officials and administrators from one site of captivity to another.[19] It is in terms of this Western ideological milieu that the essays here generatively consider Russian serf narratives, American slave narratives, Barbary captivity texts, and prison accounts by both prisoners and wardens in the United States, Britain, and Ireland, collectively investigating these writings' reproduction of and challenge to the discourses of captivity, which were formed, cemented, and disseminated throughout the nineteenth century.

Captivity and Subjectivity: The Problem of Citizenship

At stake here is not only the pragmatics of empire but also the Occam's razor which defined citizenship for some men, but not for others – and not at all for women. The modern idea of the nation arose in the late eighteenth century in part out of an Enlightenment notion of (male) subjectivity. This construct claimed for the nation what it would claim for the individual, including sovereignty and the potential for self-development. David Lloyd and Paul Thomas thus find in Matthew Arnold's *Culture and Anarchy* (1867–9) an enduring 'model' with the 'capacity to integrate the formation of the subject with the emergence of the state as a form so that the identification of the ethical subject with the state is enabled by their identical logic: both are historical forms that develop, that provide sites of reconciliation and disinterest, and are mutually representative.'[20] This 'identical logic' also required that autonomy, or political sovereignty, had to extend (albeit in different terms) to the nation's citizens: free citizens constitute a free nation. Those who are not free, then, are tacitly if not explicitly removed from the nation, and vice versa.

Well-ordered prisons, in addition to being guarantees of security from kidnapping and enslavement, emerge as the uncomfortably entangled requirements of national power and freedom, as the essays in the third section of this volume demonstrate. This is especially important to a definition of the colonizing nation from within the colonized space. As Harlow writes,

> Whether renarrated as 'civilizing mission' or admitted as abusive exploitation of land, people, and natural resources, the practices of territorial colonialism in the nineteenth and early twentieth centuries, and their later variations in the postindependence period and in neocolonial contexts, have underwritten longstanding cultural paradigms of the colonized as either prelapsarian innocents or unschooled ignorants, the most 'deserving' among whom still await tutoring by their more politically advanced, 'developed' colonizers.[21]

In myriad cases, those among the colonized who refuse to be defined by any of the limiting terms Harlow lists are subsequently 'tutored' by imprisonment, slavery, or captivity, acts that serve the further purpose of entrenching the colonizing nation's sense of power, control, and stability, even while the apparent necessity of punishment and confinement belies these assurances. The modern nation must simultaneously guarantee the liberty of its subjects and laud its power to forcibly contain or 'transform' improper citizens and those excluded from citizenship.

This vexed demand on the modern nation emerges in part as a solution to the tension between the private and the public in nineteenth-century Western societies. While Jürgen Habermas's influential account of the development of the public sphere synergetically unites the private and the public – again for the male subject, who can move between and determine both – Bruce Burgett's summary of the central debate in post-Revolutionary American notions of citizenship reveals some of the tensions in this model. If 'republicanism requires active citizens who participate within public debate and decision making, while liberalism tends to produce passive subjects secure in their ability to defend themselves against publicity,'[22] then the valuation of captivity pivots on the difference between these positions. Domestic forms of captivity distinguish between those people deemed capable of participating in the public sphere and those who are excluded from such participation – as debates even now over the access of prisoners to voting, forms of public communication, and kinds of training attest. If slaves are denied access to literacy or inmates are denied access to pen and paper, at stake is not only their access to personal expression and development but also their ability to participate in public debate in a century when that debate was dominated by print culture (just as debates surrounding inmates' access to the Internet are characteristic of our current computer age).

Captives operate beyond the limit of the ethical state in the Gramscian sense: 'The function of the ethical as opposed to the night-watchman state is to form citizens and gain consent, the two distinct projects being in fact the same: the subject is to be formed as one who consents to hegemony.'[23] Convicts' consent is not solicited and slaves and serfs (or, to again gesture towards twenty-first-century concerns, migrant workers) are not allowed full access to citizenship, thus, on one level, visibly highlighting the distinction between repressive and ideological state apparatuses, as Louis Althusser's refiguring of Antonio Gramsci's formulation would have it.[24] Material constraints on mobility – whether chains or chain-link fences – in this regard serve, for those on the outside, as a protective boundary which limits the participatory public sphere to those with privilege. Forms of captivity that are imposed from beyond the nation's borders pose a threat to both models of citizenship: the 'active citizen' can no longer participate in his nation's 'public debate' and the 'passive subject' is produced within a violence to privacy rather than a security 'against publicity.'[25] This threat is in part a consequence, however, of the nation's always-troubled reliance on the identification of subjects as being either 'inside' or 'outside.' In the introduction to their special issue, *Interiority in Early American Literature*, Christopher Castiglia and Julia Stern address 'a long historical contest over the autonomy of the individual subject (measured in terms of private ownership, purity of soul, political consent, sensual ingenuity) and possession by others, a contest that reveals the ongoing anxiety that the "self" may never be entirely self-owned (even in its more private aspects), but neither is it entirely controlled, since the subjects discussed maintain the power of narration, analysis, and often dissent.'[26] Captivity is the extreme case that proves the rule: from enslavement to incarceration, captivity marks the terminus of external control and yet the authors considered here do indeed 'maintain the power of narration, analysis, and often dissent.' This is not solely a matter of an interiority that evades physical and legal controls over the subject's exteriority. Our focus in this volume is on the alternative affiliations, among them the transnational categories of gender and diaspora, which challenge the dominant order from within its field of vision. Whether a serf pleading in court or a well-to-do dissident arguing in print, such speech acts – in the fullest sense of the term – circulate in the public domain on terms recognizable to that domain.

As a number of essays in this volume suggest, these sites of resistance emerge in concert with the class system, political struggles against what are sometimes termed 'internal colonies' (such as Ireland), and groups subject to forced servitude (slaves, serfs). But our focus on citizenship's tacit reliance on captivity has inevitably produced a certain weighting in this volume towards captive men. Captive women are an important area of inquiry in captivity studies and have been addressed widely elsewhere.[27] Our overarching engagement with writings by male captives is not intended to ignore the importance of this area of inquiry, but our emphasis on the problem of citizenship and nationality in the long nineteenth century does lead to a focus on male subjectivities. Thus, our only paper on a female captive discusses a text written at the very end of that period, one which addresses the ways in which the relationship between gender and citizenship emerged in the context of institutionally formed practices and claims about the subject in terms of class, criminality, and embodiment. The text *Prisons and Prisoners*, by British suffragette Constance Lytton, therefore draws on established modes of resistance that can frame the subject's relationship to alternatively constructed communities – in this case, a community of women that, in Lytton's view, attempts to cut across the boundaries of class and criminality. The relative silencing of women, especially in discussions of citizenship, within an already silenced space thus highlights that the prison experiment (for such it was), colonial expansion, peonage, and slavery functioned in part as supports for a masculinist ontology. Discussing writers who are to whatever degree simultaneously invested in *maintaining* that chain of being, while also involved (from one direction or the other) in *containing* subjects who are in other ways at odds with the system, points to the slippery and yet deeply entrenched nature of practices of captivity.

Masculinity may not be the focus of our book, but it is, to echo Barbara Johnson, our ground to the figure of the problematics of the dominant ontological constructions supported by captivity.[28] We consequently begin the volume with the chapter concerning Lytton and women's suffrage as a means of reminding the reader of the paradoxical centrality of this ground. The attempted silencing of women captives in this time frame is only one difficulty (perhaps among many) within this discursive framework, and it is our hope that this volume will, in part, open up further discussions of the particular problems of women captives who were, by reason of their gender, permanently excluded in nineteenth-century Western cultures from citizenship but not from the disciplinary structures that citizenship invoked and demanded, as Lytton so forcefully demonstrates.

The volume is divided into three sections. The chapters in 'The Subject of Captivity' deal with the central problem of the formation of captured identities across a variety of carceral spaces, establishing key ideological continuities between different institutionalized forms of confinement. As this section demonstrates, these disparate institutions raise similar problems for writers who claim a subjectivity that exceeds the institution's authority to define them. The writing subject – particularly in light of autobiography studies – emerges as a sign of crisis, a breach in the categories that captivity worked to reinforce and police. The writing subject raises the possibility of the imaginative and discursive transcendence of confinement, belying the aims of captivity to control all aspects of the captive's subjectivity. The chapters in the second section, 'Captivating Discourses,' examine the disciplinary operation of discourses of nation, class, and genre in prison. Expanding on the conclusions of the previous section regarding the larger social determinations that intersect with those of captivity, these contributors deal with texts that place the prison at the centre of a critique of a larger social confinement and within a larger set of discursive practices that explicitly tie the prison writing subject to a larger social sphere. This analysis of the relationship between the captive subject and a social group beyond the prison also serves as a prelude to the final section, 'Captivating Otherness.' In this last section, contributors chart the ways in which national identity was predicated on the management of otherness in relation to captivity. The trajectory from section to section is thus not historical, but telescopes outward, from an emphasis on identifying the writing subject by gender, class, and race, to identifying groups within the nation by class or political affiliation, to classifying nations within an international (and orientalist) framework.

The first section, 'The Subject of Captivity,' traces the formation of identities that are institutionally subject to containment (women and enslaved peoples) across three spheres: the prison, transatlantic slavery, and Russian serfdom. In his chapter, Jason Haslam examines the prison narrative of suffragette Lady Constance Lytton, *Prisons and Prisoners* (1914). Lytton's text helps to highlight the prison's reliance on the categories of gender and class in its attempt to construct a normative subjectivity in ways that mimic similar attempts in the wider social space. The prison is thus not a space apart, but the site for the attenuated discipline of gender and class norms – norms that, Lytton suggests, not only constrain individual subjectivity but also divide larger communities. To participate in a larger community of women Lytton must set aside the marks of her aristocratic class position – her name, her fashionable clothes, her powerful family connections – and 'pass' as the working-class suffragette Jane Warton through a mimicry of the stereotype of the working-class suffragette. But, this engagement in the larger community through an act of mimicry runs the risk of engaging in a second order of silencing that once again endangers the voice of the working-class woman prisoner, thus highlighting the prison's complexly reinforcing constructions of subjectivity in terms of class, gender, and citizenship. While Haslam considers the ways in which the bifurcation of subjectivity via class and gender norms can be both transgressed and underscored through mimicry, John MacKay attends to the power of performative speech acts to expose captivity's reliance on the classification of subjects as a reliable predictor of subjectivity. In his chapter, MacKay questions the place of discourse in prison by focusing in part on the use of autobiographical narratives by Russian serfs across the nineteenth century as legal depositions and on the use of prayer in these narratives in constructing the quest for freedom from bondage as a movement towards Christian redemption. MacKay pivots his analysis on the performativity of the authors' creation of an alignment or 'consubstantiality' with some form of authority figure, attending in particular to the trope of 'standing before judgment.' Charting the features of the serf narrative as a subgenre of autobiography closely related to the transatlantic slave narrative, MacKay's chapter reveals the ways in which narrative and rhetorical forms drawn from religious and legal discourse can be employed to contest the reduction of persons to property. Continuing the discussion of slavery, Tess Chakkalakal's paper asks us to consider the captive subject in the context of the physical mobility but deterministic identifications of the slave trade. She refocuses discussions of Olaudah Equiano's *Interesting Narrative*, a text frequently addressed as a slave narrative, by situating it not within a genre *per se* (which itself, she argues, is a confining practice), but as a text written out of the 'captivity phenomenon,' thus establishing some of the historical connections between different forms of confinement. Chakkalakal argues that Equiano's text functions performatively, as do MacKay's serf narratives, to invoke an act of mutual recognition between reader and author that cuts across the *a priori* status of both subjects, and creates, as MacKay also argues, an uncomfortable position for the text's readers, one in which they recognize their implication in the confining practice. Further, this act is one that, through a range of performative utterances throughout the text, undermines the racial discourse with which the text has traditionally been identified. Chakkalakal thus argues that the *Narrative* undermines part of the identity-determining structures of captivity, slavery, and criticism and genre themselves, echoing Haslam's and MacKay's discussions of performance and performativity as the means by which such structures can be challenged. Together, then, the contributors in this section address the construction of the subject in a variety of forms of captivity, and also examine the ways in which the performance of autobiographical writing or speech can vex that construction.

In the second section, 'Captivating Discourses,' we turn to an investigation of the ways in which discourses of group identity – particularly class and nation – are grasped through carceral containment. In his chapter, Frank Lauterbach examines the representation of the late Victorian prison as an 'imagined community' (invoking Benedict Anderson's phrase for the nation) that calls attention to the economic underclass and criminal underworld; he further situates the prison as a 'socially delimiting marker' that facilitates the distinction between these groups and the 'respectable' classes – a distinction that frequently draws on racist discourses as well, highlighting the imbrication of class and race in the Victorian imaginary. Discussing a series of narratives by so-called gentlemen convicts, figures who by their very literacy challenge the assumption that the prison is just another slum for the urban poor, Lauterbach attends to the complex class dynamics in which the discourse of the prison participates. Lauterbach's closing discussion of the 'rhetoric of alienity' leads into Monika Fludernik's discussion of the tensions between material practice and literary representation in relation to the gentleman convicts' varied alienation from the world of the prison. Fludernik stresses prison writers' engagement with the conventions of narrative practice, such as the exotic travelogue and the sentimental polemic – a practice that demands that the text solicit particular responses from readers, especially in arguing that prison discipline wounds rather than reforms the captive subject. Fludernik thus reveals the fraught ways in which literary concerns of audience and genre condition both nominally fictional and non-fictional texts. Julia M. Wright's chapter continues this interest in politically motivated literary sentimentality by examining the terms on which Charles Hamilton Teeling – in his account of his incarceration during the 1798 Irish Uprising against British colonial rule – solicits his readers' support for the Irish nationalist cause. As Wright argues, Teeling constructs the prison as permeable to the morally sanctioned national feeling of the Irish people: while the prison is an imposing edifice in which many political prisoners are held without trial, its power is repeatedly compromised by the Irish community within and beyond its walls on terms that evoke Enlightenment notions of 'moral sentiments' and subjectivity. The colonial administration is thus represented as practically inadequate to the task of containing Irish nationalist sentiment, as well as morally inadequate to the task of establishing a legitimate judicial system.

In the final section, 'Captivating Otherness,' our contributors continue with these concerns about national and identificatory cohesion and legitimacy, but do so through the lens of the association of captivity with the category of the 'foreign.' While some of the authors considered by Fludernik construct the domestic prison as an exotic space, the writers considered in this section do not domesticate such otherness even that far. Defensive rather than subversive, these texts define the nation's power with reference to its control over captivity. In the context of the newly formed United States, as Jennifer Costello Brezina notes, fears of Barbary pirates raised anxieties about the nation's ability to defend its citizens abroad. Until the Revolution, Americans were protected by British treaties; after the Revolution, Britain modified and largely withdrew its protection, leaving Americans fearful of their vulnerability along the Barbary coast specifically. Brezina suggestively details the relationship between this anxiety and an American orientalist discourse unrecognized in Said's account of pre–Second World War America. As she demonstrates, this orientalist discourse surrounding Barbary captives was crucial to the formation of American national identity in the post-Revolution period; this importance is especially relevant today, since, as Brezina thoughtfully concludes, discussions of the September 2001 attacks on the World Trade Center in New York and the US Pentagon in Virginia, and the war in Afghanistan, continue the very process of nation formation which she defines. Christine Marlin continues this interest in orientalist and racist discourse, focusing on the captured 'other' in her examination of the writings of British prison warden and reformer Major Arthur Griffiths. She demonstrates that Griffiths draws extensively on orientalist discourse to characterize the British prison system as civilized and superior, ameliorating the barbs only when addressing 'oriental' nations that are colonized by or allies of Britain. Griffiths's writings on prison, then, help to construct the cultural hierarchy that buttressed British imperialism. The other of Griffiths's prison writings, therefore, is not only the Western prisoner, but also the oriental prison as the embodiment of the rule which itself must be supplanted by British imperial authority. Just as notions of American manifest destiny were enforced in the wake of the nervous years of Barbary piracy, the favourable comparison of the British prison to its orientalist others supported claims of British imperial right, thus showing, as the volume as a whole demonstrates, the ways in which confinement not only has intersected with critical notions of identity but also occupies a crucial role on the world stage.

The notion of the 'world stage' arises here from the transnational focus of our volume – a transnationality centred in 'the West,' but dealing, as the final section demonstrates, with the West's construction of various global others. In the transitions that shadow our grouping of papers into sections – specifically the volume's movement from performance, to classification, to simple oppositionality – we can see some of the ways in which the desire for control is manifested in processes of simplification. As Haslam, Lauterbach, and Fludernik show, the upper-class prisoner was nearly a contradiction in terms, fitting into neither the class system nor the prison's expectation that criminals arise from the underclasses. Moreover, the radical uses of genre by serfs and former slaves in MacKay's and Chakkalakal's accounts bear comparison to Marlin's discussion of Griffiths's fairly conventional use of the genre of romance and its moral simplicities. Similarly, the two papers in this volume that address the problems that arise as nations emerge from Britain's control, namely Brezina's and Wright's, both point to their central texts' refusal to submit to the documentary imperatives of post-Enlightenment history; the truth of these texts lies elsewhere, in the empowerment they offer rather than the proofs they duly note. The authors addressed in this volume thus attend to the overlapping processes of exclusion in which the writer functions by making choices not only of content but also of form, for form presumes content – from the epic's demand for an empire to narrate to the prayer's requirement of the existence of a god to praise.

Thus, the scope of the volume is also intended to aid in avoiding the problematic determination of our subject matter into an overly delimited 'genre' – a problem pointed to in our epigraph by Christopher Castiglia, and by several of our authors. Tied to the difficulty of textual and political authority, such a determination would necessitate a construction of metaphorical boundaries, walls, and constraints that would work directly against the aims of many of the authors studied here, replicating the discursive and material traditions of captivity which our contributors so effectively highlight. As Samuel R. Delany writes in another context (to continue once again Castiglia's 'chain of appropriative allegories'), this volume's project 'is not to provide "a good read" but – indeed – to provide several, some sequential, others simultaneous';[29] we do not offer a totalizing definition of captivity or restraint, or of a 'genre' that somehow 'contains' this definition, in an explicit effort to avoid overly constraining the subject at hand.

NOTES

1 H. Bruce Franklin, *Prison Literature in America: The Victim as Criminal and Artist*, expanded ed. (Oxford: Oxford University Press, 1989), 124.
2 In a recent issue of *Workplace: A Journal for Academic Labor* dedicated to prison issues, for example, the prison and the university were linked as two of the institutional centres of contemporary American society. Bruce Simon writes that the issue's 'contributors refused to treat prisons and universities simply as institutions competing for state support in a conceptual vacuum,' pointing out that both institutions function 'within a larger political economy'; see Bruce Simon, 'Introduction: The Prison Issue,' *Workplace: A Journal for Academic Labor* 3.2 (December 2000): par. 6; available at http://www.louisville.edu/journal/workplace/issue6/prisonintro.html. Furthermore, Franklin, in his contribution to this issue, argues that 'just as we now assume that one cannot intelligently teach nineteenth-century American literature without recognizing slavery as context, one cannot responsibly teach contemporary American literature without recognizing the American prison system as context'; see H. Bruce Franklin, 'The American Prison in the Culture Wars,' *The Prison Issue*, ed. and intro. Bruce Simon, feature issue of *Workplace: A Journal for Academic Labor* 3.2 (December 2000): par. 11; available at http://www.louisville.edu/journal/workplace/issue6/franklin.html.
3 Bruce Franklin, *Prison Literature in America*, 235.
4 On the emergence of modern nationalism in the late eighteenth century, see, for instance, Benedict Anderson, *Imagined Communities: Reflections on the Origin and Spread of Nationalism*, rev. ed. (London: Verso, 1991); Ernest Gellner, *Nations and Nationalism* (Ithaca: Cornell University Press, 1983); E.J.

Hobsbawm, *Nations and Nationalism since 1780: Programme, Myth, Reality* (Cambridge: Cambridge University Press, 1990); and especially the very useful cultural analysis in Anthony D. Smith's 'Neo-Classicist and Romantic Elements in the Emergence of Nationalist Conceptions,' in *Nationalist Movements*, ed. Anthony D. Smith (London: Macmillan, 1976), 74–87. See also Smith's important book-length studies, among them, Anthony D. Smith, *National Identity* (rpt., Reno: University of Nevada Press, 1991); and *Theories of Nationalism* (1971), 2nd ed. (London: Duckworth, 1983). The notion of the nation exists prior to the 1780s, of course, but what distinguishes modern nationalism from 'patriotism' and its cognates is an emphasis on the nation as inclusive of and dependent on the people and the wider popular culture, and so modern nationalism is arguably heavily reliant on the rise of literacy and the proliferation of print in the wake of the Industrial Revolution in the mid-eighteenth century (see Gellner, in particular, on this point).

5 Angela Y. Davis, 'Racialized Punishment and Prison Abolition,' in *The Angela Y. Davis Reader*, ed. Joy James (Oxford: Blackwell, 1998), 96, 99.

6 Ibid., 99.

7 See, e.g., Davis, 'Racialized Punishment and Prison Abolition'; Joy James, *Resisting State Violence: Radicalism, Gender and Race in US Culture* (Minneapolis: University of Minnesota Press, 1996); H. Bruce Franklin, *Prison Literature in America* and 'The American Prison in the Culture Wars'; and Adam J. Hirsch, *The Rise of the Penitentiary: Prisons and Punishment in Early America* (New Haven: Yale University Press, 1992).

8 Angela Y. Davis, 'Race, Gender, and Prison History: From the Convict Lease System to the Supermax Prison,' in *Prison Masculinities*, ed. Don Sabo, Terry A. Kupers, and Willie London (Philadelphia: Temple University Press, 2001), 39, 40.

9 Jason Haslam, '"They locked the door on my meditations": Thoreau and the Prison House of Identity,' *Genre* 35 (3/4): 453n5. Davis quotes Matthew Mancini in listing whipping as 'the preeminent form of punishment under slavery; and the lash, along with the chain, became the very emblem of servitude for slaves and prisoners' (Mancini, quoted in Davis, 'Race, Gender, and Prison History,' 39).

10 Haslam, '"They locked,"' 452–3.

11 Orlando F. Lewis, *The Development of American Prisons and Prison Customs, 1776–1845* (1922; Montclair: Patterson Smith, 1967), 323. See Gustave de Beaumont and Alexis de Tocqueville, *On the Penitentiary System in the United States and Its Application in France* (1833), trans. Francis Lieber (Carbondale: Southern Illinois University Press, 1964).

12 Haslam, '"They locked,"' 417. Also see Frank Lauterbach's contribution to this volume.
13 See Ioan Davies, *Writers in Prison* (Oxford: Basil Blackwell, 1990). Also see J. Thorsten Sellin, *Slavery and the Penal System* (New York: Elsevier, 1976); Sellin also examines the relationship between slavery, prison, and other forms of punishment from classical times through to the modern period.
14 See H. Bruce Franklin, *Prison Literature in America*.
15 Barbara Harlow, *Barred: Women, Writing, and Political Detention* (Hanover: Wesleyan University Press, 1992) and *Resistance Literature* (New York: Methuen, 1987).
16 Julia Kristeva, *Powers of Horror: An Essay on Abjection*, trans. Leon Roudiez (New York: Columbia University Press, 1982).
17 Peter Mackenzie, *The Life of Thomas Muir ... Who was Tried for Sedition before the High Court of Justiciary in Scotland, and Sentenced to Transportation for Fourteen Years, with a Full Report of his Trial* (Glasgow: W.R. M'Phun, Trongate, 1831), 17, 33.
18 See the online database maintained by the National Archives of Ireland http://www.nationalarchives.ie/search01.html.
19 To take just one illustrative instance: the colony of freed slaves established by the British in Sierra Leone had, as governors in the late eighteenth century, 'William Dawes and Zachary Macaulay. Dawes had just served three voluntary years in Botany Bay; Macaulay had recently returned from overseeing a slave plantation in Jamaica'; see Deirdre Coleman, introduction to *Maiden Voyages and Infant Colonies: Two Women's Travel Narratives of the 1790s* (London: Leicester University Press, 1999), 21.
20 David Lloyd and Paul Thomas, *Culture and the State* (New York: Routledge, 1998), 117–18.
21 Harlow, *Barred*, 37.
22 Bruce Burgett, *Sentimental Bodies: Sex, Gender, and Citizenship in the Early Republic* (Princeton: Princeton University Press, 1998), 21. See Jürgen Habermas, *The Structural Transformation of the Public Sphere: An Inquiry into a Category of Bourgeois Society* (Cambridge, Mass.: MIT Press, 1989).
23 Lloyd and Thomas, *Culture and the State*, 21.
24 Louis Althusser, 'Ideology and Ideological State Apparatuses (Notes towards an Investigation),' in *Lenin and Philosophy*, trans. Ben Brewster (London: New Left, 1971), 121–73.
25 Burgett, *Sentimental Bodies*, 21.
26 Christopher Castiglia and Julia Stern, introduction to *Interiority in American Literature*, ed. Christopher Castiglia and Julia Stern, a special issue of *Early American Literature* 37 (2002): 3.

27 See, to take just a few examples, Christopher Castiglia, *Bound and Determined: Captivity, Culture-Crossing, and White Womanhood from Mary Rowlandson to Patty Hearst* (Chicago: University of Chicago Press, 1996); Karlene Faith, *Unruly Women: The Politics of Confinement and Resistance* (Vancouver: Press Gang, 1993); Elissa D. Gelfland, *Imagination and Confinement: Women's Writings from French Prisons* (Ithaca: Cornell University Press, 1983); and Anna Norris, *L'écriture du Défi: Textes Carcéreaux Féminins du XIXe et du XXe Siècles* (Birmingham, Ala.: Summa Publications, 2003). For discussions of the history of women's prisons in particular, also see Nicole Hahn Rafter, *Partial Justice: Women, Prisons, and Social Control*, 2nd ed. (New Brunswick, N.J.: Transaction, 1990) and Estelle B. Freedman, *Their Sisters' Keepers: Women's Prison Reform in America, 1830–1930* (Ann Arbor: University of Michigan Press, 1981).
28 Barbara Johnson, 'Is Female to Male As Ground Is to Figure?' in *Feminism and Psychoanalysis*, ed. Richard Feldstein and Judith Roof (Ithaca: Cornell University Press, 1989), 255–68.
29 Samuel R. Delany, *Longer Views: Extended Essays* (Hanover: Wesleyan University Press, 1996), xii.

The Subject of Captivity

CHAPTER 1

Being Jane Warton: Lady Constance Lytton and the Disruption of Privilege

Jason Haslam

While the origins of the modern prison are generally posited in the late eighteenth and early nineteenth centuries, the exact workings of the prison went through a distinct change as the nineteenth century came to an end. From the late eighteenth century through to the Victorian period, prisons were constructed as institutions which could help to bring about the moral rehabilitation of the criminal. This rehabilitation was to take place through isolation and silence, which, according to the humanist philosophy undergirding the practice, would allow the prisoners to reconnect with their innate ethical characters.[1] This reformative process has been construed by critics – most famously by Foucault – as a disciplinary mechanism that, rather than allowing inmates access to the self-contained individuality of the dominant society, instead creates docile and productive subjects who serve to help perpetuate the structures of power within the larger mechanisms of society. Such a disciplining of people is, in Foucault's words, part of the 'technologies of power' for which the prison is the major synecdoche. For Foucault, these technologies are figured as attempts to 'determine the conduct of individuals and submit them to certain ends or domination, an objectivizing of the subject.'[2]

As the prison system moved into the twentieth century, prison practices began to shift according to new principles of a 'welfarist administration' geared towards a 'therapeutic rationale' that focused on sociological causes of crime – a change which resulted in more explicitly socio-ideological methods of redemption.[3] Nevertheless, as John M. Sloop argues about later American prisons, the redeemable nature of the inmate was still discussed in terms of the inmate's relationship to the dominant society.[4] Ontological assumptions about the nature of certain groups – members of the lower classes, for example, or women – alter their relationship to the category of 'redeemable' simply because their natures are seen as differing from, or in some cases as simply removed from, the category of the Enlightenment individual. Thus, the early twentieth-century prison's emphasis on 'build[ing] up force of character'[5] coexists with revised methods of further classifying and separating 'types' of prisoners, including the mentally ill, children, and women. These people, then, become subject to severe and stringent forms of prison discipline, as a means of supposedly transforming them into 'useful' objects for the dominant society, rather than giving them access to dominant forms of subjectivity.[6]

Lady Constance Lytton's *Prisons and Prisoners: Some Personal Experiences* (1914) details the author's experiences in the fully developed modern prison system of Edwardian England, where she was incarcerated for her suffragette activity. As Lytton shows, for women the typing and disciplining of prisoners was a means of reinforcing gender roles, which are tied up with other identity constructions within the disciplinary practices of the larger society. Lytton describes how women's activities in prison focus on cleaning and sewing; in one of her prison stays, two books are provided: the first is a devotional text, the second 'an instructive book on domestic hygiene, "A Perfect Home and How to Keep It."'[7] The emphasis on rehabilitating women as proper domestic subjects reaches its height in the prison's role in attempting to break down the women's suffrage movement.

Lytton was arrested several times for her activities as a member of the suffragette organization, the Women's Social and Political Union (WSPU). While the upper-class Lytton was disguised as the working-class 'Jane Warton' during her third imprisonment, she was forcibly fed several times while on a hunger strike. This violent act, which was visited on numerous suffrage activists (both men and women), resulted in a stroke that partially paralysed Lytton, forcing her to write *Prisons and Prisoners* 'laboriously, with her left hand.'[8] Lytton's class passing not only exposes the prison system's unequal treatment of people from different economic positions, but also highlights the larger social connections between class and gender oppression. The narrative demonstrates how a person can be conflictingly identified within different but contiguous ideological frameworks. Depicting her class privilege as something that should be viewed as a part of the same ideological matrix that results in gender oppression, Lytton struggles in her text to remove herself from her class position, while at the same time making her unprivileged position as a woman visible and active. By portraying her existence as both Jane Warton and Lady Constance Lytton, neither of which can be the authentic or complete Enlightenment individual, Lytton's text forces one to go beyond readings of suffragette prison writings that foreground either their engagement in the collective voice of resistance to the patriarchy, or their reproduction of the silencing of the working-class woman.[9] Lytton attempts to create a position for herself in which she is disempowered as a member of the upper class but empowered as a member of the parallel communities of women and prisoners, and she does so in order to offer a powerful critique of the interconnections of identity construction and class and gender oppression within both prison and the social structure that it supports.

The Role of the Prison Narrative in the Suffragette Movement

Lytton's imprisonments occurred within the context of political action for the enfranchisement of women, and specifically concerned her militant activities as a member of the WSPU.[10] Concerted militant action started with marches to political sites such as the House of Commons, which led to arrests for disturbing the peace. Organized mostly by the WSPU and its offshoot, the Women's Freedom League (WFL), these campaigns eventually escalated to mass window-breaking events and arson, and to hunger strikes by those who had been imprisoned. The WSPU's militant campaigns largely came to a halt with the beginning of the First World War, when many, though by no means all, suffragettes rallied behind the government. The vote was given to propertied women after the war in the Representation of the People Act of 1918 and was extended to all women in 1928.

The militant campaigns were extraordinarily well documented by both the popular press and the suffragettes themselves. The suffragettes were invested in publicizing their movement as much as possible through both the spectacle (to appropriate a phrase used by both Barbara Green and Lisa Tickner) of their demonstrations and the representation of themselves in newspapers, pamphlets, and literary and other artistic works.[11] These publications served to offset the negative portrayal of the movement by the popular press and other media. Maroula Joannou writes that the suffragettes' depictions of themselves and other positive portrayals 'were welcomed and read avidly by women who had become habituated to seeing the behaviour and motives of the suffragette maligned in public elsewhere.'[12]

Among the suffragette materials, prison narratives and the related accounts of forcible feeding hold a prominent place, in part because they undermine the effects of the silencing that imprisonment imposed. As Green writes, 'in moving from street to the prison, [the suffragettes] left the realm of the exhibit ... and arrived at a realm of surveillance, voyeurism, and invisibility. They countered that invisibility with autobiography, bringing life-writing to the service of feminist activism.'[13] The goals of the suffragette prison narrative thus mimic those of the movement: to replace enforced silence with active voices, and oppression with agency.

Lytton's *Prisons and Prisoners*, and the experiences on which it was based, were among the best known and most publicized accounts of imprisonment and forcible feeding. Because of Lytton's family's fame, and its social status as part of the aristocracy (her brother, Victor, was an outspoken and pro-suffragette member of the House of Lords, while her grandfather was Edward Bulwer-Lytton, the famous novelist), her story was repeated *ad infinitum* in the press, in parliamentary speeches, and in suffragette-controlled media. Lytton's own work transforms the general content of such suffragette texts, however, in order to deal not only with gender oppression, but also with the implications of her class and its privileges.

Glenda Norquay writes that women's suffrage writing is constructed as 'a direct intervention in public and political debate' and is 'aimed at altering the structures of society.'[14] This being the case, the manner in which these texts construct the society that they wish to change takes on a certain primacy. The representation of the patriarchal system of late Victorian and Edwardian England forms the discursive ground to which suffragette authors respond. In addition to displaying the overt manner in which their society oppressed women, through depictions of scenes such as domestic abuse and forced feeding, many of the texts show the ways in which their authors were made to realize more subtle forms of oppression. These realizations generally culminate in the depiction of the author's conversion to the feminist cause.[15] Lytton's text is no exception to these generic conventions. These moments in the text both provide the reasons for her suffragette action and encourage the reader's sympathy, while at the same time offering a conceptual matrix for the understanding of the patriarchy's system of oppression. Through these formulations, Lytton reconstructs the ideological underpinnings of the definitions of women's subjectivity, including her own.[16]

Class Privilege and Patriarchy

The second chapter of Lytton's text, 'My Conversion,' describes her lengthy stay with a group of suffragettes that included two of the leaders of the movement, Emmeline Pethick-Lawrence and Annie Kenney. Once she is made aware of their militant allegiances, she tells them that 'although I shared their wish for the enfranchisement of women, I did not at all sympathise with the measures they adopted for bringing about that reform' (10). Lytton goes on to describe the logical arguments used by Pethick-Lawrence and Kenney to attempt to sway her opinion.[17] Her conversion is only achieved, however, through her sympathetic identification with an animal:

> All kinds of people were forming a ring round a sheep which had escaped as it was being taken to the slaughter-house. It looked old and misshapen. A vision suddenly rose in my mind of what it should have been on its native mountain-side with all its forces rightly developed, vigorous and independent. There was a hideous contrast between that vision and the thing in the crowd. With growing fear and distress the sheep ran about more clumsily and became a source of amusement to the onlookers, who laughed and jeered at it. At last it was caught by its two gaolers, and as they carried it away one of them, resenting its struggles, gave it a great cuff in the face. At that I felt exasperated. I went up to the men and said, 'Don't you know your own business? You have this creature absolutely in your power. If you were holding it properly it would be still. You are taking it to be killed, you are doing your job badly to hurt and insult it besides.' The men seemed ashamed, they adjusted their hold more efficiently and the crowd slunk away. (12–13)

After this passage, Lytton explicitly compares the treatment of the sheep to that of women: 'But on seeing this sheep it seemed to reveal to me for the first time the position of women throughout the world. I realised how often women are held in contempt as beings outside the pale of human dignity ... I was ashamed to remember that ... I had been blind to the sufferings peculiar to women as such' (13–14). Lytton's epiphany about the status of women is echoed by such later writers as Susan Hekman, who writes that women, through the way in which they are defined, do not have discursive access to the normative, Enlightenment identity, since this identity 'is defined in exclusively masculine terms.'[18] On the one hand, this masculine identity, as Sidonie Smith argues, 'suggests the certitudes of stable boundaries around a singular, unified, and irreducible core.'[19] On the other hand, women's identities, as Lytton makes explicit, are portrayed as existing 'outside the pale of human dignity' (13). Looking forward to Smith's conclusion that 'the woman who would reason like a man becomes "unwomanly," a kind of monstrous creature or lusus naturae,'[20] Lytton states that any woman who fights against sexist definitions of women's identity is treated as 'a distortion, an abnormality, an untidiness of creation' (41).

If the sheep in the above scene is to be read as a metaphor for the position of women in Lytton's society, then the portrayal of the sheep's handlers and of the crowd inform her depiction of the structures of that society. The passage relates the two sheep handlers to the policemen or gaolers who, later in the text, violently enforce the patriarchal decisions of the Liberal government. The more informative section of the scene in terms of Lytton's construction of general society involves the representation of the crowd encircling the sheep. Functioning as both spectators and imprisoning fence, the crowd does not just reconfigure the handlers' violence as entertainment, but in fact enables that violence, cutting off the sheep's means of escape. Lytton here turns around contemporary anti-suffragette depictions of the 'unruly feminine crowd.'[21] This spectre was used by the popular press not only in order to discount the suffragettes' demonstrations and the reasons for them, but also to elide the violent suppression of those demonstrations by the police.[22] Lytton's metaphorical depiction of a crowd being entertained by violence against women thus serves to counteract anti-suffrage propaganda by turning the 'unruly crowd' into an image of a society that enables such violence through its silent gaze and subsequent slinking support of the patriarchy.

Lytton explicates the populace's support of the oppression of women in a later passage that could allude to Henry David Thoreau's statement in his famous essay 'Resistance to Civil Government' that 'There are thousands who are *in opinion* opposed to slavery and to the war, who yet in effect do nothing to put an end to them.'[23] She writes that, early in the process of her conversion,

> I was much concerned with the arguments of Anti-Suffragists. I wrote a pamphlet to refute their points of view, as generally presented in newspapers and magazines. I was always, as it were, stopping on my road to combat their attitude. It was only after considerably longer experience that I realised the waste of energy entailed by this process, since the practical opposi-

tion which blocks the way to the legal removal of sex disability is not due to those men or women who have courage to publicly record their opposition, but to those who take shelter in verbally advocating the cause, while at the same time opposing any effective move for its achievement. (15) [24]

The oppression of women is not enabled by the robustious (to resurrect an appropriate archaism) support of patriarchal institutions and social practices, but through the silent, hypocritical consent of the generalized crowd, which renders its engagement in oppression invisible by mimicking the suffragettes.

Lytton demonstrates that this silent consent by the public to the subjugation of women and to the violent suppression of suffragettes makes itself visible, however, in everyday acts committed by 'average' people across society. Writing of her first involvement in a WSPU Deputation, in a march to the Prime Minister, she again depicts violence in the gaze and taunts of a crowd:

> I heard for the first time with my own ears the well worn taunt 'Go home and do your washing.' ... From the moment I heard that 'washing' taunt in the street, I have had eyes for the work of the washers. If there is one single industry highly deserving of recognition throughout the world of human existence and of representation under parliamentary systems, it surely is that of the washers, the renewers week by week, the makers clean. I determined, if I should find myself the solitary representative of the Deputation and its untrained spokeswoman, I should point to the collars and shirt fronts of the gentlemen who received me and claim the freedom of citizenship for the washers. (42–3)

Followed by a description of the violent force used by the police against the Deputation, this passage illuminates the relationship between everyday oppression and the actions taken against the suffragettes. Not only do the sexist taunts of the crowd serve to highlight the means through which women are oppressed on a daily basis, but the very apparel of the men in the crowd and in the government serves a similar function. Lytton realizes that the 'proper' social appearance of the men who control the State is made possible by the politically unrepresented labour of women.

The passage concerning the washers also points to one of the central tensions in Lytton's text. Her worry about speaking to the government, she suggests, is due to a feeling that she is 'not equipped to represent' working-class women (42). In questioning the legitimacy of her representational ability, Lytton challenges her own position within the suffrage movement, which to her, if not all suffragettes (as I discuss below), is ultimately concerned with the complete political representation of all women. Lytton thus perceives her class privilege in terms of its reinforcement of gender hierarchies: if the men in parliament illegitimately 'represent' the women of the nation, Lytton wants to avoid replicating this illegitimacy, to avoid participating in the oppressive milieu because, as a 'member of a prominent aristocratic family, sister of a peer, and a "chronic invalid,"' she was, in the words of Mary Jean Corbett, 'wary of special treatment from the authorities.'[25]

Despite this wariness, Lytton's class consistently frustrates her attempts to be a representative feminist figure. This is especially apparent during her first imprisonment, when the prison authorities regularly accorded her better treatment than the other prisoners. At one point, Lytton is approached by one of the women wardens, who asks, 'What have you been complaining about?' Lytton replies, 'I haven't been complaining,' but the wardress responds, 'Yes you have – you complained of something to a visitor.' Lytton then remembers that,

> when reassuring my sister as to my health and to prove to her the genuineness of my statements as to prison conditions being in no way harmful to me, I had mentioned two things which proved rather trying, viz., that my underclothes and stockings were too short to cover my knees, and the fact that one small towel had to do service for all purposes during a week. I reported this to the wardress, but explained that I had mentioned these not in complaint but to prove to my sister that my discomforts were insignificant. 'Well,' she retorted, 'next time you have anything to complain of come to me with it – if not I shall get into trouble.' ... From that time forward I was supplied with two towels, one of them renewed every week, and two rolls of flannel bandages were brought to me to cover my knees. (112–13)

Lytton learns after her release that these privileges were accorded to her because her brother 'had interviewed the head of the Prison Commissioners Department' (113). Lytton's family's social position seems to disrupt the prison's specific mechanisms of power, forcing the officials to treat her differently, and therefore partially reverses the power dynamic between Lytton and her gaolers – but this reversal could in turn result in the punishment of yet another woman, the wardress.[26]

And yet, such privileges highlight for Lytton the mistreatment of lower-class prisoners. She describes the prison chaplain who, during this same period of imprisonment, made the distinction between her and the other prisoners explicit:

> He instanced how wrong it would be if, when we were hungry, we yielded to the temptation of stealing bread. At this remark an old woman stood up. She was tall and gaunt, her face seamed with life, her hands gnarled and worn with work. One saw that whatever her crimes might have been she had evidently toiled incessantly ... The tears streamed down her furrowed cheeks as she said in a pleading, reverent voice, 'Oh, sir, don't be so hard on us.' The wardresses immediately came up to her took her by the shoulders and hustled her out of the ward; we never saw her again. The Chaplain did not answer nor even look at her, and continued his address as if nothing had happened. (120–1)

Despite his callous indifference towards the woman, he treats Lytton with deference and respect, referring to her as 'your ladyship' (122). This leads Lytton and others to 'compare[] the attitude of the Chaplain towards the prisoner who had appealed to him during his address and towards myself. It was on this occasion I first noticed that the dress-jacket I wore was different from those of my companions' (122). Afterwards, 'it became a sort of game to watch for the privileges that were accorded to me' (122). This situation, in which an upper-class prisoner was treated with more respect than others, was common in the late Victorian and Edwardian prison. As Wiener writes, 'The very drive to subject all criminals to uniform discipline made prisoners who, for whatever reason, did not fit the criminal stereotype for which that discipline had been devised into a problem requiring new and special measures.'[27] Recognizing the special care taken in her own case, Lytton uses it to highlight the improper treatment of the other prisoners, as a means of making a larger social point about class distinctions.

At the same time, Lytton's membership in the generalized group of prisoners in the chapel, evidenced by her use of 'we' in the chapel scene, is invalidated by the chaplain's deference to her, and by the prison's definition of her as a person who exists outside of the stereotype of the common criminal. Her recognition of this invalidation creates a division between Lytton's perception of her prison experience and that of other suffragettes. Even though she was arrested as a militant, and even though she serves her prison time with other members of the cause, she feels that she is not 'shar[ing] the lot of the bulk of my Suffragette companions' (123). This split is reinforced at the trial for her second arrest, where she and another well-known figure are given special consideration: 'The whole "trial" was unworthy of the name – it was a device whereby Mrs. Brailsford and I should be separated from the others and treated with more respect, I having been the only one to do a glaring act and an, apparently, harmful or greatly risky one' (225). Despite Lytton's 'harmful' act of throwing a rock at a moving car, she is separated from the majority of the women who share her beliefs. This separation is indicative for Lytton of the interdependent relationship between class structures and gender divisions, in that both effectively silence the majority of women.

Lytton's portrayal of her arrest and imprisonment is one in which class prevents her from having an 'authentic' suffragette prison experience, further keeping her from being representative of the movement and from being able to have any lasting effects. She makes this problem explicit when she describes a group of prisoners marching in the yard, and compares them to an upper-class social gathering:

> As I had watched the prisoners I saw before me a counter-procession of women of this leisured class, herded as I have so often seen them at ballrooms and parties, enduring the labours, the penalties, of futile, superficial, sordidly useless lives, quarrelling in their marriage market, revelling in their petty triumphs, concerned continually with money, yielding all opinion to social exigencies, grovelling to those they consider above them, despising and crushing those they consider below them, pretending to be lovers of art and intellect, but concerned at heart only with the appearance of being so. ... And immediately the procession of Holloway yard seemed human, dignified, almost enviable by the side of that other. ... Whether or not the women alive to-day in the ruling class can be cured is of comparatively little importance, but clearly the causes which have brought them forth must be altered at the root. (135–6)

For Lytton, the women of the leisured class may be equally creations of the patriarchal system as the lower class, but their active involvement in the social processes of their own privilege not only makes them ill equipped to engage themselves in the feminist movement, but also renders them contemptible. Somewhat working against what Marie Mulvey-Roberts sees, in her critical-biographical essay about Lytton, as the latter's understanding of 'the constraints of the feminine role imposed on aristocratic women,'[28] Lytton portrays these women as also actively participating in (re)creating their own social position at the expense of the members of the lower classes. And it must be remembered that, despite Lytton's distancing of herself from these women through the use of the third person, she herself is a member of their order, one of the group that forms 'the weakest link in the chain of womanhood' (135). Despite Green's assertion that 'In the prison Lytton gained access to those disenfranchised women from whom she had been separated,'[29] at this point in her imprisonment Lytton can only attempt to understand those disenfranchised women through a comparison to women of her own class. Even the privileged women's preoccupation with appearance is a mimicry of 'how much appearances were respected by officials' of the prison (164). Lytton's concern, then, with representation and participation within the suffrage movement as a whole, but more specifically in suffragette prison experiences, replicates the women's larger concern with representation and participation in the political process. Lytton thus demonstrates how privilege, patriarchy, and prison all function as divisive forces that alienate people from each other and reinforce the ruling group's power through that alienation.

Being Jane Warton

As Green notes, the models upon which Lytton bases her text could result in another reinforcement of some of the oppressive functions of what Foucault calls the 'carceral city,' the disciplinary social structure in which the prison 'is not alone, but linked to a whole series of "carceral" mechanisms which seem distinct enough – since they are intended to alleviate pain, to cure, to comfort – but which all tend, like the prison, to exercise a power of normalization.'[30] Using 'the gaze of the social investigator'[31] to validate her readings of inmates and of the prison system, Lytton occasionally constructs the 'common prisoner' within a set of stylized and often silent types instead of dealing with particulars. Quoting an early passage in Lytton's text (33), Green writes that, 'Throughout, Lytton is the protector of other imprisoned women – through activism the "superfluous spinster" finds a way of exercising a maternal instinct after all. This model of womanly reform, however, threatens to infantilize and silence the "common criminal."'[32] In this role of protector, Lytton falls into a general group of middle- and presumably leisure-class women who 'were encouraged to become involved in the provision of "improving" recreations for the working class as a whole. Here was one area of activity where the ideal virtues attributed to women ... could be put to a good social use.'[33] As these critics point out, such activities necessitate an infantilization of those whom they would help. Therefore, to be effective, Lytton must attack class privilege in order to attack the patriarchy; she must decry the class structure not only as it appears in favours given to her, but also as it exists in her own gaze and perception. In her early attempts to disrupt the system of privileges that favours her, she focuses on changing people's perception of her. For example, when she notices that her prison dress is better than others, she switches jackets with another suffragette prisoner (122). But, she realizes that this early and superficial cross-dressing does not have much affect on her status as *Lady* Lytton. In order to attack fully the image of her that privilege, she must attack the embodied image of privilege – herself.

Her first such attack is a physical attempt to rewrite the text of her classed body. In an effort to ensure her movement from the relatively undisciplined infirmary to the more rigorous 'other side' (173) of the prison, Lytton decides to carve the words 'Votes for Women' onto her body, 'beginning over the heart and ending it' on her face (164). She only manages to cut a deep 'V' into her chest before she is discovered, but this is enough to effect her transfer. Green writes that 'Knowing that the physicians employed a medical gaze to limit hers (as an "observation case" Lytton, with her heart condition, could not join the other prisoners in the general cells), Lytton exaggerated her position as spectacle, literally engraving her body's secrets onto her skin so that medical inspection was made moot.'[34] In fact, the oppressive medical gaze was strongly directed at the suffragettes as a whole. The movement itself was occasionally figured as the result of vaguely worded medical problems in the women's bodies.[35] Lytton's attack on her own body can be read as an attempt to subvert not only the medical gaze directed at her, but also that directed at all suffragettes, since, as Foucault argues, the medical gaze is part of the larger institutional matrix of society.[36] Lytton's actions not only disrupt the medical gaze (which functions as one of the prison's regulatory systems), but also rewrite the status of her body within the classificatory regimes of her society (regimes which the prison serves to protect and produce).

Since the specific phrase 'Votes for Women' is associated with the WSPU and other such organizations, it also carries with it some resonance of the non-aristocratic classes.[37] Lytton's attempt to carve this phrase into her flesh, then, functions both to attack her embodied upper-class femininity and to rewrite that femininity into the larger community of suffragette activists. This victorious 'V' (unintentionally mimicked years later by Liberal Prime Minister, and friend of Lord Lytton, Winston Churchill) places Lytton in opposition to the culture from which her privilege arises. This rebellious or contrary position is even evidenced typographically, with Lytton's 'V' appearing as the inverse of the phalanx of police that attacked the suffragette deputation, inscribed in Lytton's text as '∧' (44). The act of cutting herself in order to be moved is, in Lytton's words, a direct 'analogy' for the entire women's movement: 'a reasonable demand, continuously pressed in a reasonable way and with great patience; result, blank refusal on the part of responsible powers. Militant action, by means of strike and protest; result, anger, condemnation, and the request is granted' (174). Lytton's violence against her own body, which takes the form of the act of writing, repeats in miniature the actions of the group from which she has been separated by her status and, in so doing, allows her more visibly and actively to join that community. Her secondary textual portrayal of the act in turn allows her to direct the reader's attention away from herself and onto the aims of the group.

Lytton's attempts to deny her class position and to become a full member of the suffragette society are most forcibly portrayed in her class passing as a seamstress named Jane Warton. After another imprisonment, this time in Newcastle, Lytton decides that the only way to remove herself from the privileges of her class is to dissociate herself from her name. She decides this mostly because of the onset of suffragette hunger strikes and the resulting forcible feeding ordered by the government. Suffragettes began these strikes as a means of protesting the government's refusal to treat them as political prisoners, who, after the influx of Irish gentleman political prisoners in the late nineteenth century, were accorded different status in the prison.[38] The first such strike was committed in February 1909 by Marion Wallace Dunlop, who was released early, as were several subsequent hunger strikers. In September of the same year, however, the government ordered the forced feeding of all hunger strikers. The first woman to be forcibly fed was Mary Leigh. The government justified this action by assuring members of parliament and the public that it was the only way to save the striking prisoners' lives. Howlett describes the way in which the bill for forcible feeding was introduced:

> On September 29 Herbert Gladstone (the home secretary) informed the

House of Commons of his decision to introduce forcible feeding. It was, he declared, his duty to do so: forcible feeding was the only way the women's lives, which were 'sacred,' could be preserved (without releasing them and thus making a mockery of the law). However, as the Liberal journalists Brailsford and Nevinson argued in a letter to the *Times*, Gladstone was thus discounting the alternative option of granting the WSPU's demand and officially recognizing the suffragettes as political prisoners.[39]

Indeed, in a December 1909 statement concerning the 'Suffragist Women Prisoners,' the Home Secretary provided statements from doctors testifying to the safety and necessity of forcible feeding, while also going to great lengths to explain why the women could not be considered political prisoners. Howlett, however, discusses how the home secretary's reasoning is further flawed by the fact that, rather than being a life-saving measure, forcible feeding was 'a brutal and life-threatening procedure' which was used 'as a deterrent'; 'its value to the government was not that it saved life but that it inflicted pain and had a perceived ability to decimate the movement.'[40] As I have argued elsewhere, the type of masking language that the government is employing is characteristic of modern prison discourse: the violent and brutalizing effects of the prison are housed within statements of benevolence and, more importantly, of discipline geared towards the 'proper' reconstitution of the subject.[41]

It is in this context that Lytton decides to pass as Jane Warton. Following some discussion of the brutal treatment of the strikers, and of the horrors of forcible feeding, she writes, 'The altogether shameless way I had been preferred against the others at Newcastle ... made me determine to try whether they would recognise my need for exceptional favours without my name' (235). In order to do this, she engages in an extended and effective masquerade. Lytton reconceives her outward appearance, beginning by rejoining the WSPU as Jane Warton, and by buying new apparel: 'I accomplished my disguise in Manchester, going to a different shop for every part of it, for safety's sake. I had noticed several times while I was in prison that prisoners of unprepossessing appearance obtained least favour, so I was determined to put ugliness to the test' (239). By putting her costume together in piecemeal fashion, and by scouring Manchester to do so, Lytton becomes what she depicts as an amalgamation of all the working-class women of the area. She writes, 'On inquiry for a "cheap" draper, three different people recommended me to a certain shop named "Lewis." ... So many Miss Wartons were of the same mind that the street was blocked with customers for some distance down' (241). Lytton turns the sociologist's gaze (which Green discusses) upon herself, using the same patronizing language, but this time in order to transform herself into a spectacle for others. She writes that, upon entering the house where she is to stay as Jane, 'The daughters were zealots and welcomed Jane without a sign of criticism. I saw the mother gasp a little when I entered her drawing-room, but she was nevertheless most courteous and kind' (242). Performing working-class 'ugliness,' the opposite of her previous fashionable appearance, Lytton effectively removes the social barriers of privilege that protect her from the judgmental gaze of others.

This removal causes a split in Lytton's depiction of herself. As the social reformer who had 'always been interested in prisons and ... prison reform' (10), Lytton objectifies her new identity as Jane Warton much as she does the 'common criminal,' resulting in a depersonalized, third-person account of her shopping trip to the aforementioned shop: 'A sale was on there and Jane found that it was the very place for her. ... The hat was a special difficulty; every article of millinery was of the fashionable order, warranted to cover half the body as well as the head. This did not suit Jane. Finally she succeeded in getting the right one of stitched cloth, with a plait of cloth round the crown' (241). Jane, as a woman with no social barriers between her and the rest of society, is always already open to the derogatory gaze of those around her. Thus, Lytton can classify her alter-ego in the third person, and note Jane's divergence from acceptable norms (in this case those of fashion). Jane's dress embodies this openness; whereas fashionable women (such as Lytton, presumably) can cover themselves with their hats, such shielding does 'not suit Jane.'

But such an easy distinction between Constance and Jane is untenable. The passage above concludes, 'Before leaving Manchester I realised that my ugly disguise was a success. I was an object of the greatest derision to street-boys, and shop-girls could hardly keep their countenances while serving me' (241). The sudden shift from the third-person description of Jane to a first-person account of Lytton's treatment by street-boys and shop-girls demonstrates that Jane's ugliness also exposes Lytton to the gaze from which her privilege had protected her. The success of the disguise does not lie in its ability to fool others, but in the performative function of turning Lytton into an object of derision. The abuse hurled at working-class Jane is received by the upper-class Constance.

The instability of identity created by Lytton's performance continues after Jane's arrest.[42] Jane is again treated as an object open for abuse, but this time she functions as a synecdoche for all suffragettes. As she walks up to be booked in, Lytton writes that Jane's 'standing out in the room was the signal for a convulsed titter from the other prisoners. "It's a shame to laugh at one of your fellow-prisoners," said the policeman behind the desk, and the tittering was hushed. It was all I could do not to laugh, and I thought to myself "Is the *Punch* version of a Suffragette overdone?" As I got back to my companions they too were laughing, but I thought it wonderfully kind of the policeman to have spoken on my behalf.' (249). In analysing the 'status of Lytton's (suppressed) laughter' in this passage, Howlett writes that it does not matter whether she is laughing 'at the success of her mimicry' or 'at the sheer ridiculousness of Jane's appearance,' and thus whether she identifies with the other suffragette prisoners or with the common prisoners. 'In either case,' argues Howlett, 'what Lytton is clearly *not* doing is identifying herself, the subject of the laughter, with Jane, the object of the prisoners' contempt and the policeman's pity.'[43] This point is in fact emphasized by Lytton's referring to Jane as a *Punch* version of a suffragette. The cartoons of suffrage activists, regularly published in *Punch*, were heavily stereotyped and negative, so Lytton's reference to her version of the working-class suffragette as a *Punch* image could work to reproduce the magazine's 'comic' dismissal. While I agree with Howlett that Lytton's subjectivity is ambiguous here, I believe that this is due precisely to the fact that Lytton recognizes herself *both* as Constance and as Jane. Thus, Lytton can write of Jane in the third person at the beginning of the passage, and at the end write that the policeman spoke 'on my behalf.' This shifting use of pronouns is not so much a transformation in her understanding of herself as it is a signal of the problems raised by her class passing. She alternates between the subject laughing and the object of the laughter. The pronoun shifts in this passage serve to signal the problems of subjectivity created by the class distinctions of her society, but they also point towards the problematic nature of her masquerade. As in the description of the taunting she received when buying her outfit, Lytton's text struggles at the moment of public scrutiny whether to depict Jane as object or as subject.

The ostensible reason for her class passing is to effect the removal of privilege in her treatment as a prisoner. As Constance Lytton, she is told that the official justification for these privileges was the diagnosis of a pre-existing heart condition. The Home Office, quoting its own letter to the Fabian Society, stated that Lytton 'was released solely because she was suffering from serious heart disease, and because violent resistance on her part to the medical treatment appropriate to her case would have involved some risk to her life,' and that any 'statement that Lady Constance Lytton's release had anything to do with her rank or social position' was 'a wilful and deliberate misrepresentation.'[44] That Lytton did have a heart condition was not disputed; rather, she wanted to demonstrate that without having the privilege of her name, this condition would not have any effect on her sentencing or treatment. This is proven to be true during Jane's second forcible feeding:

> I told him [the doctor] I should not faint, that I was not liable to this or any form of collapse; I did not mention the slight chronic debility of heart from which I suffered. He called in the junior medical officer, who happened to be passing at the time, to test my heart. The junior doctor, who was in a jovial mood, stooped down and listened to my heart through the stethoscope for barely the space of a second – he could not have heard two beats – and exclaimed, 'Oh, ripping, splendid heart! You can go on with her' ... (275)

When imprisoned as Constance Lytton, she is given thorough medical tests and treatment. As Jane Warton, she notes that a careless and superficial test is enough to prove her health. Going beyond what Mulvey-Roberts argues is a distinction between Jane's 'private' medical history and Constance's 'public one,'[45] this passage demonstrates that Lytton's disguise changes the very way in which she is embodied by changing her relationship to the prison through removing the signs of her privileged status. In other words, Jane Warton is, as far as Constance Lytton is concerned, as different on the inside as she is on the outside, despite their sharing of one body.

The dual subjectivity, which continues throughout Jane's imprisonment, reaches its apex during Jane's first forcible feeding, making the political effectiveness of Lytton's passing clear. Lytton ends her detailed description of the process of the feeding and the horrendous physical suffering it creates by writing that

> The horror of it was more than I can describe. I was sick over the doctor and wardresses, and it seemed a long time before they took the tube out. As the doctor left he gave me a slap on the cheek, not violently, but, as it were, to express his contemptuous disapproval, and he seemed to take for

granted that my distress was assumed. At first it seemed such an utterly contemptible thing to have done that I could only laugh in my mind. Then suddenly I saw Jane Warton lying before me, and it seemed as if I were outside of her. She was the most despised, ignorant and helpless prisoner that I had seen. When she had served her time and was out of the prison, no one would believe anything she said, and the doctor when he had fed her by force and tortured her body, struck her on the cheek to show how he despised her! That was Jane Warton, and I had come to help her. (269–70)

Lytton refigures herself as the 'common woman' so well that the doctor presumes her suffering to be 'assumed,' since, as an official of the prison and of the cultural structures it represents, he cannot accept the self-sacrifice in which the working-class Jane is engaging. Looking on his actions from her privileged position, Constance wants to laugh at the doctor who is, even though a professional, still her social inferior. However, because Lytton refers to herself during the forcible feeding in the first person – the suffering happens to the 'I' that is both Jane and Constance – Lytton can reinterpret the doctor's slap as a direct and contemptible act upon Jane, in a direct parallel to her reaction to the treatment of the sheep, which is also hit in the face by a man who 'resent[s] its struggles' (13). Redirecting the reader to the knowledge of the dual nature of the 'I' by reverting to the third-person depiction of Jane in the above passage, Lytton creates a powerful political moment where, as the working-class woman, she experiences the full violence of the patriarchy and, as the upper-class woman, she can talk about it in public.[46] This section of *Prisons and Prisoners* looks forward to Shoshana Felman's figuration of women's autobiography, wherein the author can only have access to her own 'story' through an act of reading. Felman writes, 'Trained to see ourselves as objects and to be positioned as the Other, estranged to ourselves, we have a story that by definition cannot be self-present to us, a story that, in other words, is not a story, but *must become* a story. And it cannot *become* a story except through the *story of the Other.*'[47] While this structure would be problematic for authors in even more oppressive situations than Lytton's, who do not have access to class or other privileges, and whose otherness is forced upon them and thereby threatens to silence their suffering, Lytton does gain 'access,' to use Felman's term, to her own autobiography and to her voice as representative only at the moment when she can read herself as other.[48] By placing Jane and Constance in a cell together, Lytton uses her dual identity as a privileged suffragette to disrupt the prison's attempt to isolate the prisoner from the public, thereby silencing her outraged voice, while also disrupting the patriarchy's attempt to isolate the upper-class woman from the larger community of women, thereby silencing her potential political force. Through an effective denial of her privilege, Lytton joins the suffragette community and can speak on their behalf.

This politically effective moment, where a community is formed despite the oppressive forces arrayed against it, is solidified by the writing of *Prisons and Prisoners* itself. According to Howlett, the generic duplication of narratives of forcible feeding demonstrates that 'the ordeal is not an isolated and isolating bodily experience but a point of identification and union between many women.'[49] Corbett takes this further: citing Michael Sandel, she argues that suffragettes refigure the self-contained individual as a more communal, 'intersubjective' construction, leading 'beyond an individualist paradigm for identity and toward a collectivist model.'[50] The production of texts becomes one of the central means of creating this collectivist suffragette identity. The repetition of the formulae of narratives of imprisonment and forcible feeding, which Howlett discusses,[51] is a space for the construction of this multiple, fully participatory subjectivity.

With this use of text in mind, Lytton's description of her attempted carving of 'Votes for Women' on her body can be read as an intradiegetic representation of the act of writing *Prisons and Prisoners*. Lytton recognizes that the act of writing does more than allow her to join her fellow prisoners, and is more than a symbol for the movement. Her act reconstructs her own being as a function of the larger collective identity. This reconstruction of the ostensible autobiographer is emphasized by the author's signature – or rather the authors' signatures, for the book is coauthored by 'Constance Lytton and Jane Warton, Spinster.' The splitting of the author into both Constance and Jane serves the dual purpose of giving Jane a voice and of allowing Constance to speak as a member of the collective (while also removing both from a direct male influence, since 'Spinster' could describe either 'Constance Lytton' or 'Jane Warton'). This retooling of the traditional signature of the single author is also indicative of Lytton's and other suffragettes' communal reworking of the traditional autobiography. Comparing women's autobiographies in general to the male-dominated genre as a whole, Mary G. Mason writes that

> the egoistic secular archetype that Rousseau handed down to his romantic brethren in his *Confessions*, shifting the dramatic presentation to an unfold-

ing self-discovery where characters and events are little more than aspects of the author's evolving consciousness, finds no echo in women's writing about their lives. On the contrary ... the self-discovery of female identity seems to acknowledge the real presence and recognition of another consciousness, and the disclosure of female self is linked to the identification of some 'other.' This recognition of another consciousness – and I emphasize recognition of rather than deference to – this grounding of identity through relation to the chosen other, seems ... to enable women to write openly about themselves.[52]

Lytton paradoxically embodies Mason's paradigm of a referential subjectivity by attempting to become the other through and, more importantly, *with* whom she identifies herself. In a way, Lytton's text can be seen as a reversal of Boethius's seminal prison autobiography, *The Consolation of Philosophy*. Rather than intellectually or spiritually renewing herself through reference to an ephemeral Lady Philosophy, Lytton instead secularly renews herself as a member of the suffragette collective through an identification with the embodied and tortured Jane Warton. Taking both Lytton's renewal and the repetitive nature of suffragette textual practice into account, Caren Kaplan's reading of this type of identification is especially pertinent. Writing that this identification is a subversion of the 'institution of literature,' she argues that 'One form of subversion can be identified as the deconstruction of the bourgeois author (the sacred subject of autobiographical narrative) and the construction of a collective authorial identity – a kind of collective consciousness that "authorizes" and validates the identity of the individual writer.'[53] Lytton's passing and the dual authorship of the text can be seen as an engagement in the communal critique of the patriarchy and its tradition of autobiography, a tradition which, as Smith and Rita Felski both argue, is engaged in the (re)production of the self-contained, Enlightenment individual.[54] Lytton's acts of writing on her body, of passing as Jane Warton, and of writing *Prisons and Prisoners* are means through which she attempts to transmute her privileged individual identity into membership in the suffragette collective identity.

Working Silence

Notwithstanding her text's potential for dissidence, the repetition of suffragette narrative in which Lytton engages – and the communal subjectivity that it represents – can reproduce the system of privilege, and the silencing of the voices of working-class suffragettes, that Lytton is attempting to escape. Drawing on the contemporary critiques of the WSPU by ex-member Teresa Billington-Grieg and others, Corbett states that dissidents 'charged that WSPU leaders exploited willing women by subjecting them to violence at the hands of the government, and then capitalized on their victimization for publicity's sake.'[55] Portraying the Pankhursts as commercially minded autocrats, Billington-Grieg complained that 'the WSPU had taken up revolution as a performance and appropriated the methodology of advertising culture ... thus mechanizing feminism.'[56] Billington-Grieg argues that such a reproduction of dominant forms of discourse may create a communal identity, but that identity is ultimately still subjugated to the dominant culture. In the process of this subjugation it is only the middle- and upper-class leaders of the WSPU autocracy who are allowed to speak.[57] Corbett writes that some working-class activists desired to have the opportunities of middle-class women given 'to other women of their class, and not to promote a political ethic that would reinscribe women's cultural disposition to self-sacrifice.'[58] Within this reading of the suffragette movement, the mass reproduction of narratives of imprisonment and forced feeding, representative as they are of the violent acts perpetrated against the bodies of women, serve only to recreate that very violence for the benefit of those in positions of privilege, thus working against the members of the community that it purports to represent. The emphasis on similarity can fall into the trap of generalization and essentialism which underpins the discourse supporting the oppression of women and prisoners.

Despite her attempt to engage in a communal critique of patriarchy and privilege, Lytton's masquerade as a working-class woman, when combined with her stylized portrayal of forced feeding, may only succeed in further silencing the people whom she is attempting to represent. The scene of her first feeding, in which a disembodied Constance looks at the 'tortured,' embodied Jane Warton, could be interpreted as a duplication of the Enlightenment ontological hierarchy discussed by Smith,[59] in which the privileged members of society gain access to the 'universal,' disembodied transcendent self, while the unprivileged are embodied. Sue Thomas, indeed, reads this particular scene in exactly this way, using language that closely echoes what Victor Brombert has called the 'happy prison' motif, wherein prison authors portray the prison as a space that strengthens the authors' spiritual or transcendent freedom.[60] Thomas writes that Lytton occupies the space of 'spectator of the violence,' which is also the space 'of the transcendent spirit,' arguing that in Lytton's taking up 'the position of spectator of Warton's person there is a distancing of narcissistic libido from the body image and a refusal of the spirit to submit.'[61] Constance may read Jane in Felman's terms, but she is also writing her, subjecting the image of the working class to the violence that the upper-class woman literally stands above. Corbett does not take her argument this far, instead stating that Lytton's masquerade 'made her own point of view more authentically if not wholly representative.'[62] Such a reading of the representative nature of Lytton's passing can be supported, though, by the fact that Lytton's book became an authoritative text that lower-class women used in their own depictions of prison, a conclusion further supported by the fact that Olive Schreiner dedicated *Woman and Labour* (1911) to Lytton.[63] And yet, as Thomas's reading shows, such a representation can cut two ways, for the authenticity that Corbett lauds is tied to Lytton, thereby belying the 'representative' nature of her text by making it an authority that suppresses, rather than enables, the voices of working-class suffragettes and prisoners. Indeed, Regenia Gagnier sees such a suppression as a generic figure of working-class autobiographies that deal closely with gender. Writing about nineteenth-century British examples of these texts, Gagnier argues that while their authors 'extensively adopted middle-class ideology,' and 'Although they attempt self-analysis,' still 'their experience cannot be analyzed in the terms of their acculturation. This gap between ideology and experience leads not only to the disintegration of the narrative' but also 'to the disintegration of personality itself.'[64] The use of Lytton's text as a model by working-class suffragette prison authors could, according to Gagnier's theory of textual production, lead to the disintegration of the working-class voice.

There is a further tension created through the use of what Green refers to as 'spectacular feminism,' that is, the textual and visual displays – including parades – that the suffragettes used for their political ends. While the elision of difference by the autocracy of the Pankhursts and the authority of Lytton's text may reinscribe the silencing of working-class women, the emphasis on difference, which Billington-Grieg espouses, could have equally damaging effects, since prisons function along lines of alienation and isolation, denying any form of prison community or even communication. In this context, Howlett notes that 'Difference was deadly; to be different was to be isolated, both experientially and politically.'[65] Smith sees such a dangerous difference as a possible result of the autobiographical strategy of 'self-fragmentation'; she writes, 'shattering the old notion of the unitary individual in favor of the split and multiply fragmented subject may not always serve emancipatory objectives; rather it may serve further oppressive agendas.'[66] Suffragette prison writing, including Lytton's text, is locked into a conundrum, where the elision of difference threatens to silence many women, but the emphasis on difference allows the continued destruction of feminist community, both of which, therefore, reproduce the ideological effects of the prison and the carceral city as a whole.

Lytton's prison narrative, I argue, is precisely an attempt to discuss and effectively remove the difficulties raised by such readings. Her effort to do so does not lie in her ability to make her upper-class voice authentic or to objectify 'Jane,' but, rather, relies on a decentring of her own authenticity and on a construction of her identity in which 'Constance' is as much an act as is 'Jane.' In order to make Jane representative of the working-class suffragette, *Prisons and Prisoners* must wash out the taint of privilege by erasing the identity of Constance. Mulvey-Roberts points to a similar movement throughout Lytton's life, in which she reacted 'against being a member of a family whose conspicuous display of wealth epitomized colonialism and aristocracy.' However, rather than allowing Lytton, in Mulvey-Roberts's words, 'to go beyond empathy to identification'[67] with working-class women, and rather than solely reinscribing 'class difference through discriminatory gazes,'[68] *Prisons and Prisoners* instead lends Jane a voice by trying to remove that of Constance. Lytton's inscription of the 'V' on her body was an early attempt at such an erasure, because this act of rewriting herself as a member of the larger suffragette community is, in some ways, a 'violent splitting of the subject of her autobiography' which 'can better be read as violence against herself than against the object(s) of her mimicry' of the working class.[69]

I would take this splitting one step further. In opposition to Mulvey-Roberts's assertion that 'Through incarceration the image [Lytton] held of her own imprisoned self could eventually be released,' I argue that Jane's ordeal gives her a voice, but results in the erasure of Constance.[70] The final three chapters of the text function to remove Lytton's claim to authorship and, indeed, to any form of action. Chapters 14 and 15, 'The Home Office' and 'The Conciliation Bill,' are composed primarily of quotations from newspapers, letters, and medical and governmental reports, with most of the original text serving solely to introduce the other material. The last chapter, 'Holloway Prison Revisited: My Fourth Imprisonment,' offers much less detailed descriptions than the earlier prison chapters and ends with depictions of the actions of others. In addition, we learn that Lytton suffers a stroke and is partially paralysed, resulting in her inability to serve the WSPU physically: 'From that day to this I have been incapacitated for working for the Women's Social and Political Union, but I am with them still with my whole soul' (335). Lytton's emphasis on the words and actions of others and her portrayal of her stroke are placed at the end of the narrative not only for reasons of chronology, but also for the purpose of removing Constance Lytton's voice from the authoritative prominence of the narrative's conclusion. *Prisons and Prisoners* does engage in the communal project, but does not allow Constance's voice to become fully representative or determinative of that community. As Susan Stanford Friedman argues, 'In taking the power of words, of representation, into their own hands, women project onto history an identity that is not purely individualistic. Nor is it purely collective. Instead, this new identity merges the shared and the unique.'[71] Rather than reproducing through her class the ontological dominance and oppression of the masculine Enlightenment identity and the disciplinary practices involved with it, Lytton uses *Prisons and Prisoners* to enact a dual movement of self-silencing and self-creation that allows for an engagement with a communal statement that works against the imprisoning discourses of the patriarchy.

NOTES

1 P.Q. Hirst details this reconstruction, writing that 'Prison regimes were intended ... to produce a self-governing and industrious' subject who exhibited 'orderly habits.' P.Q. Hirst, 'The Concept of Punishment,' in *A Reader on Punishment*, ed. R.A. Duff and David Garland (Oxford: Oxford University Press, 1994), 277. The 'self-governing' aspect of this reformed subject points to the prison project's relationship with dominant constructions of the Enlightenment individual, the 'undivided and whole' person who is the source of 'conscious action.' Paul Smith, *Discerning the Subject* (Minneapolis: University of Minnesota Press, 1988), xxxiii–xxxiv.
2 Michel Foucault, 'Technologies of the Self,' in *Technologies of the Self: A Seminar with Michel Foucault*, ed. Luther H. Martin, Huck Gutman, and Patrick H. Hutton (Amherst: University of Massachusetts Press, 1988), 18.
3 Martin J. Wiener, *Reconstructing the Criminal: Culture, Law, and Policy in England, 1830–1914* (Cambridge: Cambridge University Press, 1990), 379–80.
4 John M. Sloop, *The Cultural Prison: Discourse, Prisoners, and Punishment* (Tuscaloosa: University of Alabama Press, 1996), 60.

5 1912 Fabian tract, quoted in Wiener, *Reconstructing the Criminal*, 379.
6 For Foucault's discussion of this use of prison discipline, and its relation to larger social processes, see his *Discipline and Punish: The Birth of the Prison*, trans. Alan Sheridan (New York: Vintage, 1979), esp. 231–56, 293–308. For discussions of the social history of the prison, see, in addition to Foucault and the others mentioned, David Garland, *Punishment and Modern Society: A Study in Social Theory* (Chicago: University of Chicago Press; Oxford: Clarendon Press, 1990); Michael Ignatieff, *A Just Measure of Pain: The Penitentiary in the Industrial Revolution, 1750–1850* (New York: Pantheon, 1978); and Christopher Harding and Richard W. Ireland, *Punishment: Rhetoric, Rule, and Practice* (New York: Routledge, 1989).
7 Constance Lytton, *Prisons and Prisoners: Some Personal Experiences* (London: William Heinemann, 1914), 86–7. Subsequent references to this text will be cited parenthetically.
8 Barbara Green, *Spectacular Confessions: Autobiography, Performative Activism, and the Sites of Suffrage 1905–1938* (New York: St Martin's Press, 1997), 67.
9 June Purvis summarizes some of these readings, as well as many of the prison narratives, in her article 'The Prison Experiences of the Suffragettes in Edwardian Britain,' *Women's History Review* 4.1 (1995): 103–33.
10 The WSPU was formed in 1903 by Emmeline Pankhurst, whose daughter, Christabel, would effectively go on to lead the group for the next ten years. Not being satisfied with the Liberal government's continued inaction on the issue of women's suffrage, the WSPU began a militant campaign in 1905. The militants were subsequently labelled 'suffragettes' by the press in order to differentiate them from such groups as the National Union of Women's Suffrage Societies, who avoided 'illegal' action, and were generally labelled 'suffragists.' The militants appropriated the derogatory term, with the WSPU even naming one journal the *Suffragette*. For a discussion of the complexities of these terminological distinctions see Green, *Spectacular Confessions*, 185, note 1; Gertrude Colmore offers a contemporary depiction of the differences between 'suffragette' and 'suffragist' in *Suffragettes: A Story of Three Women* (London: Pandora, 1984, rpt. of *Suffragette Sally*, 1911), 21, 24, 43–56, 60–1. The *Suffragette* also discusses the difference, in a brief 1914 editorial titled 'Suffragist or Suffragette?':

> We have all heard of the girl who asked what was the difference between a Suffragist and a Suffragette, as she pronounced it, and the answer made to her that the 'Suffragist jist wants the vote, while the Suffragette means to get it.' The matter has attracted some attention in the ordinary Press, and the 'Yorkshire Post' says, after dealing with the origin of the word 'Suffragette':

['] The militants of the Women's Social and Political Union, with their usual aptitude for effects, saw that the word with its suggestion of youth and daintiness was an asset rather than the reverse, and they promptly adopted it and paraded it.['] ('Suffragist or Suffragette?,' *Suffragette*, 1 May 1914: 56)

The history of women's suffrage in Britain and elsewhere has been detailed by several critics, including, Green, *Spectacular Confessions*, esp. 1–27; Susan Kingsley Kent, *Sex and Suffrage in Britain, 1860–1914* (Princeton: Princeton University Press, 1987); Jill Liddington, *The Long Road to Greenham: Feminism and Anti-Militarism in Britain since 1820* (London: Virago, 1989); Andrew Rosen, *Rise Up, Women! The Militant Campaign of the Women's Social and Political Union 1903–1914* (London: Routledge and Kegan Paul, 1974); and Lisa Tickner, *The Spectacle of Women: Imagery and the Suffrage Campaign 1907–14* (Chicago: University of Chicago Press, 1988). Also see Sandra Stanley Holton, *Suffrage Days: Stories from the Women's Suffrage Movement* (New York: Routledge, 1996). For early representations of the movement's history, see, among the myriad examples, Annie Kenney, *A Militant*, ed. Marie Mulvey Roberts and Tamae Mizuta (London: Routledge/Thoemmes, 1994, rpt. of *Memories of a Militant*, 1924); Jane Lewis, ed., *Before the Vote Was Won: Arguments for and against Women's Suffrage* (New York: Routledge and Kegan Paul, 1987); Joyce Marlow, ed., *Votes for Women: The Virago Book of Suffragettes* (London: Virago, 2000); Glenda Norquay, ed., *Voices and Votes: A Literary Anthology of the Women's Suffrage Campaign* (Manchester: Manchester University Press, 1995); and Emmeline Pethick-Lawrence, *My Part in a Changing World* (London: Victor Gollancz, 1938).

11 For discussions of these representations see, for example, Green, *Spectacular Confessions*; Norquay, *Voices and Votes*; Tickner, *Spectacle of Women*; and Caroline J. Howlett, 'Writing on the Body? Representation and Resistance in British Suffragette Accounts of Forcible Feeding,' in *Bodies of Writing, Bodies in Performance*, ed. Thomas Foster, Carol Siegel, and Ellen E. Berry (New York: New York University Press, 1996), 3–41.

12 Maroula Joannou, 'Suffragette Fiction and the Fictions of Suffrage,' in *The Women's Suffrage Movement: New Feminist Perspectives*, ed. Joannou and June Purvis (Manchester: Manchester University Press, 1998), 104. Anti-suffrage material appeared in papers and pamphlets, and even in novels, such as W. Burton Baldry's *From Hampstead to Holloway: Depicting the Suffragette in Her Happiest Moods* (London: John Ouseley, 1909).

13 Green, *Spectacular Confessions*, 84.

14 Norquay, *Voices and Votes*, 3.

15 For descriptions of these generic categories, see Norquay, *Voices and Votes*, 13–16, 39–40.
16 For discussions of gender and power in Victorian and Edwardian England see the collection edited by Linda M. Shires, *Rewriting the Victorians: Theory, History, and the Politics of Gender* (New York: Routledge, 1992), especially the following: Christina Crosby, 'Reading the Gothic Revival: "History" and *Hints on Household Taste*'; Ina Ferris, 'From Trope to Code: The Novel and the Rhetoric of Gender in Nineteenth-Century Critical Discourse'; and Judith Newton, 'Engendering History for the Middle Class: Sex and Political Economy in the *Edinburgh Review*.' Also see Rita Felski, *The Gender of Modernity* (Cambridge: Harvard University Press, 1995), and Angela Ingram and Daphne Patai's introduction to their edited volume, *Rediscovering Forgotten Radicals: British Women Writers, 1889–1939* (Chapel Hill: University of North Carolina Press, 1993).
17 Kenney describes this same meeting, writing that before Lytton's conversion to militancy, the upper-class woman was 'understanding and sympathetic even in her opposition' (*Militant*, 87).
18 Susan Hekman, 'Subjects and Agents: The Question for Feminism,' in *Provoking Agents: Gender and Agency in Theory and Practice*, ed. Judith Kegan Gardiner (Urbana: University of Illinois Press, 1995), 195.
19 Sidonie Smith, 'Resisting the Gaze of Embodiment: Women's Autobiography in the Nineteenth Century,' in *American Women's Autobiography: Fea(s)ts of Memory*, ed. Margo Culley (Madison: University of Wisconsin Press, 1992), 76.
20 Ibid.
21 Green, *Spectacular Confessions*, 31. Baldry's anti-suffrage novel depicts just such an 'unruly feminine crowd': 'Trafalgar Square was crowded with women. Never had London seen many of the unfair sex congregated in one place before. And London was annoyed for it wanted to get home to its tea – and the huge crowd had stopped the traffic. ... There was not a smile among the whole of that assembly. All their faces looked as though they were draped in black.' The crowd then begins a deputation, leading to a conflict with the police, which makes the statue of 'Poor Lord Nelson nearly [fall] off his monument!' (Baldry, *From Hampstead to Holloway*, 119–21, 123).
22 Comparing these popular depictions of suffragettes to the representation of rape, Howlett writes that such an elision of violence 'is associated with a displacement of the violence, which is attributed to the raped woman rather than to the rapist' (Howlett, 'Writing on the Body,' 11–12). Furthering this displacement, 'Images of women being punished or silenced were ... a staple of contemporary cartoon humour'; 'Ridicule' of the suffragettes and comic

denials of their abuse at the hands of the police were used as 'potent weapon[s] in the maintenance of hegemony' (Tickner, *Spectacle of Women*, 163).

23 Henry David Thoreau, 'Resistance to Civil Government,' in *Reform Papers*, ed. Wendell Glick (Princeton: Princeton University Press, 1973), 69. Lytton begins the chapter 'Jane Warton' with another quotation from 'Resistance to Civil Government,' which she alters to make gender nonspecific: 'Under a Government which imprisons any unjustly, the true place for a just man (or woman) is also a prison' (234; Thoreau, 'Resistance,' 76). In the following chapter, 'Walton Gaol, Liverpool,' she recounts that while imprisoned as Jane Warton she wrote the same phrase, along with 'Votes for Women' and a biblical passage, on her cell wall (264). In an unpublished letter (dated 10 January 1908) kept in the British Library, Lytton tells a Mr Broadbent that Thoreau is one of her 'favourite authors' (the letter is folded into the Library's copy of *Marah*, a book of poetry written by her father, Robert Bulwer-Lytton, under the pseudonym Owen Meredith [3rd ed., London: Longmans, 1893]). For a discussion of Thoreau's essay in relation to the nineteenth-century prison and prison writing, see my '"They locked the door on my meditations": Thoreau and the Prison House of Identity,' *Genre: Forms of Discourse and Culture* 35 3/4 (2002): 449–78.

24 The pamphlet Lytton refers to is her *'No Votes for Women': A Reply to Some Recent Anti-Suffrage Publications* (London: A.C. Fifield, 1909).

25 Mary Jean Corbett, *Representing Femininity: Middle-Class Subjectivity in Victorian and Edwardian Women's Autobiographies* (Oxford: Oxford University Press, 1992), 165.

26 Marie Mulvey-Roberts describes the social position of Lytton's family in some detail in her article, 'Militancy, Masochism, or Martyrdom? The Public and Private Prisons of Constance Lytton,' in *Votes for Women*, ed. June Purvis and Sandra Stanley Holton (London: Routledge, 2000), esp. 162–3.

27 Wiener, *Reconstructing the Criminal*, 309.

28 Mulvey-Roberts, 'Militancy, Masochism, or Martyrdom,' 160.

29 Green, *Spectacular Confessions*, 54.

30 Foucault, *Discipline*, 307–8.

31 Green, *Spectacular Confessions*, 58. Some contemporary observers also criticized Lytton in this way: a 1914 editorial in the *Egoist* (unattributed, but likely written by Dora Marsden) tries to 'make clear' to Lytton and others who are 'Saviours' that they 'are misguided more than willingly by erring; that their avocation is futile and distressful; that they in concrete fact actually spoil the landscape for those whom they believe they serve.' 'Views and Comments,' in *Egoist: An Individualist Review*, 10.1 (15 May 1914): 184. For a discussion of

some other, much more positive public responses to Lytton's story, see Sue Thomas, 'Scenes in the Writing of "Constance Lytton and Jane Warton, Spinster": Contextualising a Cross-Class Dresser,' *Women's History Review* 12 (2003), esp. 61–5.
32 Green, *Spectacular Confessions*, 62.
33 Chris Waters, *British Socialists and the Politics of Popular Culture, 1884–1914* (Manchester: Manchester University Press, 1990), 167.
34 Green, *Spectacular Confessions*, 99.
35 Susan Kingsley Kent cites one medical doctor's opinion that the suffragettes' militancy was the result of a '"mental disorder" caused by "physiological emergencies" within their reproductive systems.' See *Gender and Power in Britain, 1640–1990* (New York: Routledge, 1999), 269. Lytton's attack on the medical gaze strongly echoes that of Charlotte Perkins Gilman, especially as portrayed in 'The Yellow Wallpaper.' Lytton refers to reading Gilman's *The Man-Made World* during her last imprisonment (333). Gilman's narrator in 'The Yellow Wallpaper' equates the pseudo-medical 'rest cure' with imprisonment in order to expose the oppression of traditional gender roles. Charlotte Perkins Gilman, 'The Yellow Wallpaper,' in *Daughters of Decadence: Women Writers of the* 'Fin de Siècle,' ed. Elaine Showalter (New Brunswick, N.J.: Rutgers University Press, 1993), 98–117. So too does Lytton expose the hypocrisy of the medical profession's classification of women in order to highlight the specific oppression of the prison and the larger social subjugation of women. At one point, Lytton sarcastically reminds the governor and the prison doctor that 'prison was not a "rest cure"' (145).
36 Foucault, 'The Politics of Health in the Eighteenth Century,' in *Power/Knowledge: Selected Interviews and Other Writings 1972–1977*, ed. Colin Gordon, trans. Colin Gordon, Leo Marshall, John Mepham, and Kate Soper (New York: Pantheon, 1980), 166.
37 Joannou ('Suffragette Fiction,' 110) notes that the phrase 'no surrender' was 'made famous by the militant suffragette Mary Leigh,' who, as Michelle Myall writes, was 'a working-class suffragette.' Myall, '"No Surrender!": The Militancy of Mary Leigh, a Working-Class Suffragette,' in *The Women's Suffrage Movement: New Feminist Perspectives*, ed. Maroula Joannou and June Purvis (Manchester: Manchester University Press, 1998), 174. For a general overview of working-class involvement in suffragette activity, see Purvis, 'Prison Experiences.'
38 See Wiener, *Reconstructing the Criminal*, 310–13.
39 Howlett, 'Writing on the Body,' 6.
40 Ibid., 5, 7. The Home Secretary's report to which I refer is Departments of

States and Official Bodies, Home Office, 'Suffragist Women Prisoners,' 18 December 1909, in *Home Office Papers and Memoranda,* 1889–1910.

41 For further analysis of this use of institutional language in a prison context, see my 'Discovering Identity in James Tyman's *Inside Out: An Autobiography of a Native Canadian,*' *English Studies in Canada* 26.4 (2000): 473–92, as well my essay on Thoreau ('"They locked"').

42 While my use of the word 'performance' in this context recalls Judith Butler's theoretical reading of the linguistic category of the performative in terms of gender, I am using the term in its more mundane dress. Butler's theoretical frame, in which gender is itself an unconscious performative social structure, could provide a valuable reading of Lytton's text, not only in terms of gender but also of class. In my more general use of the word, Lytton's act of becoming Jane is performative in that she is Jane Warton as far as society is concerned – the various signs she uses to represent the working class are in themselves the act that makes her Jane Warton in the eyes of others. Unlike Butler's performative, Lytton's sign/act is very much a conscious one. See Judith Butler, 'Imitation and Gender Insubordination,' in *Inside/Out,* ed. Diana Fuss (New York: Routledge, 1991), 13–31.

43 Howlett, 'Writing on the Body,' 31.

44 'Suffragist Women Prisoners,' *Home Office Papers and Memoranda.*

45 Mulvey-Roberts, 'Militancy, Masochism, or Martyrdom,' 167.

46 As Mulvey-Roberts writes, 'By embracing anonymity through her Jane Warton disguise, Lytton was better equipped not only to identify with women across the class divide but also to draw attention to the ordeals endured by forgotten women' ('Militancy, Masochism, or Martyrdom,' 162).

47 Shoshana Felman, *What Does a Woman Want? Reading and Sexual Difference* (Baltimore: Johns Hopkins University Press, 1993), 14.

48 Lytton's dual subjectivity functions against Maud Ellmann's assertion that, despite the hunger strikers' 'refus[al] to be influenced by the authorities ... their sufferings reveal that this denial of the other necessarily entails the isolation and annihilation of the self.' Ellmann, *The Hunger Artists: Starving, Writing, and Imprisonment* (Cambridge: Harvard University Press, 1993), 93. The value of Ellmann's construction of 'hunger artists' (women who use self-starvation as a means of gaining power) is belied by her occasional denial of historical context and textual evidence in order to further an overly general psychoanalytic point. This lends to potential misreadings of hunger strikes. For example, after discussing Lytton's text, she writes, 'Nonetheless, it is hard to silence the suspicion, unwelcome as it is, that these women are obeying an unconscious *wish* to be force-fed and to experience the shattering of subjectivity it entails. Indeed, what makes these episodes particularly harrow-

ing is that they reawaken a trauma familiar to us all. Our first experience of eating is force-feeding: as infants, we were fed by others and ravished by the food they thrust into our jaws. We eat, therefore, in order to avenge ourselves against this rape ... *All eating is force-feeding*' (35–6). The slippage between the forcible feeding of the suffragettes (an act of violence largely without value as a food source) and the everyday feeding of a child could be seen as dangerously denying the violence perpetrated against these women. The pathologizing of 'all eating' also could be read as denying the suffering of people who have eating disorders, whom Ellmann also discusses. Mulvey-Roberts offers a more contextualized reading of Lytton as a masochist, and similarly notes that 'Ellmann is over-stating the case' (Mulvey-Roberts, 'Militancy, Masochism, or Martyrdom,' 179).

49 Howlett, 'Writing on the Body,' 9.
50 Corbett, *Representing Femininity*, 161.
51 Howlett, 'Writing on the Body,' 7.
52 Mary G. Mason, 'The Other Voice: Autobiographies of Women Writers,' in *Life/Lines: Theorizing Women's Autobiographies*, ed. Bella Brodzki and Celeste Schenk (Ithaca: Cornell University Press, 1988), 22.
53 Caren Kaplan, 'Resisting Autobiography: Out-Law Genres and Transnational Feminist Subjects,' in *De/Colonizing the Subject: The Politics of Gender in Women's Autobiography*, ed. Sidonie Smith and Julia Watson (Minneapolis: University of Minnesota Press, 1992), 121.
54 Sidonie Smith writes that traditional autobiography 'involves a contractual obligation in which the autobiographer engages in a narrative itinerary of self-disclosure, retrospective summation, self-justification'; see *Subjectivity, Identity, and the Body: Women's Autobiographical Practices in the Twentieth Century* (Bloomington: Indiana University Press, 1993), 162. Felski sees the critique of the traditional autobiographical subject as a condition of what she refers to as feminist confessions. She writes, 'the shift toward a conception of communal identity which has emerged with new social movements such as feminism brings with it a modification of the notion of individualism as it is exemplified in the male bourgeois autobiography'; see Rita Felski, *Beyond Feminist Aesthetics: Feminist Literature and Social Change* (Cambridge: Harvard University Press, 1989), 93–4.
55 Corbett, *Representing Femininity*, 170.
56 Green, *Spectacular Confessions*, 90.
57 Billington-Grieg's and other dissidents' problems with the non-democratic practices of the WSPU led to the formation in 1907 of the Women's Freedom League. See Claire Eustance, 'Meanings of Militancy: The Ideas and Practice of Political Resistance in the Women's Freedom League, 1907–14,'

in *The Women's Suffrage Movement: New Feminist Perspectives*, ed. Maroula Joannou and June Purvis (Manchester: Manchester University Press, 1998), 51. Billington-Grieg's questioning of the WSPU looks forward to contemporary critiques of patriarchal culture – a culture which still exists and in which, as Judith Kegan Gardiner writes, 'the woman laborer [is] all too often exploited and ignored.' 'Introduction,' in *Provoking Agents: Gender and Agency in Theory and Practice*, ed. Gardiner (Urbana: University of Illinois Press, 1995), 3.

58 Corbett, *Representing Femininity*, 173.
59 Sidonie Smith, 'Resisting.'
60 Victor Brombert, 'The Happy Prison: A Recurring Romantic Metaphor,' in *Romanticism: Vistas, Instances, Continuities*, ed. David Thorburn and Geoffrey Hartman (Ithaca: Cornell University Press, 1973), 62–79.
61 Thomas, 'Scenes in the Writing,' 60.
62 Corbett, *Representing Femininity*, 169.
63 On this use of Lytton's text, see Howlett, 'Writing on the Body,' 33. On Schreiner's dedication, see Felski, *Gender*, 156.
64 Regenia Gagnier, *Subjectivities: A History of Self-Representation in Britain, 1832–1920* (Oxford: Oxford University Press, 1991), 45–6.
65 Howlett, 'Writing on the Body,' 36.
66 Sidonie Smith, *Subjectivity*, 155–6.
67 Mulvey-Roberts, 'Militancy, Masochism, or Martyrdom,' 162–3.
68 Thomas, 'Scenes in the Writing,' 65.
69 Howlett, 'Writing on the Body,' 34.
70 Mulvey-Roberts, 'Militancy, Masochism, or Martyrdom,' 161. Shortly after making this point, Mulvey-Roberts writes that 'the secularised religiosity that pervaded the WSPU ... filled an emotional void for Constance following an unhappy love affair' (161). Mulvey-Roberts makes this point within the overall context of her strong efforts to 'break[] down the hagiographic approach' that she sees in some readings of Lytton's text and life ('Militancy, Masochism, or Martyrdom,' 176). Even within this context, though, and despite the overall excellence of her analysis, the phrasing of the statement above could risk reducing Lytton's motives for her suffrage activities to gendered stereotypes.
71 Susan Stanford Friedman, 'Women's Autobiographical Selves: Theory and Practice,' in *The Private Self: Theory and Practice of Women's Autobiographical Writings*, ed. Shari Benstock (Chapel Hill: University of North Carolina Press, 1988), 40.

CHAPTER 2

Form and Authority in Russian Serf Narratives

John MacKay

It has been argued that autobiography cannot be regarded as a 'literary genre,' inasmuch as the term 'genre' refers to distinct, consistent, and recognizable formal properties allowing for discriminations between 'kinds' of imaginative writing.[1] And apart from assuming the presence of narrative chronology itself – and certainly keeping in mind chronology's signal malleability, how often it's subjected to condensation and projection into flashes forward and back – it's true that we don't find it easy to map autobiography onto any of the standard narrative genres. Of course, even narrative temporality can be abandoned for long stretches within autobiographies. Augustine provides perhaps the best example, as he stops his narrative of spiritual/political struggle for an extended meditation on nothing less than – temporality itself.

In part, the problem has to do with the traditional subordination of autobiography to the representation of 'interesting' social and historical milieux. Such subordination often yields a wedding of life-writing to some larger narrative paradigm, or what Bakhtin in a related context calls biographical 'rubrics.'[2] Thus, the famed or inveterate traveller tells a story closely linked with the rhythms of specific journeys; the soldier writes in accordance (or, more rarely, out of accordance) with some public narrative of specific war; the celebrated detective recounts his famous cases 'from within,' and so on. Autobiography, it might be said, has no formal genre, but is a kind of receptacle – though not, to be sure, an infinitely capacious one – in which narrative types can find temporary lodging. In a sense, therefore, the 'fictionalizing' of autobiography begins prior to its composition, and perhaps especially when the writer in question is a famous person: that person has narrational promises to keep to his or her public.

This points to another, less formal aspect of genre broadly considered, namely its role in defining 'horizons of expectations.' Fredric Jameson, developing one of Northrop Frye's ideas, has called genres 'literary *institutions*, or social contracts between a writer and a specific public, whose function is to specify the proper use of a particular cultural artifact.'[3] This other aspect, which we might call (following Jameson) the 'contractual imperative' of genre, assuredly does have a place within ordinary conceptions of autobiography, although the demands of life-writing are of a different, severer and more epistemological kind than those required by any merely generic template (which mainly come down to questions of subject matter and style, or literary conventions as such). For what is expected of the autobiography, of course, is truth: not just any old truth, but truth about the writing subject, about what made him or her what he or she is. This shifts the orientation of autobiography away from the literary and towards (on the one hand) the historical, the political, and the legal, and (on the other) towards the philosophical (the 'ontology of the self'). The autobiographical declaration is intended to validate the author as a public authority, as one whose voice is at once veracious, unique, and comprehensible, and who can even be taken in turn by readers/listeners as a figure for *their* understanding of world and self – as a new genre of subjectivity, in other words.[4]

Within most theoretical accounts of autobiography, we detect a tendency to separate the two sides of 'genre,' putting narrative shape on one side, contractual or performative aspirations on the other. Thus Bakhtin, in his account of ancient biography and autobiography (in the third section of the great essay on the chronotope),[5] divides the 'two essential types of autobiography in classical Greece' into an opposition of predominantly *narrative* and predominantly *performative*. The first type, the 'Platonic,' centres on 'the life course of one seeking true knowledge,' passing 'from self-confident ignorance, self-critical skepticism, self-knowledge and ultimately authentic knowing.'[6] The form of the writing is that of a journey, a 'course' or 'path,' ranging over time and space and 'broken down into precise and well-marked epochs or steps.'[7] The second type, the 'rhetorical' autobiography, is grounded not in the chronotope of the 'path' but rather that of the Athenian *agora* or public square, the site of political debate, and the place where verbal tribute (*encomium*) was paid to 'civic and political *acts*.'[8] Here the dominant metaphor is not one of travel but of revelation or laying-bare. Bakhtin stresses the punctual, political, and (most of all) public nature of this kind of writing: 'In ancient times the autobiographical and biographical self-consciousness of an individual and his life was first laid bare and shaped in the public square. ... To be exterior meant to be for others, for the collective, for one's own people. A man was utterly exteriorized, but within a human element, in the human medium of his own people. Therefore, the *unity* of a man's externalized wholeness was of a *public* nature.'[9] The rhetorical autobiography is thus precisely an act, a happening, and the 'authorization' of the speaker by and through the public mirroring of that 'externalized wholeness.'

Expressed in this way, the formal and performative sides of autobiography remain conceptually separate, divided by the all-too-familiar barriers separating 'intrinsic' and 'extrinsic.' Contemporary theories of subjectivity, however, enable us to bring the structural and the rhetorical aspects of autobiography into a speculative (i.e., conflictual) unity. Aspects of this relationship have indeed been traced out by earlier, dialectically inflected literary criticism. For example, Marxist critics have shown how and why some forms of expression (i.e., the bourgeois novel) emerge as 'authoritative' at specific times and places, while demonstrating at the same time how 'authority' in turn depends on expressive forms both for self-representation and to reproduce itself on the ideological level.[10] Much recent theory, however, has stressed the instability of the relationship of (political, legal, patriarchal) authority to the forms it uses to underwrite and propagate it. The non-convergent multiplicity of interpellating authorities, and the diversity of forms available, make possible a host of *qualifications* of existing norms. Still operating within the Marxist tradition (and with a method enriched by psychoanalysis), Göran Therborn provides one of the clearest summaries of this dynamic, stretched between the poles of 'subjection' and 'qualification':

> The formation of humans by every ideology, conservative or revolutionary, oppressive or emancipatory, according to whatever criteria, involves a process simultaneously of subjection and of qualification. The amorphous libido and manifold potentialities of human infants are subjected to a particular order that allows or favors certain drives and capacities, and prohibits or disfavors others. At the same time, through the same process, new members become qualified to take up and perform (a particular part of) the repertoire of roles given in the society into which they are born, including the role of possible agents of social change. ... Although qualified by ideological interpellations, subjects also become qualified to 'qualify' these in return, in the sense of specifying them and modifying their range of application.[11]

There can be no question that authority, stretching up to the state and down to basic structures of kinship, permeates the autobiographical process from the very beginning, and partially determines the 'rubrics' with which the autobiographer writes him- or herself.[12] And yet subjection never creates a 'whole' subject, and at the same time provides subjects with tools whereby they might fabricate alternative models of identity. Sidonie Smith summarizes the consequences of 'qualification' for our thinking about life-writing: '[T]he autobiographical subject finds him/herself on multiple stages simultaneously, called to heterogeneous recitations of identity. These multiple calls never align perfectly. Rather they create spaces or gaps, ruptures, unstable boundaries, incursions, excursions, limits and their transgressions. ... Through tactical dis/identifications the autobiographical subject adjusts, redeploys, resists, transforms discourses of autobiographical identity.'[13] In other words, the subject does not stand within the Bakhtinian public square, but rather *happens* within it; and mutations of any given chronotope do not emerge independently of the qualifications of subjects who are always living within several 'time-spaces.'

'Public square' is just a metaphor, of course, and it suits the Athenian context insofar as it points to the fluidity of audience and speaker in the *agora*: any participant could at any moment potentially be considered as part of the 'public' *or* as self-baring 'individual.' However, there is another, related metaphor more suited to the kind of writing I'll be focusing on in this paper, namely autobiographical narratives produced approximately between 1785 and 1911 by Russian serfs and former serfs. I would call this the trope of 'standing before judgment.' This heuristic preference has to do with more than the sheer fact that some of the earliest serf narratives are in fact legal depositions (including the very earliest I'll be discussing, Nikolai Smirnov's 1785 'Autobiography'), as a number of the earliest New World slave narratives also are.[14] Autobiography virtually always bears the anxious traces of the 'apologia pro vita sua'; there is a (usually subliminal) appeal to some kind of institutional authority – whether the institution be a readership, a literal judge, or a divine judge.[15] The setting of *judgment* allows for productive reversals and complications, especially when the supposedly superior, 'judging' position of the (hypothetical) auditors paradoxically exposes them *as* judges, rather than as 'neutral observers.' This allows the autobiographer to point to dissonance and contradiction, as readers themselves – who are no less assailed by 'multiple calls' of interpellation – fall under the scrutiny of some 'outside term' of evaluation.

Already in the early eighteenth century,[16] the majority of Russian autobiographers (who were invariably members of the nobility) presented their 'lifetimes' as essentially coterminous with the time spent in government or military service. Consequently, the distance between the writing subject and legitimate authority almost collapses, as the autobiographical protagonists acted as near-functionaries of law, army, or state. In an excellent article on the roots of autobiography in Russia, Alois Schmücker points out how some eighteenth-century autobiographers saw their work in life-writing as a virtual continuation of their state service. Memoirist Petr Ivanovich Rychkov (1712–77) argued that all noblemen in service should write their memoirs for the sake of their 'usefulness' to those who would occupy the same positions in the future.[17] Within their narratives, noblemen also linked the rich variety of their experiences and interests to their education and more general *Bildung*, thereby offering their recounted lives as a testimony to and culmination of the great state-driven projects of Enlightenment.[18] In these texts, the writing of self is at once an affirmation of and contribution to a larger 'public sphere' within which the autobiographer works.

What happens, however, when 'consubstantiality' with authority is less easy to assert; when a radical limitation of the subject's proximity to authority is an essential part of the way that subject is defined socially? This, of course, was the situation of those rare Russian serfs who wrote autobiographical texts, inasmuch as they wrote them *as* serfs.[19] Like other people in bondage in modern times, Russian serfs were largely illiterate, rural, usually very far removed from the centres of power, and for the most part prevented from voicing effective protest. Also like other people in bondage, Russian serfs had in a sense already been 'judged' by authority and found wanting; thus serfdom constitutes an unusually pure example of Orlando Patterson's 'extrusive' mode of slave recruitment, where the slave is *an insider who has fallen*.[20] Indeed, life-writing by serfs constituted in itself a kind of affront to authority.

It should be added that this writing lacked the supplementary support of an explicit *alternative* secular authority, like an abolitionist movement.[21] Nonetheless, Russian serfs did seek out other ways to align themselves with, and thereby *qualify*, 'authority,' whether earthly (the Tsar, the peasantry as a whole) or unearthly (Christ, religious history). That is to say, the serf, like any other autobiographer, could both appeal to and make use of some supposedly common substratum of belief as the basis for a justification of the autobiographical project. But where was this 'substratum' to be found within the reality of bondage, and how might it be manipulated to clear some greater space of freedom for the serf? The remainder of this essay is dedicated to outlining how various strategies of qualification affect the shape that these autobiographies take. Those rhetorical strategies – including appeals to religion, to the 'myth of the Tsar,' to natural propensities, and to quasi-bardic powers of insight and prophecy – constitute the dialectical link between form and authority within these Russian serf texts, and frequently work to disrupt the constructions of subjectivity imposed by the dominant ideology.

The four works I'll be examining were composed between 1785 and roughly 1911, and are very diverse in character.[22] Chronologically, they stretch from Nikolai Smirnov's 1785 deposition[23] to the long narrative poem *News about Russia* (composed by the anonymous peasant poet 'P' sometime before 1849),[24] to Nikolai Shipov's 1881 account of his repeated attempts to escape bondage (culminating in his liberation in 1845, highly unusual for being mediated by a period of captivity in Daghestan),[25] and finally to M.E. Vasilieva's fragmentary account of her girlhood in serfdom on an estate near Voronezh (1911).[26] Through an analysis of the form of these writings in relation to authority I aim to highlight some of the salient 'deep structural' characteristics of these texts. This is a challenge in more ways than one: none of the texts I'm looking at has been considered as a 'kind of writing' or collected (even in Russian), much less used directly as material for novels in the manner that Harriet Beecher Stowe used slave narratives for the construction of *Uncle Tom's Cabin*. Of course, serfs do appear in nineteenth-century Russian prose works as 'characters' – but *that*, of course, is a very different kind of appropriation of the bondsman's voice from what we see in *Uncle Tom's Cabin*, which reworked actual slave testimony to its own ends (as revealed in the famous 'Key').[27] My use of the term 'serf narratives' is thus informed by the generic categorization of the 'slave narrative' within studies of African-American literature. I concentrate almost exclusively here on the far less well-known Russian productions, but it will be important to understand what we might call the contrasting 'mechanisms' of slave and serf narratives (as distinct from their obviously different content) in order to give theoretical breadth to the notion of 'slave narrative' as such. Eventually, comparative reflection on slave/serf narratives might have something to contribute to our notions of autobiography more generally, and in what follows I make a few gestures in that direction.

I would make a preliminary division of the serfs' strategies of qualification into three categories: alignment with or towards dominant authority; alignment with only a select part of that authority; and alignment with some other (hypothetical) authority against the dominant. Falling into the first category are appeals to religion, to common humanity, to cultural commonality, and to some shared sense of the autobiographer's 'bardic' or writerly authority. The second category, crucial in Russia, primarily concerns the use made by the peasantry of the 'myth of the Tsar': the idea that the Tsar was the father/protector of the peasantry, *their* leader rather than that of the mostly hated nobility.[28] Finally, we find indications that the narrators sometimes grope towards a specifically 'serf peasant' understanding of the culture and mode of production in which they live. This is effected, first, through the thick insertion of testimonies from other serfs into a putative 'autobiography,' and second, by characterizing the entire nobility as 'other' in the sense of *alien*, as non-Russian.

This is not to say that these categories can provide a scheme for a truly exhaustive account of the narratives. As my final example (M.E. Vasilieva's text) will show, writings from the late post-emancipation period require a different conception of form and authority, one that demands in turn an abandonment or radical modification of the 'standing before judgment' metaphor. Nonetheless, the categories both help to sketch out the ideological perimeters of serf thought and enable some preliminary comparisons with what we find in the US South. For example, American slaves upheld no equivalent to a 'myth of the Tsar' but did indeed look, in John Ernest's words, 'for the authority of a transcendent author to support their own narratives of progress, hope, responsibility, and community.'[29] Indeed, the relative degree of imaginative connection to the *state* – however fictive and mystified that connection might be – is one of the crucial features distinguishing the memoirs of Russian and US bondsmen, and is of great consequence for the manner in which they conceive of their individual and collective relationship to the place where they live.

II

Predictably enough, religious faith is the main ground of authority to which serf narrators – like many slave narrators – appeal. Divine authority has a unique flexibility and power: not only can it be assumed that 'God's will' carries weight for everyone involved; God is the God of judgment *and* of mercy, 'King of Kings' *and* protector of the meek. This breadth, this abstraction we might say, provides a shape for totality, a 'third term' through which the emergence of earthly authority might be understood. 'In the context of divine authority,' writes Albert J. Raboteau *à propos* of US slaves, 'the limited authority of any human was placed in perspective. By obeying the commands of God, even when they contradicted the commands of men, slaves developed and treasured a sense of moral superiority and actual moral authority over their masters.'[30] Faith, however, can also generate outsiders, namely infidels, those not 'consubstantial' with this most basic of unities; and rallying against the infidels is as internally binding an act (for a community of believers) as rallying for them is a disruptive and disunifying one. Taken together, all of these attributes help produce a kind of grid or topography with 'faith' at the centre, wherein a narrator can be situated at varying distances from the (not-ultimately-reachable) authority.

Such oscillations are crucial in Smirnov's autobiography, written in a 'God-forsaken' prison setting. Smirnov was a serf belonging originally to Andrei Mikhailovich Golitsyn (1729–70), a prominent member of one of the foremost Russian aristocratic families. All the villages belonging to this particular Golitsyn household were managed by Smirnov's father (also a serf, of course), who was able to pay for his son's education in (among other subjects) 'Russian grammar and spelling,' 'the basic rudiments of the French and Italian languages,' 'English, history, geography, mythology, iconology ... the rudiments of physics and chemistry ... draughtsmanship, painting, architecture, geodesics and the fundamentals of mathematics.' Unable to enrol in Moscow University, Smirnov studied informally with at least one professor from that institution, namely Semyon Desnitskii, the founder of Russian secular jurisprudence and a former student of Adam Smith in Glasgow. Clearly endowed with an extraordinary desire and aptitude for learning, Smirnov was in fact destined to work for his father, helping to manage the various villages as scribe and accountant. When his repeated requests for manumission were rejected one after another, he decided to flee, first stealing 3500 rubles from his father, then trying escape Russia by posing as 'the Italian merchant Camporesi.' He claims that he eventually hoped to join up with the three young Golitsyn sons, who were on a 'Grand Tour.' Deceived and robbed by a couple of con artists, Smirnov contracted an illness and was captured in St Petersburg. He indicates that he expected clemency. However, after pronouncing hanging as its initial verdict, the chamber of the criminal court decided that Smirnov should be given ten blows with the knout, have his nostrils ripped open, be branded (presumably on the forehead) and sent in shackles to perpetual hard labour in Riga. It was at this point that Smirnov composed his narrative, as both an explanation of his deeds and a desperate if rather ambivalent expression of penitence.

Of course, the exigencies of the deposition require that Smirnov speak of himself as having acted *in opposition to* God's will, in order to save his life. At its simplest, his story is one of his proximity to God, as he and God move closer to or further away from each other. The first mention of God within the narrative comes only at the point of action, after Smirnov has already suffered rebuff and resolved to flee: 'Finally, forgetting honour, the sacred duty of family, the laws of God and state, and turning my ear away from the wailings of conscience, I stole 3500 rubles from my father.' Here, though, 'the laws of God' are but one of the codices against which he transgresses. As he plunges further into 'crime' (including disguising himself as an army officer, itself a serious offence), and as family and society are left behind, the figure of 'God' absorbs the punishing authority into itself. But 'God,' as we will see, becomes a device with which the subject can convert (hostile) earthly verdicts into more self-legitimizing forms.

At the outset, Smirnov's God is subjectivized into a kind of presiding nemesis, enabling the terrified but still (as we will see later) fundamentally unrepentant narrator to acknowledge the Law while complicating his own guilt with an account of circumstances and an admission of folly. Smirnov moves to acknowledge the legitimacy of the divine 'Judge':

> At first this exploit [of theft and flight], the first step I had ever taken towards crime, succeeded in accord with God's will, and satisfied my desires in every particular; until I reached Pskov, I encountered no obstacles to my unhappy enterprise. But in that city righteous God, who takes vengeance against the dishonest and those who transgress his commandments, put a stumbling block in my unlawful path.

In fact, a certain ambiguity already clouds the representation of 'righteous God,' whose 'will' seems to sanction Smirnov's 'first step ... towards crime.' But God's apparent acquiescence, we learn, conceals a sternly judgmental attitude. Smirnov, adopting the defendant's posture, immediately provides the Judge with extenuating information that might mitigate the harshness of the sentence. Here the appeal is made to common human rather than religious sympathies:

> There I had the misfortune of encountering one of those cunning and artful people who, gifted from birth with all intellectual and physical qualities except honesty and wealth, live at the expense of their neighbors, and in the shrewdest way transfer into their own pockets the wealth of all those simpletons who happen to fall into their hands.

(The 'person' is a charming land-surveyor named Paul, who manipulates Smirnov and eventually robs him blind.) God, as it turns out, is appealed to both as judge and as just, as good and as 'all-knowing,' with the tacit implication that Smirnov's own earthly judges (and his readers) should follow suit.

This careful balance of explanation – hovering between a confession of guilt and a more 'empirical' explanation of failure – persists throughout the text:

> [Paul's] falsehearted amity was but a mask, concealing the perfidious intention of transferring that money, which I had secured through dishonest means myself, into his own pocket. My responsiveness [to him] was, by contrast, a consequence of my simple-heartedness and sincerity, as well as of the acquiescence of God, who had thus determined to lead me to the edge of that dreadful and bottomless abyss into which my unreflecting youth and haste had plunged me.

Here, Smirnov's insistence upon his own essential innocence – his 'simple-heartedness and sincerity' – nearly casts a shadow of judgment upon God himself, whose rigours seem excessive in light of the young serf's naïvely erring character. Yet God is by definition 'just,' of course, and so the trope of 'leading' Smirnov 'to the edge of the abyss' is at once a way for Smirnov to gain sympathy and to admit his guilt. God, who orders all things rightly but also sees into the hearts of men, offers Smirnov both the role of 'the justly accused' necessary for some minimal communication with his earthly accusers, and the possibility of qualifying that role.

It would seem, for instance, that he ascribes his downfall entirely to God when he identifies the sources of his Petersburg malady in divine, punitive action: 'Our almighty Creator, punishing me for my innumerable crimes, exacerbated my illness to such a degree, that it became impossible for me even to leave my room, much less set off on such a long trip.' At the same time, however, he reports that he had been sick *before* his trip – a nervous illness brought on by his failure to secure his manumission – and was generally of a 'weak constitution.' Again,

Smirnov uses religious rhetoric to admit wrongdoing, and appeals to human sympathy to elicit compassion; he is both transgressor and victim of circumstances.

This space between these two poles is filled at the end by God's sudden shift in posture from aloof and punitive to merciful, just as 'the most terrible hour arrived':

> Our almighty Creator looked with an eye of mercy on my sincere and clean-hearted regret, and accepted my ardent prayers, sent up to Him from the depths of my soul. Into the heart of the officer on duty there at the city prison, He instilled pity. The officer observed that I was already barely breathing, and postponed my transfer for a short time.

This led to the first postponement of Smirnov's sentence, and eventually to its entire cancellation.[31] Of course, the urgency driving his narrative – this is 'life-writing' in a literal sense – distinguishes it from most serf texts. But we can still discern within it several crucial functions of the 'God' trope: as the site of that moral knowledge to which the serf submits; as the prototype for a rigorous yet compassionate earthly justice; and as an authoritative form that creates a kind of meeting place for oppressor and oppressed, a form that accounts for the bondsman's inner life.

Prayer is perhaps the main conduit between the serf and 'the Lord,' as it is generally in discursive traditions concerning communication between humans and gods. God is commonly invoked at narrative cruxes, the prayer stalling the narrative like a new beginning (or threatened end), a reminder that the narrative would not ever have been written, were it not for outside support. Generally these incantations have a stereotypical quality, like these words 'quietly muttered' by Nikolai Shipov on the cusp of escaping from his Circassian captors, and after having just evaded the jaws of a wild and enormous mountain hog: 'Lord! Deliver Your sinful slave. Don't allow beasts or enemies to tear at my unclean body on alien ground. And bring me to stand at Your holy tomb in Jerusalem, so I may pour out all my heartfelt tears, for all Your rich and generous mercies.' Smirnov's entire text *is* a prayer, a double prayer spoken to divine and (mainly) earthly authority,[32] during the course of which the desperate bondsman tries to bring God 'on-side' without alienating the representatives of the law. This is possible because prayer (like God) is a 'property' shared by serfs and their masters; in different circumstances, it can become the site of tenser discursive struggle. I have in mind the wonderfully corrosive invective against the 'pious master' familiar from US slave narratives: Frederick Douglass's 'reverend slave-driver, Rigby Hopkins,' who 'prayed earlier, later, louder, and longer' than any other;[33] and Henry Bibb's open contrast between his own prayers for protection (against wolves, in this case), and those of the vicious Deacon who owns him:

> My little family were looking up to me for protection, but I could afford them none. And while I was offering up my prayers to that God who never forsakes those in the hour of danger who trust in him, I thought of Deacon Whitfield; I thought of his profession, and doubted his piety. I thought of his hand-cuffs, of his whips, of his chains, of his stocks, of his thumb-screws, of his slave driver and overseer, and of his religion; I also thought of his opposition to prayer meetings, and of his five hundred lashes promised me for attending a prayer meeting.[34]

Smirnov's 'prayer' is uttered in a different context entirely, of course, but it is worth noting that the open and ringing denunciation of specifically religious hypocrisy found in Douglass and Bibb is much harder to find in the Russian narratives. This is largely because religious life in Russia had quite different discursive and historical outlines: peasant religious practice was never forbidden in Russia under serfdom, nor could such a prohibition even have been contemplated; nor did opposition to bondage have anything like the combined religious-and-sectional quality so central to American abolitionism. In the US, the heightened volatility of religion as discursive weapon (along with slave authors' somewhat 'sectionally' protected status, of course, in non-slaveholding states, at least before the passage of the Fugitive Slave Act) enables the slave narrators to wrest away religion from their opponents, rather than (as in Smirnov's case) using it to shape some alternative and redemptive, yet publicly comprehensible, self-image.[35] On the other hand, the question of who owns, not 'true faith,' but the nation, becomes a more open field of ideological contention between serfs and masters.

The importance of the nation within the 'imaginary' of serfdom is well illustrated by Nikolai Shipov's remarkable 'multiple-captivity' narrative. Shipov (b. 1802) was a serf peasant who, along with his father, was much engaged in trading rams and other livestock. He attempted both flight and the purchase of himself and his family out of serfdom, to no avail. Shipov was literate, however, and in 1844 he found an odd statute in the ninth volume of the 'Code of Laws,' indicating that a serf captured by 'mountain bandits' would become free in perpetuity, along with his entire family, upon being liberated. Already accustomed to trading with non-Russian mountain peoples in the northern Caucasus, he deliberately fell into bondage on 8 February 1845, escaping his captors – and serfdom – eleven days later.

Shipov's prayers ('deliver your humble slave!') were thus substantially answered, though it's doubtful he ever got to Jerusalem; as strategies within the narrative, however, these prayers demonstrate a strong religious identification that persisted through the most trying of tribulations. That Shipov possesses a 'solid' peasant Orthodoxy is stressed throughout his travels, legal and illegal, and particularly at those moments when he encounters various religious 'others,' from Jews and Muslims to Orthodox dissenters/schismatics like the Old Believers and 'skoptsy' (self-castrators). In the passage below, he describes a moment during his eight-year-long flight from the home village (1832–40) when he and his wife ended up in a Bessarabian village (in present-day Moldova), waiting for foreign passports:

> [I] hired a Yid[36] to take us to the small town of Brichani. The sleigh-trail had already disappeared, but it was impossible to travel on wheels; it was, in short, that time of year when roads are bad, and only with difficulty did we make it to Brichani. It turned out that there wasn't a single Russian in the town – they were all Jews, but there was nothing to be done; we rented an apartment from a Jew. The room was highly unpleasant, with a heavy and peculiar smell; my wife had never seen such a nasty chamber, and it disgusted her. We lived there for over a week, and the boredom was unbearable. Shrovetide arrived, and somehow my wife contrived to bake *bliny*[37] – and that gave us both great pleasure.

While a Jewish merchant will later become Shipov's mentor and indispensable benefactor, we see here how Shipov presents himself as a profoundly traditional, 'mainstream' Russian man, for all his upwardly mobile strivings. After all, his liberation is based on an 'illegal' exploitation of Russian law, and the ruse, brilliant as it is, carries the risk of exposing the state and its laws to ridicule. This is a rhetorical danger that Shipov deftly avoids throughout. Though apparently 'knee-jerk' in character, Shipov's anti-Semitism also helps to seal his contemporary readers' sense of his allegiance to the hegemonic faith and the *patria* despite all of his transgressions.

Nonetheless, Shipov's very predicament leads him into contradictions between his professions of 'nationality' and his need to change his status within the 'nation.' His Circassian captors are at war with Russia (1845), and in a sense his escape from them is a heroic act of service to the fatherland – presumably, the desire to promote such heroism motivated the creation of the strange law that Shipov discovers. For this reason, his narrative has much of the shape and generic feel of a classic 'oriental captivity' narrative. Indeed, some of the Circassians reveal, during a card game called 'fools,' that they believe him to be a captured soldier: 'The Circassians played badly, but I played "the fool" deliberately; they were pleased [with my ineptitude] and laughed at me, saying "saldat ten'tiak" ("this soldier's a fool").' In Shipov we often sense strange doublings of the classic serf/slave tactic of 'playing dumb' to authority. In the course of executing a plan of enormous cunning, the serf is compelled at once to pretend to be a trader, to commit the 'foolish' act of falling into captivity, to seek opportunities to escape, and to 'play the fool' before his captors – the last being a performance for which he has had a lifetime to prepare. Shipov is anything but a fool, of course – he knowingly takes advantage of both Russian law and an imperialist war in order to win his 'personal' victory against the imperial nation, his own. Both the mountaineers and the Russian invaders become pawns in his deadly earnest game of hide-and-seek; his liminal situation, tense though it is, provides him with a wider range of discursive alternatives than he had enjoyed in the Russian heartland.

To be sure, Shipov in captivity never ceases to represent himself as a patriot and entrepreneur. On one occasion, left alone for just a moment by his captors, he makes a 'discovery' that reveals to him why the Russian incursions are so necessary. Here the patriot's and the tradesman's eyes fuse together:

> I sat there looking at the ground and suddenly noticed something shiny, like a little star. It struck me that this must be some kind of metal in mineral form! I thought: 'May God enable our Tsar quickly to subjugate Shamil and his plundering peoples, and to conquer this rebellious land, where no small amount of wealth and abundance might be found. If God wills it, an end will come to this never-ending fighting and bloodshed, and our Tsar will take possession of this wonderful land ...'

At the same time, the 'wonderful land' possesses attractions that unconsciously seem to draw Shipov's sympathies towards the Caucasian 'other.' An 'orientalized' sexuality plays its role here: Shipov is clearly entranced by the beauty of the wife of one of his captors' ('her fast-moving, fiery black eyes'), never failing to mention her bringing him his daily gruel; and the idea of alternative family structures comes to fascinate him, especially when he is invited to get married to a Caucasian woman and stay in the mountains forever. (He refuses on the quite correct grounds that he 'already had a wife and children, and that [Orthodox] law forbade marrying again with another wife still alive.') Shipov seems genuinely moved when he reports how his abductors, on their way back to deliver their catch, make a detour and stop to pay homage to their 'dead relatives' at the site of a village that had been annihilated by the Russians. The care with which Shipov reports on the familial bonds among his captors suggests that the mountaineers' life represents for him the kind of 'organic community' for which the serf can only yearn.

And at one crucial moment during the captivity, he reads the struggle of his 'enemies' as a struggle for liberty, in an interpretation that seems to beg for an allegorical reading:

> [One] Circassian glared at me fiercely, like a beast; it seemed that he wanted to devour me with his darting eyes. His glance was hardly a surprise to me, however, for only rarely did any of the savages look at me with pity or a smile. This was understandable. All mountain peoples had lived freely and independently from time immemorial; only with Russians did they have to struggle so continuously and for so long. During that time a lot of Russian blood had been spilt. But from among the mountain people, you might find only one of ten who hadn't had a grandfather, a father, a son, or some other relative killed by Russians. So how could a savage stare at me, other than with hate?

Although the Caucasians summarily vanish from the narrative (though not from Russian history) after Shipov's escape, it is tempting to read the passage as both a conventional assertion of oriental 'savagery' and as an expression of genuine fellow feeling. After all, his captors are also the underdogs in a colonial war with Russia, a war managed by nobles and fuelled by peasant cannon fodder. Indeed, I would suggest that we read Shipov's words as a 'screen' image of the *internal* colonization of peasant Russia itself by the elite: if we substitute 'nobility' for 'Russian' and 'peasantry' for 'mountain people,' we can clarify (albeit a bit crudely) the unconscious ideological roots of Shipov's sympathy. Here, the language of anthropological description betrays doubt about that state authority with which Shipov seeks to align himself.

It was possible, however, for serfs to take a more 'separatist' tack, by beginning with a clear distinction between their submission to divine authority and their compelled submission to landowners. The opening lines of the long narrative poem *News about Russia* make this distinction blatant:

News about Russia

Gathered from the life of the mir.[38]
From the deeds and words of the people
Set in verses
By the half-literate peasant P.,
Belonging in body to a landlord,
But in soul, to Christ.

Similarly, references to biblical history are used as frames for interpreting the predicament of Russian bondsmen in 'agonistic' ways that recall the subversions of religious rhetoric by such writers as Equiano, Douglass, and Bibb. *News about Russia* occasionally even deploys the great Mosaic mythology of bondage and deliverance so important in US slave religion:

by what
Strange turn of fate did Rus'[39] become so like
The ancient folk of Israel? And how
Were we enthralled in evil, the evil
Of Egyptian bondage? It would seem
That we are Christians, hardly devotees
Of idols – so whence came all these tyrants?
From our world they exclude the light
Of Christ, require that the people pray
To them and venerate, through them,
The golden calf.[40]

The speaker here is one of many anonymous peasant voices in the poem, a young serf man who functions as a kind of momentary 'double' for the narrator. *News about Russia* was written by a serf from the Iaroslavl' area, who refers to himself only as 'Petr O.' or 'P.' The tale is loosely centred on the serf narrator's failed attempt to marry a free peasant girl, but the simple frame-structure of the poem is richly complicated by the generous insertion of dream visions, songs, and especially 'side' narratives told in what appear to be semi-fictionalized voices other than the narrator's. (Thus, within a tale told by one character, another character will begin to tell a tale about someone else, who will also in turn set off on his or her own independent narrative, until the reader finds himself at several removes from the main narrator, 'P.') This proliferation of story can be confusing at times, as each tale threatens to sprout into a theoretically infinite number of branches. It also makes *News about Russia* into a kind of 'omnibus' testimonial work, where a host of serf voices are linked into a single structure – rather like the famous 'matrioshka' dolls, one inside the other.

The cumulative effect of the poem is the representation of a large, diverse peasant population united in its antipathy to the landowning class – a multi-voiced peasant *authority*. We might think of 'P''s creation as a narrative counterpart to the symbolic construction of African-American community achieved in Frederick Douglass's *Narrative*, when the 'root' given Douglass by the conjure man Sandy Jenkins (prior to Douglass's decisive physical encounter with Edward Covey) becomes a token of black people's collective opposition to white domination.[41] *News about Russia*'s strategies of qualification are grounded in both a sense of deprivation and a proprietary relationship to Russia, insofar as it characterizes landowners as radically 'other' and irredeemably depraved. Indeed, landowners are associated a few times with the Mongols, as in this ironic toast uttered by one of the narrator's neighbours:

'Let's drink to the court of Shemiaka,
And to our brave voivodes!
And to the blossoming of Asiatic customs,
And to the income taken from us by force!'[42]

The same movement can be seen when the narrator's father points to more ubiquitous Tatar 'impurities' within Russia, to the 'pagan blood (brought us by the yoke),' of which 'we've hardly been purged at all.'[43] Thus, apart from the constant and crucial appeals to the Tsar, the poem's ultimate addressee ('God and Tsar will be with us, / And the hearts of Russians will blossom'), the poem makes few appeals to any beliefs or qualities putatively shared by lord and peasant.

It stands in this respect opposed to Smirnov's narrative, where overt appeal is made to both religious and what we might call 'human' commonalities – notions of pleasure and pain, hope and disappointment, that might be assumed to be universal:

> I persevered in [a regime of home-learning] for a year or more, despite the fact that my studies were interrupted almost daily by various matters pertaining to the estate and the house. I would have gone on even longer if I hadn't been compelled to go to the master's village to help carry out various plans having to do with waste lands and settlements. ... Then, after returning to my father's house, I was occupied for several months with the government census. The result was that, for almost a year, I left my studies untouched, and forgot the better part of what I had begun to learn. ... In spite of my bad health I tried with all my strength to renew my now-lapsed studies. My efforts were fruitless, however, for every day I was compelled to write and copy orders and expense sheets for the village, to work on the account books, and to do many others things concerning the house and the [estates]. For these things I had not the slightest ability or inclination.

Even a serf, it is implied, has 'abilities' and 'inclinations' which merit consideration and which may even justify resistance; even a serf is 'also a man,' in the language of US abolitionists. How daring this strategy of obstinacy seems in the context of this deposition, seeking as it does to ward off a death sentence. Smirnov seems to assume in his audience a kind of ethic of 'self-realization,' as well as certain 'cultural values' which transcend in importance any rigorous commitment to serfdom. Indeed, in revealing the intentions behind his flight, he aligns himself with the 'Europeanizing,' 'meritocratic' and 'state service' culture of his immediate audience, of which of course he had an intimate and (for a serf) utterly exceptional knowledge:

> My greatest desire was to perfect my knowledge of Italian (in which I had already had a good amount of success) and of architecture and painting, and I continued to dream of studying these subjects in Rome or in Naples. I intended to return to my fatherland afterwards and register in the civil service.

Near the end of the deposition, he gives the same description of his intention, clearly revealing his persistent confidence in the cultural (if not legal) legitimacy of his actions.

In his poem's penultimate lines, 'P', too, seems to imagine that his literary achievement might command general acclaim, though not until after emancipation, when

> ... the son of a single peasant man
> Will cry out with a poet's voice,
> And soon thereafter himself receive
> Honour and rank from the world.

However, in the case of 'P', a related but more autonomous source of authority is drawn upon: the visionary authority of the bard. This figure is not simply the craftsman but the *magician* of words; the writer who can tell his story *and* that of 'peasant Russia' in metrical language and on epic scale;[44] the prophet to whom special insight into the human and natural worlds is given, not infrequently (in *News about Russia*) in the form of dream. In the section quoted below, the narrator is riding in a cart, on the last leg of his journey home after seven years of working in St Petersburg:

> One could tell where the nightingales sang,
> Hearing their song. Loudly their voices rang out
> In the green groves next to the brooks,
> And flowed together with streams of pure water,
> And with the breeze that played amid the leaves.
>
> 'Ah, deaf midnight guardians!
> O native streams and groves,
> Are you near my village?'
>
> A nightingale warbled in response, and through
> The fragrant languor of the trees
> A breeze blew upon my face –
> This breath of wind laid me to the soundest sleep
> Of all the passengers upon the cart.

In these lines, the peasant poet is clearly claiming a kind of mastery of secular poetic language, of a language accessible only to the most educated members of the society. Poetic diction – 'nightingales,' 'native streams and groves,' 'fragrant languor' and so on – announces his ability to speak *as an artist* to the 'advanced' culture of the nobility. He seems to claim a more radical distinction, however, by suggesting both a special connection to the natural surroundings ('a nightingale warbled in response') and to a heightened (or deepened) kind of sleep. The very next lines clearly raise the poetic and larger cultural stakes beyond those of mere craftsmanship towards questions of true *visionary* authority:

> But my immortal soul slept not:
> Dejected inside the dark body, from which
> It seemed already to await separation,
> My soul imagined things as in a daydream.
> It wandered, it seemed, upon a high mountain
> In dark autumn, above a deep and rapid river
> In a gully far below, opening before my eyes
> Like an abyss. In the distance, beyond the span
> Of water, flowers in the meadows released
> Their scents, and there were gardens on green hillocks
> Where little birds were sweetly singing.
> The ceaseless light of the sun shone through
> These halls of glory, and people clothed in splendour
> Took joy in blessings everlasting. My soul
> Overheard no meek conversations,
> Saw only hands ceaselessly clapping.

Again, part of the claim to a 'bardic' mantle is conveyed by the (naïve) use of conventions: 'green hillocks,' 'halls of glory,' and so on. But the narrator is also clearly selected for visionary experience, for a heightened encounter with both nocturnal nature (his companions are asleep) and with sleep itself. He is eventually able to see both the grand visionary alternative and (in an ironic oscillation) all aspects of the sordid serf reality (the 'abyss').

His credentials as representative of the people and as prophet of future calamity and triumph are vital to the success of his greater, wildly ambitious project: through his poem and his voice to convince the Tsar (Nicholas I) to end serfdom. At the very end of *News about Russia*, he switches to prose for a note to his presumed royal audience, indicating the kind of political and legal authority to which he aspires:

> When my verses have been read up to this page by the most high Romanov family, there will be [nothing] to prevent them from meeting with the writer. To arrange a meeting, I will have to be commanded to come

through a call conveyed by the postal service. ... I will ask God that he give me the boldness to stand before the face of the Tsar! And receiving [that call], I will appear.

'P''s address to the Tsar represents the strongest mode of 'appeal to authority' possible within serf narratives. The distinctive ideology of 'naïve monarchism' allowed the serf imaginatively to leap over the middle layers of oppression to the pinnacle of power – a pinnacle always defined as aligned with village interests. This link (on the level of ideology) to a possibly understanding or forgiving State distinguishes 'P''s tale particularly clearly from the US narratives, where a free State appears, if at all, in the non-personified form of the *territory* of the North, of Canada, and occasionally of Europe and Africa. Of course, the Tsar, the ultimate *padrone*, can chastise his children just as (or more) readily than he supports them. Nonetheless, the serf, extrusively enslaved on his/her 'home turf' and massively in the majority position, can convert that 'fallen insider' status into something like a proprietor's relationship to the 'land' as a whole, especially when energized by the myth of the monarch.

III

But what happens to the serf voice when the need for such justification has been removed – by success, by accident, or simply by the passage of time? I would like to close this essay with a brief reflection on this question, using M.E. Vasilieva's extraordinary late fragment, 'Notes of a Serf-Woman' (published 1911). Vasilieva's autobiographical self, named 'Akul'ka' in the text, never emerges from her childhood, spent in the village of 'Dubovoe.'[45] The author includes no conventional comparisons between a previously enslaved and currently free condition; nor is the child-serf bent towards some future moment of liberation. Vasilieva's account is dryer, more dispassionate, as in this section devoted to a description of the character of the landowner's (or 'barin's') son, Egor Petrovich. The resulting text offers a reflection on authority and submission, rather than a submissive performance for authority. Indeed, I shall read the passage as a two-part allegory of autobiographical understanding and misunderstanding.

Like his vicious grandfather (of whom a portrait hangs inside the manor-house), Egor Petrovich is 'the very picture of a barin: tall, slender, with black arching eyebrows and an oblong pink face':

'As far as appearance is concerned, Egor Petrovich and [the] portrait of his grandpa, Georgii Nikolaevich, are as alike as two drops of water,' said [the estate steward] Nikanor Savel'evich. 'And his character, too, will be exactly like that of his grandpa, who flogged people to death. Once, when he was eight, the young barin tried to set me on fire. I was his tutor at the time and had a terrible time with him; and I dared neither to put a stop to his behaviour nor complain about him to the mistress. In the maid's room, he once crawled under the tambour[46] and began piercing the girls' bare legs with pins. The maids were crying and didn't know what to do: they couldn't complain to the mistress, because she'd only slap them across the face and wouldn't stop her son in any case.'

The steward pulls the boy out by the ear, telling him to 'go and complain to [his] mommy' about the punishment. This was risky; the steward himself had long since been rendered deaf because of his mistress's frequent blows to the head. But the eventual outcome was less predictable:

'The whole day I awaited the mistress's blows, but what ended up happening was something different. At dusk I laid myself down on the leather sofa in the footmen's room and nodded off. Luckily, I soon woke up and noticed that my head felt hot and that the room was filled with a stench like that of burned hair. I grasped my head and, finding it aflame, seized a sofa cushion and extinguished the fire. I was thinking "how did my head catch fire?" – when I looked around and saw the barin's son standing behind a wardrobe, watching me and laughing; he had a box of sulphur matches in his hand.'

Here, lordly authority is malicious, infantile, and (in the steward's account) *hidden* – quite precisely *not* a force with which any kind of 'alignment' is possible. It is notable that the maids' complaint elicits a piece of autobiography, from Nikanor Savel'evich, in the context of a chat about the young master. The testimony begins with an act of 'dragging out' or exposing authority, but culminates with a kind of shrug of the shoulders. The young barin is said simply to *be* a certain way, a certain kind of person, almost a natural force that can always conceal itself again from serf eyes (Egor Petrovich stands at the end 'behind a wardrobe,' just as earlier he'd been 'under a table'). The fatalism of the steward's understanding, which is also an admission of his inability to do anything about the situation, is underscored by the reference to the grandfather's portrait. The story is one of well-nigh natural continuity, going back to the forefathers and beyond; the barin can't finally be seen, but he can be closed up in a story or portrait, in a 'representational' understanding.

But the second part of the description, Akul'ka's own testimony (which I necessarily quote at length), would seem to invert this structure:

> After such stories, I began to fear the young barin, but wanted to look at him all the same. I would run over to the fence surrounding the master's garden, hide in the bushes and observe how Egor Petrovich trained his dog to carry things along the path lined with lime-trees. The young master harassed his dog as well; he carried an iron-tipped lash that left a bloody stripe each time it touched the dog's shaved hind-quarters. And God protect the dog if he were ever to snap or show his teeth: then Egor Petrovich would flog him with all his might, and the animal could do nothing but yelp and howl. The young master would eventually throw the lash down and, after walking up and down the path for a couple of minutes, called the dog (who was hiding in the bushes) and began petting him.
>
> My arms and legs would sometimes shake with fear as I watched the young barin beat his dog; but I still remained at the fence, and would run there again to await him the next day.
>
> On another occasion, Egor Petrovich came to the garden with a rifle in order to shoot birds. He preferred wounding them to killing them immediately. When a bird would fall to the ground, its little wings quivering, the young barin would bend over and stare as though he were feasting his eyes on it; he would then grab the bird by its legs, shake it, and hurl it against the fence. He killed my tomcat in the same way.
>
> Vas'ka (the cat) got into the habit of following me to the master's garden. While I stood by the fence, he would climb onto it and sit there sunning himself.
>
> At first the young barin didn't notice Vas'ka. But one day he suddenly took aim and fired in my direction, and the cat fell over into the garden like a thunderbolt. At first I thought that Vas'ka had jumped off the fence, but when the young barin lifted him by his legs and hurled him in my direction against the fence, I realized that Vas'ka had been killed and ran over to him.
>
> Seeing that the cat was goggle-eyed like a crayfish, I began to howl at the top of my voice.
>
> The barin saw me and shouted:

>'Come here, pretty little girl, come over to me!'
>
>I picked the cat up in my skirt, took to my heels and ran to the cattle-yard without looking back once.

Authority is precisely *not* concealed from Akul'ka, for she *sees* the barin from afar, spying on him as he had spied on the steward. But hers is a frozen looking, fixated, it would seem, on the barin's hapless dog. The dog, it is clear, is her 'figure of [self]-understanding': faithful, submissive, and suffering. That rapt identification – involving who knows what desires and fears of rebellion! – persists until the fateful moment when she finds herself close to the real position of that suffering animal, the position of mute non-understanding and (ultimately) death. Egor Petrovich fires 'in her direction,' but hits the cat instead, who is instantly made 'goggle-eyed,' unable to see. All that she can do is leave with the corpse, abandoning the dog, no longer a possible object of identification, to the blind vicissitudes of history.

In one way or another, the deepest genre-template underlying serf autobiography is always the 'escape from captivity' narrative, with all its resonances with both biblical history and the etymological meaning of 'redemption.'[47] Even in stories of failure, like those of 'P' and Smirnov, redemption is alluded to as a constant possibility. Yet this genre, too, is characterized by a dialectic of 'form' and performative 'authority.' The form is that of moving from a bad (serf) place to a better (free) place; and this formal *movement* is presumed to correspond to a securing or redemption of the self. In Vasilieva, however, the two halves remain disjunct. The steward's 'understanding' of the situation is a cover for his real immobility, his need to dissolve present depredations into a historical narrative; the serf-girl's 'flight' from the master is sheer blind panic, and seems to contain the seeds of yet more repetition.[48] There is no seamless linking of the enslaved past to the 'free' present; 'Akul'ka' is left behind in serfdom, just as the barin's dog is.

Readers of serf and slave narratives urgently desire a clear identity of life-chronology and social/political *meaning*, but Vasilieva blocks this by refusing any recuperation of her 'self.' In a way, this gesture recalls the refusal of many slave narrators – William Craft, Frederick Douglass, and Harriet Jacobs among others – to culminate their stories with a final 'arrival' in freedom, pointing out instead, in Douglass's words, a 'strength of prejudice against color'[49] persisting in the 'lands of liberty' to which the slaves flee, presenting new and insidious forms of authority with which the freed people must contend, a point I have discussed at length elsewhere.[50] In terms of the present argument, by refusing the teleology of redemption, Vasilieva joins Douglass, Henry Bibb, and other great slave narrators in the salutary task of making our reading of autobiographies by bondspeople as painful as possible.

NOTES

1 For a strong version of this argument, see Paul de Man, 'Autobiography as De-Facement,' in *The Rhetoric of Romanticism* (New York: Columbia University Press, 1984), 67–81.
2 Mikhail Bakhtin, 'Forms of Time and of the Chronotope in the Novel: Notes toward a Historical Poetics,' in *The Dialogic Imagination*, ed. Michael Holquist, trans. Caryl Emerson and Michael Holquist (Austin: University of Texas Press, 1981), 142.
3 Fredric Jameson, The *Political Unconscious: Narrative as a Socially Symbolic Act* (Ithaca: Cornell University Press, 1981), 106.
4 In this connection, see Georg Lukács's pages on the relationship of biographical form to the modern historical novel in *The Historical Novel*, trans. Hannah and Stanley Mitchell, intro. Fredric Jameson (Lincoln: University of Nebraska Press, 1983), 300–22.
5 Bakhtin, 'Forms of Time,' in *The Dialogic Imagination*, 130–46.
6 Ibid., 130.
7 Ibid.
8 Ibid., 131 (my emphasis).
9 Ibid., 131, 135.
10 For a classic example, see Jean-Paul Sartre, *Search for a Method*, trans. and intro. Hazel E. Barnes (New York: Knopf, 1963), passim.
11 Göran Therborn, *The Ideology of Power and the Power of Ideology* (London: Verso, 1980), 17. See also Paul Smith's distinction between the (subjected) *actor* and the (qualifying) *agent* in *Discerning the Subject*, intro. John Mowitt (Minneapolis: University of Minnesota Press, 1988), xxxiii–xxxv.
12 Bakhtin writes of the Roman 'analytic' biography, in which 'all biographical material is distributed' into 'well-defined rubrics': 'social life, family life, conduct in war, relationships with friends,' and so on ('Forms of Time,' in *The Dialogic Imagination*, 142). It is not difficult to see how these classifications would lead to a variety of narrative 'kinds' within a single autobiography.
13 Sidonie Smith, 'Performativity, Autobiographical Practice, Resistance,' in *Women, Autobiography, Theory: A Reader*, ed. Sidonie Smith and Julia Watson (Madison: University of Wisconsin Press, 1998), 110–11.
14 In connection with this, see William L. Andrews's discussion of the 'black

criminal narrative' in *To Tell a Free Story: The First Century of Afro-American Autobiography, 1760–1865* (Urbana: University of Illinois Press, 1986), 41–51.

15 To take a famous example: Rousseau shows his awareness of being judged at several points in his autobiography, most notably on the first page: 'As to whether nature did well or ill to break the mould in which I was cast, that is something no one can judge until after they have read me. Let the trumpet of judgment sound when it will, I will present myself with this book in my hand before the Supreme Judge.' Jean-Jacques Rousseau, *Confessions*, trans. Angela Scholar, ed. and intro. Patrick Coleman (Oxford: Oxford University Press, 2000), 5. The doubleness of the assertion is clear: the text's claims for radical individuality ('break the mould') are precisely the products of a hyperconsciousness of a judging, external gaze. But Rousseau is also turning the idea of 'sovereign judge' on its head, pre-emptively judging his readers' fitness for judging *him*, and essentially depriving his judges of any special religious sanction they might claim for themselves. On the surface, it seems that Rousseau is trying to find a way of coordinating self-presentation with some supposed (religious) standards of authority, and this is indeed a crucial autobiographical strategy. The self asserts that it is in some sense *on the side* of authority, whether authority knows it or not, in a gesture that might be called (following Kenneth Burke) 'consubstantializing.' Cf. Burke on persuasion/ identification: 'You persuade a man only insofar as you can talk his language by speech, gesture, tonality, order, image, attitude, idea, identifying your ways with his. ... [Y]ou give the "signs" of ... consubstantiality by deference to an audience's "opinions."' Kenneth Burke, *A Rhetoric of Motives* (Berkeley and Los Angeles: University of California Press, 1969), 55–6. But the appeal to religious scruples ('we're all sinners before God') helps to insulate the autobiographer from any earthly authority that might claim to instantiate divine authority. In other words, Rousseau actually secularizes his 'public square' here.

16 In this paper I am deliberately ignoring or bracketing earlier memoirs (like Avvakum's famous 'Life').

17 Rychkov was a member of the Petersburg Academy, and wrote his autobiographical 'Notes' ('Zapiski') ca. 1774. See Alois Schmücker, 'Anfänge und erste Entwicklung der Autobiographie in Russland (1760–1830),' in *Die Autobiographie: Zu Form und Geschichte einer literarischen Gattung*, ed. Günter Niggl (Darmstadt: Wissenschaftliche Buchgesellschaft, 1998), 414–58.

18 A great though complex example is the *Life and Adventures* of Andrei Timofeevich Bolotov (1738–1833), written between 1789 and 1816; see Schmücker, 'Anfänge,' 431–5.

19 I have found eighteen autobiographical narratives verifiably written by Rus-

sian serfs and ex-serfs, all published for the first time after the emancipation of 1861. For information on some of them (only four are discussed here), see Peter Kolchin's landmark comparative study *Unfree Labor: American Slavery and Russian Serfdom* (Cambridge: Belknap Press of Harvard University Press, 1987) and M.D. Kurmacheva's *Krepostnaia Intelligentsia Rossii: Vtoraia polovina XVII–nachalo XIX veka* (Moscow: Nauka, 1983).

20 In contrast to the *intrusive* mode, where the slave is an outsider, a defeated enemy (as in the US); see Orlando Patterson, *Slavery and Social Death: A Comparative Study* (Cambridge: Harvard University Press, 1982), 38–45.

21 For an excellent discussion of the different rhetorical context of US slave narration, see Andrews, *To Tell a Free Story*, 1–31.

22 I have recently completed an English edition of these four narratives; all translations in the present essay are my own.

23 The original text of the Smirnov's deposition is in the Russian State Archive of Ancient Documents, Moscow, section 7, file 2679, pages 66–7 recto and verso, from the year 1785. The deposition was published under the editorship of K.V. Sivkov with the title 'Avtobiografiia krespostnogo intelligenta kontsa 18-ogo veka,' in *Istoricheskii arkhiv* 5 (Leningrad: Izdatel'stvo Akademii Nauk SSSR, 1950), 288–99.

24 The poem *News about Russia* was sent as a 'letter of protest' to Tsar Nicholas I in 1849, and was first published in *Vesti o Rossii: Povest' v stikhakh krepostnogo kres'ianina*, ed. T.G. Snytko (Iaroslavl': Iaroslavskoe knizhnoe izdatel'stvo, 1961). The manuscript is in the State Archive of the Russian Federation (GARF), archive 109, file 100, from the year 1850. The poem was clearly thought to be authentic by the police who investigated its provenance (to no avail), and has been treated as such by later historians including Daniel Field (in his *Rebels in the Name of the Tsar*) and Peter Kolchin (*Unfree Labor*).

25 Nikolai Shipov, 'Istoriia moei zhizni: Razskaz byshago krepostnago krest'ianina N.N. Shipova,' *Russkaia Starina* 30 (1881).

26 M.E. Vasilieva, 'Zapiski krepostnoi,' *Russkaia Starina* 145 (1911): 140–51. My translation and introduction appeared as 'Notes of a Serf Woman by M.E. Vasilieva,' in *Slavery and Abolition* 21.1 (April 2000): 146–68.

27 To see two famous examples of authors who used serfs as characters, cf. Turgenev and Tolstoy. Among major works of Russian prose, the one that seems to be at least occasionally a 'reworking' of actual testimony is Dostoevsky's *Notes from the House of the Dead*, published in the year of the emancipation (1861).

28 The great English-language study of Russian 'naïve monarchism' is Daniel Field, *Rebels in the Name of the Tsar* (Boston: Unwin Hyman, 1989).

29 John Ernest, *Resistance and Reformation in Nineteenth-Century African-American*

Literature: Brown, Wilson, Jacobs, Delany, Douglass, and Harper (Jackson: University Press of Mississippi, 1995), 7.
30 Albert J. Raboteau, *Slave Religion: The 'Invisible Institution' in the Antebellum South* (Oxford: Oxford University Press, 1978), 318.
31 After a reconsideration of the case in the Secret Section and a report to Catherine the Great, Smirnov was sentenced (by Catherine's order) to be sent 'as a soldier to the military troops stationed at Tobol'sk.' (Tobol'sk was the city to which many of the Decembrists were exiled after their abortive 1825 revolt.) Smirnov apparently accepted this sentence as a manifestation of the 'inexpressible charity of her imperial greatness.'
32 His last paragraph makes this clear: 'Now, sending the most heartfelt prayers to almighty God for the forgiveness of my heavy sins, I submissively await the decision as to my fate, feeling quite certain that for my crimes I deserve not only the punishment prescribed by law, but even greater chastisement. All my hope and faith I place upon the infinite mercy of God, upon his goodness towards a contrite sinner, and upon the boundless mercy and compassion of our humane and most merciful monarchy.'
33 Frederick Douglass, *Narrative of the Life of Frederick Douglass, an American Slave, Written by Himself,* in *Slave Narratives,* ed. William L. Andrews and Henry Louis Gates, Jr (New York: Library of America, 2000), 336.
34 Henry Bibb, *Narrative of the Life and Adventures of Henry Bibb, an American Slave, Written by Himself,* in *Slave Narratives,* ed. Andrews and Gates, 511–12.
35 In this respect, Smirnov's use of religion more closely resembles that of a pre-abolition slave narrator, like his contemporary James Gronniosaw (whose autobiography originally appeared in 1772); see James Albert Ukawsaw Gronniosaw, *A Narrative of the Most Remarkable Particulars in the Life of James Albert Ukawsaw Gronniosaw, an African Prince, as Related by Himself,* in *Slave Narratives,* ed. Andrews and Gates, 1–34.
36 In Russian, 'zhid' (as opposed to the neutral 'evrei' ['Jew']). It is worth mentioning that the population of the small town mentioned by Shipov (Brichani) was annihilated by the Nazis during the Holocaust.
37 A kind of pancake, eaten during Shrovetide.
38 Pronounced like 'mere': the village community.
39 Old name for 'the Russian lands.'
40 'The golden calf is a symbol for money' (note in original).
41 Douglass, *Narrative,* 329.
42 'The court of Shemiaka' is an idiom meaning 'an unfair trial' or 'kangaroo court.' The expression derives 'apparently from *Shemyaka,* the name of an arbitrary and casuistic judge in a satirical old Russian tale' (Sophia Lubensky, *Russian-English Dictionary of Idioms*). A 'voivode' ('voy-uh-VODE') was either

1) a commander of an army in medieval Russia, or 2) the governor of a town or province in the Muscovite period.
43 A reference to the 'Tatar yoke,' the period of Mongol domination of the Rus' principalities (1240–1480).
44 As far as I know, *News about Russia* is the longest autobiographical poem in the Russian language.
45 Vasilieva's story ends with '*to be continued*,' suggesting that the journal intended to present additional instalments. But no more appeared, and I have been unable to locate any information either about the fate of those plans for future publication or (beyond what is contained in the narrative itself) about the putative author, 'M.E. Vasilieva.' The actual date of composition of the 'notes' is unknown; it was published exactly fifty years after the emancipation of Russia's serfs under Alexander II (in 1861).
46 An embroidery frame.
47 'The action of freeing a prisoner, captive, or slave by payment; ransom' (*OED*).
48 In the last paragraph, I sense the implication that the young barin will resume his pursuit of the 'pretty little girl' on his return from Petersburg.
49 Douglass, *Narrative*, 361.
50 See my essay '"And Hold the Bondman Still": Biogeography and Utopia in Slave and Serf Narratives,' *Biography* 25.1 (Winter 2002): 110–29.

CHAPTER 3

I, Hereby, Vow to Read
The Interesting Narrative

Tess Chakkalakal

> It is the constitution of a community of witness that makes the marriage; the silence of witness (we don't speak now, we forever hold our peace) that permits it; the bare negative, potent but undiscretionary speech act of our physical presence – maybe even *especially* the presence of those people whom the institution of marriage defines itself by excluding – that ratifies and recruits the legitimacy of its privilege.
>
> Andrew Parker and Eve Kosofsky Sedgwick, *Performativity and Performance*

When Olaudah Equiano first published the story of his life in 1789 under the title *The Interesting Narrative of the Life of Olaudah Equiano or Gustavus Vassa, the African Written by Himself*, it received considerable attention from English reading audiences.[1] Read as 'spiritual autobiography, captivity narrative, travel book, adventure tale, narrative of slavery, economic treatise and apologia,'[2] the *Narrative* appealed to various tastes and consequently, like a number of other captivity narratives of the period, was a bestseller in its day.[3] A key difference, however, between Equiano's *Narrative* and its contemporaries is that the former continues to appeal to readers today because its generic hybridity still serves multiple interests. The *Narrative* has proved essential reading for scholars working in a number of historical/national fields. For instance, such critics as Paul Gilroy and Stuart Hall rely on the *Narrative* to revise categories of racial discourse, a shift that is critical to their respective Black Atlantic and Black Diaspora Studies projects. As well, Equiano, according to recent assessments of the *Narrative*, 'has come to embody early black Atlantic self-representation.'[4] Furthermore, the *Narrative* continues to be taught in the fields of eighteenth-century British and American literature and history as well as in courses relating to postcolonial, African, and African-American literature and history.[5] Recognized as 'the capstone' of eighteenth-century black British writing as well as a 'prototype' of the African-American slave narrative, Equiano's *Narrative* has become a central document to several areas of study.

While the text is often incorporated into a number of fields, it remains foreign to each of them. That it is a text premised on the paradoxical experience of 'foreign citizenship' is made clear when Equiano refers to himself as 'almost an Englishman' (77) and recognizes his difference from the Europeans among whom he lives throughout the text. Equiano asserts that difference when he begins his narrative as 'an unlettered African' and considers Africans – not Europeans – to be his countrymen. A number of the *Narrative*'s twentieth-century readers have commented upon the implications of its author's dual identity. S.E. Ogude, for instance, questions Equiano's claim to an African identity; he contends that Equiano's British sources for his description of Africa makes the place a virtual fiction.[6] Carretta's more recent groundbreaking historical research extends Ogude's claims by establishing that Equiano 'was born in South Carolina [and] constructed an African identity to support the British one he embraced as a free man.'[7] Carretta's evidence effectively challenges Wilfred Samuels's, Paul Edwards's, and Dwight McBride's readings of the *Narrative* predicated upon Equiano's beginning in Africa and, in McBride's words, 'presenting himself in the narrative as living proof of the African's ability to reason and to master European forms of philosophy and cultural production.'[8] The tension between the identities (European versus African) raises a number of interpretive problems. Most importantly, it raises the problem of classifying Equiano's *Narrative* and being attentive both to history and to the author's intentions. While most critics attempt to solve the problem Equiano's *Narrative* raises by looking *outside* the text, I want to suggest here that solutions can be found in the rhetorical conventions employed within the *Narrative* itself.

Genre and Identity

The *Narrative* differs from, for instance, sentimental, spiritual, and autobiographical narratives. While those genres can elide the difference between the author and reader in order to achieve a union or identification, Equiano's *Narrative* retains a distinction between the two to maintain a distance between the writer's life and its reader's. That is to say, the *Narrative* does not simply tell a story of a single individual's struggle from slavery to freedom in order to gain sympathy from his reader to further the cause against slavery. Instead, Equiano *translates* the experience of captivity into a language that will be understood by an audience for whom such experiences are entirely foreign and, in doing so, the *Narrative* relies on the reader's *different* experiences to negotiate the author's own. The *Narrative* presents us with a catalogue of experiences that occur as the result of an encounter between the African and the European. Seeing himself as both rather than either European or African, Equiano transforms the terms upon which citizenship (outlined in the introduction to this volume) is defined.

In his extensive study of the African-American literary tradition, Henry Louis Gates, Jr explains that 'Equiano's strategies of self-presentation and rhetorical representation heavily informed, if not determined, the shape of black narratives before 1865.'[9] Gates's consideration of the *Narrative* is part of a broader discussion on the 'black text' – a generic category that operates according to both literary conventions and authorial identity. By identifying common tropes, issues and structural devices in various works by black writers, Gates makes these otherwise neglected texts more readily accessible to readers. Gates's theory of the Afro-American literary tradition, however, does not necessarily apply to the *Narrative*, whose immense popularity proves that it did not suffer from such problems. As Equiano was directly involved in the publication and dissemination of his *Narrative*, his book reached readers throughout Great Britain and the United States, and it was eventually translated into several languages. Gates elides these historical details, its fictional account of Africa, and the author's occupation and economic status in order to turn the *Narrative* into a 'prototype' of the African-American slave narratives which he, and others, consider to be 'the locus classicus of Afro-American literary discourse.'[10]

Subsequent critics extend Gates's reading of Equiano's 'subaltern' status by keeping their readings of the *Narrative* inside the well-demarcated parameters of the slave narrative.[11] In his essay '"I Was Born": Slave Narratives, Their Status as Autobiography and as Literature,' James Olney offers readers a quick reference guide to distinguish the slave narrative from other forms of autobiography. Olney explains that 'the most obvious distinguishing mark is that it is an extremely mixed production typically including any or all of the following: an engraved portrait or photograph of the subject of the narrative; authenticating testimonials, prefixed or postfixed; poetic epigraphs, snatches of poetry in the text, poems appended'; in spite of these differences, Olney goes on to constructs a master outline for the slave narrative.[12] Such lists, of course, cannot help but have a reductive effect on analysis; in the case of slave narratives, texts are typically read as instances of authorial biography. For critics committed to the generic category of the slave narrative, the value of this particular *Narrative* lies in the ways in which it upholds the conventions they have identified. In doing so, the *Narrative* facilitates the construction of a coherent community out of ex-slaves and literary 'Others.' But regardless of how useful such a mode of classification may be, it limits the possibilities offered to the reader by Equiano's diverse experiences. What does a reader do after having identified a given text as a slave narrative? The most common response has been to explore the specific ways in which slavery has influenced the author's life. In other words, the slave narrative, as a category, functions as a black version of the *bildungsroman*. Reading Equiano's *Narrative* as a slave narrative considers it through the subject's struggle from slavery to freedom, from illiteracy to literacy, and, finally, from childhood to adulthood. Such a reading depends on a linear, teleological mode of reading that, as I will argue, the *Narrative* resists. Equiano's argument against slavery depends upon intertwining the disparate experiences of the reader with the author's to break down the difference between the European and African. For this reason, Equiano repeatedly introjects into his *Narrative* details far removed from his experience.

And it is such details that set the *Narrative* in opposition to specific generic conventions of the slave narrative and Afro-American literary discourse more generally. 'Equiano's choice of the autobiographical mode,' Tanya Caldwell insists, reveals less about Equiano's personal experience than a long-standing tradition 'employed by eighteenth-century British writers of nonfictional, semifictional, and fictional lives.'[13] Caldwell, along with Julia K. Ward and Elizabeth Jane Wall Hinds, understands Equiano's *Narrative* as operating within – rather than against – eighteenth-century literary and rhetorical conventions.[14] In this regard, there is very little that is 'African' about Equiano's *Narrative*. However, while Equiano may very well participate in eighteenth-century literary and rhetorical conventions, he makes clear at the outset that he does not consider himself to be European. '[D]id I consider myself an European,' he writes, 'I might say my sufferings were great: but when I compare my lot with that of most of my countrymen, I regard myself as a *particular favourite of Heaven*' (31). Having attained his freedom by mastering the eighteenth-century conventions, he still understands himself as being held captive by those same conventions.

In his introduction to *Olaudah Equiano, Mary Rowlandson, and Others*, Gordon Sayre argues that 'the captivity phenomenon arises out of encounters between unfamiliar peoples, generally as a result of European imperialism in the Americas and Africa.' Importantly, Sayre marks the territory of captivity as narrating an encounter between unfamiliar peoples. According to Sayre, the captivity narrative necessarily regards this encounter as a hostile one wherein 'two cultures brought into conflict are so foreign to one another that an individual forced into the midst of the other community regards the new life as a kind of imprisonment.'[15] However, for Equiano, the new life he encounters as a result of his imprisonment is filled with multiple possibilities for self-improvement.[16] Using Equiano's text as central to the definition of the captivity phenomenon distorts the *Narrative* as Sayre's definition is disproportionately invested in Equiano's account of his birth in and capture from Africa. Although this account may initiate the *Narrative*, it is actually a very brief section of the text and Equiano offers little commentary on the circumstances of his capture. Nonetheless, Equiano does find himself in something of a double-bind. On the one hand, he enjoys his experiences of travel and trade that afford him multiple sources of increasing his wealth and acquiring new skills. On the other hand, these same encounters hold him captive and subject to unfair treatment.

Among the most illuminating parts of Equiano's account of his encounters are those in which he suffers 'ill usage' (116) at the hands of others, or witnesses others subjected to such suffering. Somewhere in the West Indies, a countryman of Equiano's saves money to buy a boat, which the governor, when he discovers that it is the boat of 'a negro,' seizes without payment in an act of 'extortion and rapine' (102). In Montserrat, 'a Creole negro' of Equiano's acquaintance is robbed of his fish by his master, and '"can't go to any body to be righted"' (110). In Santa Cruz, the oranges and limes that Equiano intends to sell are 'plundered' from him by white men (118). In Charlestown, he recalls, upon selling a 'puncheon of rum' to a gentleman, 'being a negro man, I could not oblige him to pay me' – though afterwards, the man pays him, but partly in useless copper dollars (128–9). Near the Bermudas, a captain boards Equiano's ship, insists falsely that a 'mulatto man' whom all recognize to be free is a slave, and carries the man away – for no reason other than that 'might overcomes right' among such 'infernal invaders of human rights' (121). Free blacks are stolen away in bondage even in Philadelphia, 'plundered without possibility of redress' (122). And throughout the Caribbean, Equiano finds that if a slave collects a small portion of grass in his spare time, expecting to sell it in the market, 'nothing is more common than for the white people on this occasion to take the grass from them without paying for it' (108). Having no legal means to redress the wrongs committed against him and his 'countrymen,' Equiano uses his *Narrative* as a means by which these acts of injustice can be addressed and made right. The *Narrative* attempts to negotiate the conflicts which arise between African and British subjects more equitably than Equiano experiences them.

For this reason, I read the *Narrative* as existing between, rather than within, particular discourses in order to consider the consequences of Equiano's captivating encounters on those very conventions that bind him to a single identity. Equiano's *Interesting Narrative* operates as a performance – a specific action or set of actions – whose mutual recognition between reader and author cuts across the determined status of both subjects, dissolving, ultimately, the boundaries which separate the European from the African. Reading the *Narrative*'s departures from the author's experiences, what I call its performative utterances, reveals a set of terms that accounts for the conventions Equiano operates within and also attends to those moments in the *Narrative* where the author attempts to find a way out of them.

Equiano's *Narrative* begins in Benin in 1745. Shortly after, the *Narrative* moves to the territory of the American South, where Equiano claims to have been brought by force. Once there he is sold to a British naval officer and taken to London to serve in the Royal Navy. Unlike most African men and women held captive in Europe and the Americas, Equiano is allowed to travel extensively and consequently meets and pursues relationships with diverse peoples. Unlike the majority of black slaves, he is trained to work the sea rather than the land, and although his labour is not compensated, he is granted the benefit of free travel. For this reason, Equiano does not – as do many of the captives of the captivity narratives – 'yearn to return home.' Indeed, despite African nativity he does not call it or any place in Europe 'home.'[17] Instead, he whole-heartedly embraces his new life on the sea. Unlike the impoverished and hostile conditions in which most former slaves were forced to live after they gained their freedom, Equiano enjoys a life of wealth and comfort as the result of the sound investments he made during his travels and exploratory adventures.[18]

Still, as outlined above, Equiano does encounter great difficulties on his voyages and most of these difficulties are attributed to his perceived racial difference. The response to a black man travelling as both a slave and a 'freeman' is mixed. While travelling to different parts of the world, Equiano realizes that his skin colour is used to determine his status. While he occupies a position of some prominence and wealth in European society at the time he writes his *Narrative* he was not treated as 'European'; instead, he realizes as the result of his encounters that his wealth, experience, and status do not protect him from being subjected to abuse and injustice.

Equiano becomes conscious of his skin colour as he comes into contact with people who use it to determine his value. Such experiences may result in a split subjectivity, as W.E.B. DuBois famously outlines in his theory of 'double consciousness,' but the *Narrative* proves otherwise.[19] The *Narrative* does not represent Equiano's desire to respond to or even to avenge the abuse suffered at the hands of those who would deny him the right to earn a living. By showing how he is subjected to racial prejudice in primarily legal and economic terms, Equiano manages to make his European and African identities virtually interchangeable. Equiano is the same man in all his encounters but is treated differently according to the prejudices of those he encounters. He believes that 'there are few events in my life, which have not happened to many' of his 'countrymen' (31). What sets his experiences apart – that is, what constitutes his reasons for regarding himself as 'a *particular favorite of Heaven*' (31) – is his understanding of both Europeans and Africans. He is thereby able to show that the difference constructed between these identities is harmful to both. What bonds Equiano to his African 'countrymen' is their common experience of unfair treatment by the law; yet he is set apart from his African countrymen because he has been able to travel and accumulate wealth.

Miscegenous Marriages

Equiano's *Narrative* is motivated by a desire to extinguish the difference between African and European identities. But, he cannot achieve his task without the participation of his reader. The experience of reading Equiano's *Narrative* involves Africanizing the European reader and Europeanizing Africa; it is a process predicated on intercourse between reader and author. I use the term intercourse here to distinguish it from discourse, as the latter would imply that the *Narrative* contributes to an already existing set of conventions whether they be those of British, African, or African-American literature. Intercourse, instead, refers to a relationship that comes into being as the result of a singular action between individuals, acted out most explicitly and publicly through marriage ceremonies. In terms of the *Narrative*, the marriage ceremony functions as an encounter that holds the possibility for infinite gain. Rather than operate within particular discourses, Equiano's *Narrative* functions, to borrow from Tilottama Rajan's conception of autonarration in the eighteenth century, as a 'transgressive miscegenation' between subjects.[20]

Rajan characterizes autonarration as 'a genre characterized by its transgressive miscegenation of private and public spaces [and] part of a larger discursive formation characteristic of romanticism' (153). Rajan further notes that although it is 'not exclusively a women's genre,' its use 'tends to put the writer in a female subject-position' (153). The subject of autonarration is usually female, Rajan argues, because it is the female subject who must negotiate her relationship between representation and experience without relying on the constative or performative utterance: 'either as it was, or as it becomes through the act of writing' (160). Rajan rightly assumes that the social constraints surrounding the telling of a woman's life-story impel an articulation 'in two different media of "life" and "text," as if one requires the supplement of the other' (159). She goes on to describe autonarration as 'a specific form of self-writing, in which the author writes her life as a fictional narrative, and thus *consciously* raises the question of the relationship between experience and its narrativization' (160). By emphasizing 'consciously,' Rajan draws our attention to the importance of women's writing that manipulates personal experience to serve particular socio-political interests. Rajan contends that critics of women's life-writing have failed to recognize the presence of the author's consciousness at work because women had no place thinking about or participating in political affairs; instead, their influence was restricted to the home. Reconsidering women's life-writing as autonarration foregrounds its national scope.

The premises of Rajan's argument require her to hold her discussion of autonarration along gender lines. Equiano's *Narrative* proffers another instance of autonarration, but one that occurs along racial lines.[21] Rajan's definition of autonarration can be adapted to address the eighteenth-century black subject who must negotiate a comparable tension between experience and representation. Most importantly, autonarration recognizes the ways in which a disjunction exists in the formulation of consciousness. While the miscegenation Rajan refers to in her reading of eighteenth-century memoirs by women operates primarily figuratively, miscegenation, for Equiano, is a literal matter. Equiano, in both his private and public life, was a vocal advocate of interracial marriages. In response to an article by James Tobin denouncing all forms of miscegenation, Equiano composed a letter expressing the benefits of 'the mutual commerce of the sexes of both Blacks and Whites' published in the *Public Advertiser* on 28 January 1788. Equiano's letter concerning intermarriage, alongside his explicit references to it throughout the *Narrative*, allows us to understand Rajan's formulation of autonarration both figuratively and literally.

Because Rajan's notion of autonarration arises out of a branch of linguistics that J.L. Austin terms the performative function of language, I return now to a consideration of Austin's performance. In *How to Do Things with Words*, Austin defines performative utterances by suggesting that they are utterances that are neither true nor false, but rather words that in their utterance perform a specific action. In order to elucidate this concept, Austin provides a series of instances that would constitute performative utterances, the first of which is the marriage vow. Austin explains that the words 'I do' uttered in the course of the marriage ceremony are an action and are considered to be a performative element of language because the utterance performs an action by changing the status of the marrying couple; but the words do not have the same meaning outside of the context of the marriage ceremony.[22] While there are a number of such performative utterances in daily life, the marriage ceremony is exemplary because it is both contractual (through the utterance the couple affirms a promise) and declaratory (the vow uttered by each participant changes the status of the other). The marriage ceremony, instrumental to Austin's theory of performativity, has since enabled contemporary cultural critics to analyse and subvert instances of racist, homophobic, and sexist practices in daily life.[23]

It would hardly be an overstatement then to claim that in using the marriage ceremony in 1789 to promote social change, Equiano was far ahead of his time. The relationship between reader and author of the *Narrative*, in effect, functions as a transgressive miscegenation. Equiano foregrounds problems concerning the reading and writing of his autobiography by describing his own struggle to become literate. In order to imitate the 'wisdom of white people,' Equiano turns to books 'so [as] to learn how all things had a beginning' (68). He draws a direct link between his turn to books and a desire to participate in white institutions and practices. However, the passage relating a 'curiosity to talk to books' (68) is immediately followed by an incident in which the author becomes aware of colour distinctions. Equiano realizes that he can never acquire the wisdom of white people because he is black; thus he 'began to be mortified at the difference in complexions' (69). The books Equiano reads teach him to discern differences in complexions, a practice which does not bode well for him as a black man. The reader, however, would not necessarily experience the same sense of mortification. In fact, it is unlikely that most readers would typically consider racial difference in relation to the experience of reading at all. Equiano makes this connection by relating the events of his own life in which he suffers 'instances of ill usage' (116) at the hands of whites. Such scenarios trouble the connection between white readers and the *Narrative*. White readers would be equally mortified by the position white subjects occupy in the *Narrative*. Reading, in Equiano's terms, becomes a mortifying experience for both black author and white reader as each comes to recognize the limitations of these categories. As Equiano aims to produce an experience of mortification in his reader, he creates a situation in which the two, despite historical, racial, and perhaps even ideological differences, are able to find common ground: justice.

Equiano further bridges the difference between himself and his reader by drawing upon a personal experience that would be familiar to his reader: the marriage ceremony. He uses the marriage ceremony as a vehicle to change the reader's perception of the author. In the *Narrative*, different versions of the marriage ceremony negotiate the gap between the author's African and European identities as he writes as neither a British nor an African subject, but as both at once. Through an extended discussion of marriage laws and practices, Equiano shows how his life – as both African and British – is mortifying. The reader becomes equally mortified, not as a result of sympathy or identification with Equiano, but because she mirrors Equiano's outrage when he is treated, as he so often is, as someone for whom the law does not apply.

The marriage ceremony attempts to correct this discrepancy.[24] First, Equiano uses its depictions to represent the ways in which the actions or inactions of the one affect the other. Secondly, Equiano's reading of these marriage ceremonies plays upon its contractual, progenitive, and performative conventions to create the conditions for African-British subjects like himself to be recognized and protected by the law.

Marriage marks the beginning, middle, and end points of Equiano's life. First, he articulates his earliest memories by describing the 'mode of marriage' practised by the people in Benin when he was a child (33). A second marriage ceremony marks the midpoint of the *Narrative*. Equiano is now a young man working on a ship that has arrived in the West Indies where he and his owner have stopped to acquire more slaves for England. The marriage Equiano describes on this occasion is an interracial union between a black free-woman and a white man. Not surprisingly, the third, and final, description of a marriage ceremony occurs in London when he 'chanced once to be invited to a Quaker's wedding' and concludes the *Narrative* (225). As a witness to these three ceremonies, that is, as someone who is allowed to participate but must remain silent at them, Equiano offers his reader an African-British perspective that is crucial to the success of his *Narrative*. His presentation of the marriage ceremony advances the movement against slavery and captivity by dissolving the difference between African and British identities.

Marriage in Context and in the *Narrative*

Because Equiano's views on marriage are unique to his experience as a well-travelled black man in the eighteenth century, analysis of the rhetorical function of marriage in the *Narrative* requires a brief discussion of common perceptions of marriage and interracial unions of the period. Marriage practices in late eighteenth-century England were a matter of some concern. Carolyn D. Williams points out in her article 'Another Self in the Case: Gender, Marriage and the Individual in Augustan Literature' that the 'idea of marriage in which [man and woman] become "one flesh," became increasingly alarming in the eighteenth century.'[25] The 'one flesh' clause of the marriage contract was met with alarm, as it put women and men on equal footing. The egalitarian possibilities of marriage in terms of gender met with similar alarm in matters of race as well. Outlining attitudes towards interracial unions in his *Black and White: The Negro and English Society, 1555–1945*, James Walvin shows the opposition blacks and whites had to overcome before they could form relationships with one another. Walvin explains that 'alarm, rather than curiosity was the most common response to miscegenation.'[26] He cites Edward Long, a popular polemicist in the 1770s, who describes miscegenation as a 'venomous and dangerous ulcer that threatens to disperse its malignancy far and wide, until every family catches infection from it.'[27] Walvin concludes from his study of various texts from the period that '[t]here can be no doubt, that by a substantial and influential section of English society, miscegenation was regarded as a threat to the structure of that society.'[28] Interracial marriage thus affords Equiano an opportunity to imagine a society predicated upon racial and sexual equality.[29]

The disjunction between Equiano's African and European identities necessitates a transgressive miscegenation through which the *Narrative* is written. Thus, Equiano opens the *Narrative* with the following disclaimer: 'It is, therefore, I confess, not a little hazardous, in a private and obscure individual, and a stranger too, thus to solicit the indulgent attention of the public' (31). His self-identification as a stranger alludes to his foreign status, which, by the time he writes his *Narrative*, can only be discerned by skin colour. In the *Narrative*, Equiano reveals his reasons for claiming an allegiance to Africa even though there is little evidence to support his claim that he was born there. Equiano understands his African identity through encounters in which he is treated unfairly. By including the above disclaimer at the start of his *Narrative*, Equiano marks his entry into a potentially transgressive discourse that crosses the boundaries that separate his African and European identities in order to redress the wrongs he has suffered. Equiano crosses the line between Africa and Europe, fiction and truth, to legitimize his African-British identity. He recounts his past experiences of injustice to supplement his present situation, and gives each of his experiences of injustice a sense of relevancy and immediacy for his non-African readers.

Equiano is able to describe marriage ceremonies because he has served as an exemplary 'witness' to them. While his experience of Africa rests largely on his presence at a specific ceremony, he draws numerous conclusions concerning the inner workings of that society from it. His description of the 'mode of marriage' practised in Benin in 1745, the supposed place of his birth and childhood, outlines an equitable system of justice far removed from his experience of living in England and provides him with the means by which he can begin to imagine a way of life very different from his own. Marriage, in this context, complicates an otherwise 'simple' system of relations within a community that has 'little commerce with other countries' (32). While most African men, in Equiano's recollection, respect and believe in the absolute authority of the law as decided by the 'chief men' – one of whom Equiano claims is his own father – the laws governing the 'honour of the marriage bed' are a notable exception to their principle of justice (33). 'Of this,' Equiano explains, it was only when the laws of marriage were broken that Africans condoned the practice of slavery (33). In other words, slavery signifies a transgression of law, but is not in and of itself a legally sanctioned institution.

From this notable exception to African justice, Equiano presents his childhood in Africa as a scene out of a typical English pastoral. People live peacefully and enjoy the prosperity of a fertile countryside. Much of this information does not come from the author's own recollections but from an earlier text written by an Englishman, whom Equiano acknowledges in a footnote.[30] The description of the laws which govern the sanctity of 'the marriage bed' to 'most of the nations of Africa' stands out as a point of intersection between the African and European continents, for both use the law to determine an individual's status (33). It is thus on the grounds of marriage – as both a legal and spiritual matter – that the author can begin to formulate an argument against slavery.

Equiano prefaces his description of the first marriage ceremony by recounting an instance of adultery. As an explicit sign of a breach in the marriage contract, adultery was punished by slavery or death. Interestingly, the specific instance of adultery that instigates Equiano's account of the marriage ceremony involves an extenuating circumstance. Although the practice was to kill or enslave anyone found guilty of committing adultery, Equiano centres his discussion on a situation where the guilty party was 'spared on account of the [married couple's] child' (33). Does Equiano recount the exception merely to prove the rule? More likely, the specific exceptionality in this case prepares his reader for a series of exceptions. As he begins to outline aspects of the marriage ceremony, he adds a brief comment in parentheses that offers the possibility of a marriage that diverges from the stipulated laws governing the practice: 'Their mode of marriage is thus: – both parties are usually betrothed when young by their parents (though I have known the males to betroth themselves)' (33). Because Equiano knows of some men who marry outside the 'usual' law, acting on their own desire without interference from parental bodies, he shows the possibility of individual agency despite the constraints of convention. It is through these two exceptions to the 'mode of marriage' that Equiano inserts his 'I.' Although he is not an active participant, he asserts his presence by showing that ritual practices are malleable and prone to making exceptions. The marriage ceremony usually involves two participants, a man and a woman, but Equiano subverts this cross-gender dyad by inserting a third 'I.' As witness to the union between the other two, the third 'I' becomes the broker of knowledge. For this reason, the marriage ceremony Equiano describes pays particular attention to the witnesses, those whom Equiano calls 'their friends':

> On this occasion a feast is prepared, and the bride and bridegroom stand up in the midst of all their friends, who are assembled for the purpose, while he declares she is thenceforth to be looked upon as his wife, and that no other person is to pay any address to her. This is also immediately proclaimed in the vicinity, on which the bride retires from the assembly. (33)

'Their friends,' 'the vicinity,' and 'the assembly' – although different, each of these terms is used to describe the same persons: witnesses. The iterative effect of this triple naming proffers the third 'I' with a multiple and varied perspective clearly denied to the marrying couple. Although it is the man and woman – husband and wife – around whom the ceremony revolves, Equiano's interpretation of this marriage ceremony renders their presence virtually incidental. Note that the 'bride retires from the assembly' and then is 'brought to her husband' (33). Husband and wife are able to do nothing without the consent and intervention of the witness. By first pointing to the possibility and knowledge of exceptions to marriage customs and then shifting focus from the couple to the witnesses, Equiano's rendering of the marriage ceremony shows how he, as witness and writer, possesses the ability to constitute the speech-act; hence, marriage opens up the possibility to write his life in the form of the *Narrative*. With this new-found ability, Equiano writes a new law by using the terms of the old one.

After recounting a number of Africa's 'cultural events,' Equiano acknowledges his distance from the events. The events do not provide information concerning the author's 'life,' but are significant because 'such reflections as these melt the pride of [European] superiority into sympathy for the wants and miseries of their sable brethren, and compel them to acknowledge, that understanding is not confined to feature or colour' (45). Whereas Equiano had been formerly 'recollecting' events in his life, he is now seen *reflecting* upon the circumstances of his life. The shift from recollection to reflection marks the author's self-conscious movement from his personal experience of racism towards mutual and fair exchange. Beneath Equiano's reading of the marriage ceremony lurks the possibility of the event as invention. In his meditations on marriage or, more accurately, on the exceptions to the laws which govern the practice, the *Narrative* manifests a life which does not conform to the constraints it has been assigned.

At the *Narrative*'s midpoint, Equiano forewarns his reader of a structural shift. After relating the circumstances of his captivity and subsequent enslavement, the chapter opens with a helpful summary: 'In the preceding chapter I have set before the reader a few of those many instances of oppression, extortion and cruelty, to which I have been a witness in the West Indies; but, were I to enumerate them all, the catalogue would be tedious and disgusting' (113). After having enumerated a long list of instances of 'oppression, extortion and cruelty,' Equiano decides 'that it cannot any longer afford novelty to recite them; and they are too shocking to yield delight either to the writer or the reader. I shall therefore hereafter only mention such as *incidentally* befel myself' (113; emphasis added). Up until now, the incidents of the *Narrative* have been organized randomly. From this point on, however, Equiano will relate only those events which 'incidentally befel' him. Note the double meaning implied by the adverb. Samuel Johnson's *Dictionary of the English Language*, published in 1755, offers two definitions: 'Beside the main design; occasionally.'[31] While the second meaning relates to the occurrences of Equiano's encounters, the first meaning relates specifically to the structure of the text. Equiano marks the midpoint of his *Narrative* by declaring the import of the digression; that is to say, this *Narrative* relates not only what happens to its author but also what goes on around him, those events which stray from the central subject: the life of the author.

Like the ceremony in Benin, Equiano describes the wedding at St Kitts because it is an exception. On this occasion, however, there can be no doubt: it is the exception that breaks the rule. Equiano's description of this particular ceremony is the most rigorous of all his accounts:

> While I was in this place, St. Kitts, a very curious imposition on human nature took place: – A white man wanted to marry in the church a free black woman that had land and slaves at Montserrat: but the clergy-man told him it was against the law of the place to marry a white and a black in the church. The man then asked to be married on the water, to which the parson consented, and the two lovers went in one boat, and the parson and clerk in another, and thus the ceremony was performed. (119)

It would be redundant, I think, to point out the different ways in which this passage fits in with Equiano's larger project to bridge the gap between his African and British identities. Needless to say, moving the interracial couple from the firm ground of prejudice to the unstable waters of interracial union makes it possible for the author to express his opinion of 'the law of the place' that prohibits a white and black to marry in the church. Equiano uses the wedding scene he has drawn for his reader to convey his thoughts: 'The reader cannot but judge of the irksomeness of this situation to a mind like mine' (119). This situation leaves his mind 'hourly replete with inventions and thoughts of being freed' and leaves him more confused and desperate than the incidents of injustice that he experiences directly. Where the marriage ceremony had previously signified the power of the witness to create the conditions necessary for union, in St Kitts marriage laws restrict relations between black and white. Recording the wedding at St Kitts, performed *in spite of* legal restrictions, makes Equiano a passive accomplice in this illegal act. The appeal to the reader directly following this incident transfers some of his guilt onto the reader.

The reader is in a position to pass judgment on Equiano. Why does the wedding at St Kitts cause the author such agony? Should the problem of interracial union be so pivotal in the author's desire for freedom? Equiano provides a lengthy explanation and justification for his silent participation in the illegal ceremony. But what of the *Narrative*'s reader? As a silent observer of the wedding at St Kitts, the reader must also justify her position. Since there is no loss of life or injury caused by this wedding, the stakes in the reader's judgment and position are low. The stakes are raised, however, with the entry of the 'mulatto-man' (121) into the *Narrative*.

Shortly after the interracial marriage ceremony, Equiano introduces Joseph Clipson, also known as the mulatto-man. Equiano is careful to mention that Clipson was 'born free in St Kitts, and most people on board knew that he served his time to boat building and always passed for a free man' (121). Whether Clipson is the product of the earlier interracial union is difficult to prove. But Clipson's moniker indicates his relation to *some* interracial union in St Kitts, one that is considered illegitimate and leaves Clipson vulnerable to 'infernal invaders of human rights' (121). As Equiano relates Clipson's fate, it becomes increasingly difficult for the reader to remain passive in her judgment of those who break the laws prohibiting interracial unions.

> [Clipson] was forcibly taken out of [the] vessel. He then asked to be carried ashore, before the secretary or magistrates, and these infernal invaders of human rights promised him he should; but, instead of that, without giving the poor man any hearing or shore, or suffering him even to see his

wife and child, he was carried away, and probably doomed never more in this world to see them again. (121)

Could these 'infernal invaders of human rights' include those readers who choose to do nothing to protect interracial unions and their progeny from the imposition of slavery and captivity? Whatever the response to this question, the reader must reconsider her relationship to the text. As the product of an interracial union, Clipson embodies the danger of interracial relationships, particularly those of a sexual nature. Although Equiano never comes into direct contact with Clipson, he feels it necessary to relate Clipson's circumstances. The import of this episode rests on its 'very cruel' nature and because it 'filled [Equiano] with horror' (121). This segment of the *Narrative* further shows the injustice of a culture that refuses to legitimate and respect the interracial relationship, a relationship, Equiano elsewhere contends, that 'would yield more benefit than a prohibition' to both blacks and whites.[32] Reading the marriage at St Kitts in conjunction with the Clipson episode suggests the narrator's purpose is not just to present the author's life or even enumerate 'the horrors of slavery.' Rather, Equiano uses these episodes to foreground his *Narrative* as breaking a law that governs marriage and thus prohibits mutual commerce between African and British subjects.

Shoring Up Equiano's Marriages

These instances of the marriage ceremony, alongside the Clipson episode, exhibit the inextricability of marriage and the formation of Equiano's *Narrative*. The marriage ceremony, as Equiano presents it, is paradigmatic of 'a potentially transgressive discourse' and 'claim[s] a presence and immediacy that is impossible in narrative as an account of the past' (Rajan, 153). It is this generic feature of Equiano's *Narrative* that distinguishes it from other eighteenth-century narratives written in the autobiographical mode and makes it, in Rajan's useful terms, an autonarration. The legal and progenitive aspects of marriage Equiano outlines help us to understand the broader sociopolitical purpose of the *Narrative*. Equiano's interpretation of Benin's marriage practices indicates the importance of the marital contract in determining human relations, while his description of the marriage at St Kitts shows that the terms of the contract are in the best interests of neither the marrying couple nor the society surrounding them. As such, Equiano illegitimizes the law by recording (and thereby legitimating) a union that has been deemed improper by legal codes, but not, importantly, banned by the church. The parson does, after all, agree to marry the couple, albeit outside the walls of the church. The *Narrative*'s explicit support of the marriage can therefore be seen as engaging in an attempt to change the law so that it operates for the mutual benefit of both black and white. The third and final instance calls upon the performative elements of the marriage ceremony to give Equiano's *Narrative* meaning beyond elucidating the author's identity and historical circumstance. It is here that Rajan's notion of autonarration is crucial in thinking through the relationship between the author's identity in his own time and ours.

The third and final representation of marriage takes place in London in 1785. Like Equiano's previous examples, this ceremony is noteworthy because it is atypical. In this instance, the ceremony does not reflect the conventions practised by most people living in England at the time. The mode of marriage practised in England in 1785 would have followed the conventions of the Anglican Church as established by the monarch and bishop. The marriage custom that becomes associated with England by the *Narrative* is an American Quaker wedding. The inclusion of the Quaker wedding (which Equiano also chooses for his own marriage to the white Englishwoman Susanna Cullen) in the final pages of the *Narrative* makes clear Equiano's rhetorical use of the marriage ceremony. Carretta's textual note accompanying the incident reiterates this fact: 'by inserting the letter of thanks to the Quakers and his description of the Quaker wedding, both set in London, Equiano has digressed from the chronology of his narrative (297, note 631). Again, it is by way of the digression that Equiano involves his reader in the progression of the *Narrative*'s events.

By situating the author/reader relationship through a scene of an atypical marriage arrangement, Equiano forces the reader to assess her own identity and the ways in which it has changed through her engagement with a subject who is treated unjustly by the law. Equiano inscribes the wedding vow as well as describes it. Noting that 'the man audibly declares to this purpose' (225), Equiano's account of the general event indicates that the vow can be read as well as heard. This remark is followed by an inscription of the vow itself, which, of course, the reader must read (at the very least) to herself. Reading the vow in the context of Equiano's *Narrative* gives it its performative effect and the reader and Equiano are hereafter united by the law. Describing the event, Equiano declares: 'Friends, in the fear of the Lord, and before this assembly, I take this my friend, M.N. to be my wife, promising, through divine assistance, to be unto her a loving and faithful husband until it shall please the Lord by death to separate us.' (225) The 'I' of this passage is Equiano, but the identity of the 'wife' remains unknown. Equiano uses the initials M.N. to denote the other rather than a proper name, leaving the other's identity ambiguous. Equiano also made a number of revisions to this particular passage. Carretta explains that the first five editions of the *Narrative* contain the lines 'promising, through divine assistance to be unto her a loving and faithful husband till death separate us.' In the following four editions, Equiano changes this line to read 'promising, through divine assistance to be unto her a loving and faithful husband until it shall please the Lord by death to separate us,' giving the Lord rather than any mortal man the right to separate the couple.[33] The Quaker wedding vow, fully inscribed, becomes the model for the interpretive process as a dialogue in which the text mediates a series of differences within and between author and reader so that the two might experience, in Equiano's terms, 'mutual commerce.' He further writes that '[a] commercial intercourse with Africa opens an inexhaustible source of wealth to the manufacturing interest of Great Britain, and to all which the slave-trade is an objection' (234). The marital contract bears economic fruit as Equiano ends his *Narrative* explaining the mutual benefit of African-British relations.

The marriage vow marks an intercourse between reader and author. Since Equiano's vow must be simultaneously read and heard to have its desired effect, the *Narrative*'s reader provides the necessary context for the event. Unlike Rajan's female subject, 'who must negotiate her relationship between representation and experience *without* relying on the constative or performative utterance' (153; my italics), the African-British subject employs both at once. It is with the utterance of the wedding vow that the *Narrative* performs a 'transgressive miscegenation.' As the relationship between reader and author is couched in the terms of the wedding ceremony, this miscegenous relationship is granted the stamp of legitimacy otherwise not recognized and protected by the law.

Although Equiano is the subject of the wedding vow, he does not forego his position as witness. In the Quaker ceremony, the witnesses do not remain silent. Instead, they are to sign their names to the marriage certificate that endorses the couple's union. The presence of the witness is necessary to the union. It is not surprising, then, that of the marriage ceremonies Equiano witnesses, it is the Quaker mode of marriage that he 'highly recommend[s]' (226). The Quaker ceremony not only upsets the *Narrative*'s chronology, but it provides the context and principle by which the incidents of the *Narrative*, as well as the reader's position in those incidents, must be assessed.

In marked contrast to the scenes of abuse Equiano suffers, the exchange of vows between subjects within the context of the marriage ceremony represents a space in which a just situation can be imagined. Whereas Equiano and his fellow slaves are without recourse when they are treated cruelly by the 'infernal invaders of human rights,' he finds in the marriage ceremony a contract that shields him (and his countrymen) from their actions. Moreover, if one of the subjects breaks a vow – as was the case in the first marriage Equiano described – the community will be called upon to decide upon the just punishment. In this way, the marriage ceremony enables Equiano to imagine a life and system of exchange far removed from the restrictions and practices of slavery. It is perhaps somewhat surprising to note that Equiano makes little mention of his own wedding and subsequent marriage to Cullen. He writes only that he was married to 'Miss Cullen, daughter of James and Ann Cullen' on the 7th of April after hearing the debate in the house of Commons on the Slave Trade (235). There is little evidence to suggest that either Equiano or Cullen encountered any opposition to their union and, as his will makes evident, he benefited greatly from it.[34]

Like much of the *Narrative*, Equiano's account of the marriage ceremony has little to do with his personal experience. Instead, the marriage ceremony provides Equiano with a vehicle to produce both a critique and legal end to slavery. His representation of different ceremonies calls into question the ways in which interpersonal relationships are regulated by peculiar institutions and calls for such regulations to be dismantled. The descriptions and reproductions of marriage ceremonies throughout the course of the *Narrative* help readers to understand its fictional elements and its argument against slavery. Reading the *Narrative* as an act of textual miscegenation rather than within the confines of particular historical, generic, or national literary categories makes more sense in relation to the terms of Equiano's project. Equiano concludes his *Narrative* advocating a union between Britain and Africa through 'economic intercourse' (234). Such a union is predicated, it would seem, upon terms for mutual exchange between these subjects that Equiano's *Narrative* establishes through witnessing the dissolution of difference between African and British subjects. Equiano's methodical insertions of marriage within his *Narrative* cause a rupture in the chronology of his life story. These ruptures represent the ways in which Equiano resists racial and other interpellative, captivating discourses that attempt to relegate him to the margins of political life.

The slave narrative's emphasis on communal utterances and collective tales elides the distinctive features of Equiano's consciousness; this *Narrative* offers the possibility of imagining a life outside the confines of his experience as black and oppressed. Equiano's *Narrative* is *not* a prototypical slave narrative or a British eighteenth-century personal narrative or a captivity narrative. Despite efforts to incorporate the text as foundational to old and new traditions, the *Narrative* must be read as a text that imagines a life apart from conventions committed to continuing or establishing tradition, thus conceptually evading captivity itself.

But without participating in tradition, what establishes the use and truth value of Equiano's eighteenth-century text in the twenty-first? This is a question that continues to linger. Equiano's efforts to rewrite his life on his own terms must still confront the fact of his blackness. Equiano's *Narrative* is interested in addressing the contradictions and cracks within both African and British legal systems by engaging readers in free exchange and intercourse with the circumstances of his life. It is unfortunate that twentieth- and twenty-first-century readers insist on constructing barriers to restrict the free exchange between reader and author that Equiano's *Narrative* promotes.

NOTES

1 Eight editions were printed in Great Britain during the author's lifetime, and a first American edition appeared in New York in 1791. In his introduction to the 1995 edition, Vincent Carretta reprints some of the favourable reviews the *Narrative* received upon its first publication; see Olaudah Equiano, *The Interesting Narrative and Other Writings*, ed. and intro. Vincent Carretta (New York: Penguin, 1995). All further page references to Equiano's *Narrative* will be to Carretta's edition and appear parenthetically in the body of the essay.
2 Vincent Carretta, introduction to *The Interesting Narrative and Other Writings*, xxv.
3 See John Marrant's *A Narrative of the Lord's Wonderful Dealings with John Marrant* (1785) and Michel René Hilliard D'Auberteuil's *Miss McCrea: A Novel of the American Revolution* (1784), both in Gordon M. Sayre, ed., *Olaudah Equino, Mary Rowlandson, and Others: American Captivity Narratives* (Boston: Houghton Mifflin, 2000), 203–24; 352–76.
4 Gretchen Holbrook Gerzina, 'Mobility in Chains: Freedom of Movement in

the Early Black Atlantic,' *South Atlantic Quarterly* 100.1 (2001): 44. See also Stuart Hall, 'Cultural Identity and Diaspora,' in *Identity, Community, Culture, Difference*, ed. Jonathan Rutherford (London: Lawrence and Wishart, 1990), 235; and Paul Gilroy, *The Black Atlantic: Modernity and Double Consciousness* (Cambridge: Harvard University Press, 1993), 12.

5 Adam Potkay, 'History, Oratory, and God in Equiano's *Interesting Narrative*,' *Eighteenth-Century Studies* 34.4 (2001): 602.

6 S.E. Ogude, 'Facts into Fiction: Equiano's *Narrative* Reconsidered,' *Research in African Literatures* 13 (1982): 33.

7 Vincent Carretta, 'Defining a Gentleman: The Status of Olaudah Equiano or Gustavus Vassa,' *Language Sciences* 22 (2000): 386.

8 Dwight McBride, *Impossible Witnesses: Truth, Abolitionism, and Slave Testimony* (New York: New York University Press, 2001), 135. See also Wilfred D. Samuels, 'Disguised Voice in *The Interesting Narrative of Olaudah Equiano or Gustavus Vassa, the African*,' *Black American Literature Forum* 19.2 (1985): 64–9; and Paul Edwards, 'Three West African Writers of the 1780s,' in *The Slave's Narrative*, ed. Charles T. Davis and Henry Louis Gates, Jr (Oxford: Oxford University Press, 1983), 175–98.

9 Henry Louis Gates, Jr, *The Signifying Monkey: A Theory of African-American Literary Criticism* (New York: Oxford University Press, 1988), 153.

10 Henry Louis Gates, Jr, introduction to *The Classic Slave Narratives*, ed. and intro. Henry Louis Gates, Jr (New York: Penguin, 1987), xiv. Houston A. Baker, Jr, *Blues, Ideology, and Afro-American Literature: A Vernacular Theory* (Chicago: University of Chicago Press, 1984), 31.

11 Marion Rust, 'Speaking of Olaudah Equiano,' in *Passing and the Fictions of Identity*, ed. Elaine K. Ginsberg (Durham, NC: Duke University Press, 1996), 24.

12 James Olney, '"I Was Born": Slave Narratives, Their Status as Autobiography and as Literature,' in *The Slave's Narrative*, ed. Charles T. Davis and Henry Louis Gates, Jr (Oxford: Oxford University Press, 1985), 151.

13 Tanya Caldwell, '"Talking Too Much English": Languages of Economy and Politics in Equiano's *The Interesting Narrative*,' *Early American Literature* 34 (1999): 264.

14 Elizabeth Jane Wall Hinds, 'The Spirit of Trade: Olaudah Equiano's Conversion, Legalism, and the Merchant's Life,' *African American Review* 32 (1998), 635–47; Julia K. Ward, 'The Master's Tools: Abolitionist Arguments of Equiano and Cugoano,' in *Subjugation and Bondage: Critical Essays on Slavery and Social Philosophy*, ed. Tommy L. Lott (New York: Rowman and Littlefield, 1998), 79–98.

15 Gordon M. Sayre, introduction to *Olaudah Equiano, Mary Rowlandson, and Others*, 4–5.

16 Joseph Fichtelberg's recent assessment of Equiano reads him more specifically as a 'captive of the market.' In doing so, Fichtelberg argues that Equiano 'attains his freedom by mastering the inner life of commodities, which he associates with the discipline of Christian feeling.' Equiano's 'captivity narrative' is thus read in conjunction with Crevecoeur's *Letters from an American Farmer* as both explore their 'strange encounters' as holding 'the possibility for infinite gain and infinite loss.' See Joseph Fichtelberg, *Critical Fictions: Sentiment and the American Market, 1780–1870* (Atlanta: University of Georgia Press, 2003), 29.
17 Sayre, introduction, 5.
18 Equiano's exceptional wealth can be observed most vividly in the will he composed on 28 May 1796. Carretta informs us that '[a]t a time when fewer than 5% of the male population had enough assets to merit writing a will, and when perhaps no other person of African descent in Britain left a will,' Equiano left his surviving daughter 950 pounds – the equivalent to $120,000 today (Carretta, 'Defining a Gentleman,' 398).
19 W.E.B. DuBois, *The Souls of Black Folk* (1903; New York: Fawcett, 1961), 17.
20 Tilottama Rajan, 'Autonarration and Genotext in Mary Hays' *Memoirs of Emma Courtney*' *Studies in Romanticism* 32.2 (1993): 149–76 (subsequent references will be cited parenthetically). It should be noted that while the term 'miscegenation' is now the common one for discussions of the sexual 'mixing' of races (and all of the problematics involved in such a concept), it is somewhat anachronistic here, since 'miscegenation' and related words were only coined in 1864, in the pamphlet 'Miscegenation: The Theory of the Blending of the Races Applied to the American White Man and Negro.' For critical discussions of miscegenation, see, for example, Heather Hathaway, '"Maybe Freedom Lies in Hating": Miscegenation and the Oedipal Conflict,' in *Refiguring the Father: New Feminist Readings of the Patriarchy*, ed. Patricia Yaeger and Beth Kowaleski-Wallace (Carbondale: Southern Illinois University Press, 1989), 153–67; and Shirley Samuels, 'Miscegenated America: The Civil War,' *American Literary History* 9 (1997): 482–501.
21 Within this context, it is of some interest that one of the earliest reviews of the *Narrative* was written by Mary Wollstonecraft in the May 1789 issue of the *Analytical Review*. Wollstonecraft's interest in the *Narrative* may have been motivated by the generic similarities between life narratives by women and former slaves in the eighteenth century; see Mary Wollstonecraft, review of *The Interesting Narrative*, rpt. in *The Interesting Narrative of the Life of Olaudah Equiano*, ed. Angelo Costanzo (Peterborough: Broadview Press, 2001), 262–3.
22 J.L. Austin, *How to Do Things with Words* (Cambridge: Harvard University Press, 1962), 5.

23 For example, Andrew Parker and Eve Kosofsky Sedgwick elucidate the various ways in which Austin's work has been effectively used by contemporary theorists to interrogate linguistic and cultural practices that debase queer identities in the United States; see Andrew Parker and Eve Kosofsky Sedgwick, introduction to *Performativity and Performance* (New York: Routledge, 1995), 6–7.
24 Carretta points out the significant role Equiano's own marriage plays in his 'continuous acts of social self-[re]construction' by showing how it 'gained him access to the ownership of land through inheritance on his wife's side' (Carretta, 'Defining a Gentleman,' 390). Here I am interested in the rhetorical uses Equiano makes of marriage in writing his life-story.
25 Carolyn D. Williams, 'Another Self in the Case: Gender, Marriage and the Individual in Augustan Literature,' in *Rewriting the Self: Histories from the Renaissance to the Present*, ed. Roy Porter (London: Routledge, 1997), 104.
26 James Walvin, *Black and White: The Negro and English Society, 1555–1945* (London: Penguin, 1973), 54.
27 Ibid, 55.
28 Ibid.
29 For an extended discussion on Equiano's thoughts on interracial marriage see his letter to James Tobin published in the *Public Advertiser*, rpt. in *The Interesting Narrative and Other Writings*, 328–30.
30 Equiano's note reads, 'See Benezet's *Account of Guinea* throughout.' See also Carretta's additional note for a brief description of Benezet (241).
31 Samuel Johnson, *A Dictionary of the English Language* (London: Times Books, 1979; London: W. Strahan for J. and P. Knapton, 1755).
32 Olaudah Equiano, letter to James Tobin, the *Public Advertiser*, 28 January 1788, rpt. in *The Interesting Narrative and Other Writings*, 329.
33 Carretta, 'Defining a Gentleman,' 398.
34 According to Equiano's will, through his marriage to Susanna Cullen he acquired 'Two Acres of Copyhold Pasture Ground with the Appurtenances' (354).

Captivating Discourses:
Class and Nation

CHAPTER 4

'From the Slums *to* the Slums': The Delimitation of Social Identity in Late Victorian Prison Narratives

Frank Lauterbach

Contemplating his experience of no less than seventeen Victorian prisons within twenty-five years, the anonymous ex-convict 'No. 7' concludes that the portal of every English jail should display the words 'From the slums *to* the slums.'[1] And Jabez Spencer Balfour, a former MP sentenced to penal servitude in 1895 on charges of fraud, observes on the occasion of his detention in the Black Maria that 'to a man of refinement the sudden association, on terms of equality, ... with the noisy and ribald dregs of criminal and outcast London is an experience calculated to beget despair in the most sanguine mind.'[2] Though their experiences and circumstances differ widely, both 'No. 7' and Balfour associate the 'typical' inmates of a prison with a specific social class: 'No. 7,' coming from what seems to be a lower-middle-class background, claims an almost inevitable causal 'relationship between the common lodging-house and the gaol' (129) and, thus, links the urban 'slums' of virtual homelessness outside the prison to the 'slum' made up of the jail itself. Less detached (and more conceited) in his analysis, Balfour tries to retain an air of respectability by immediately and unequivocally labelling the other prisoners as the scum of the metropolis. 'No. 7,' an experienced 'jail-bird,' as well as Balfour, a celebrated novice (who himself used to be part of the law-making process), are, then, strikingly similar in their perception of the prison as a place with specific social associations. For both writers (who, incidentally, met at Parkhurst Prison) the 'typical' inmates of a jail are of a certain class: the homeless outcasts, and hence delinquents, of the city. Consequently, the prison becomes culturally significant as a marker to delimit different social realms; that is, a criminal nether world, seen to be inevitably associated with the prison by the respectable bourgeoisie, represented by political and legal authorities at the various stages of the penal process.

Balfour's attitude is particularly revealing in this respect. His narrative gesture in the above passage of engaging the outside perspective of a middle-class politician, through the rather abstract reference to 'a man of refinement,' suggests that those inmates he describes as criminals represent social otherness. Rather than focusing on penal practices and their effects on himself and/or others, Balfour renders the prison (or, in this case, the Black Maria) meaningful as a descriptive boundary between himself and a socially different group and, thus, between opposite classes distinguished in terms of respectability, delinquency, criminality, and so forth. Despite his extreme snobbishness, Balfour's reflections can serve as a representative example for most late Victorian prison writing by convicts (as well as by prison administrators and penal reformers). In fact, the perception of the prison as a boundary – and, more importantly, the ensuing textual subjection of the convicts to a specific group identity – emerges as a central leitmotif in writing from and about imprisonment in the Victorian period. In what follows, I will primarily offer a reading of various first-hand accounts of imprisonment – accounts which were widely read as thrilling (and chilling) sensation pieces but which have rarely been the object of serious study[3] – and I will argue that the perception of the prison as a boundary allows for textualizing the differentiation between prisoners and any sort of outside authority as a means of social identification rather than personal subjection. In this process, various strategies of such textualizations of difference can be employed, depending on whether the Other is considered to belong to the same systemic category as the Self or whether it is conceived as decidedly 'alien.'

I

Because I focus on the ways in which the perception of the prison as a social boundary serves these strategies – and how they, in return, support identificatory purposes – my argument will depart from some central paradigms established by a number of penal historiographies. One of the most fundamental of these paradigms – equally prominent in Whiggish, Marxist, and (so-called) revisionist accounts – has been to view the *effect* of prisons on inmates as a key to mapping the development of carceral establishments. Whichever stance historians take towards nineteenth-century (British and Anglo-American) prison reforms, they are primarily concerned with the relationship between the confining institution and the confined individual. In liberal interpretations, this focus on the prison's effect on the individual is linked to an endorsement of the reformers' attempts to alleviate the delinquent's miseries and to allow for his/her readmission into society. Thus, even a cursory sampling of such views finds Torsten Eriksson detecting 'innumerable examples of [man's] compassion and of his will to lead the offender into a new life as a useful and responsible citizen,' while Christopher Hibbert identifies the movement towards 'relating [punishments] to each individual criminal' as *the* historical solution for combating crime.[4] Even though the revisionist rereading of prison history questioned such progressivist optimism, it retained a no less individualistic approach. Likewise concerned with the penal institution's effect on the imprisoned subject, revisionists, then, see reformatory establishments as powerful instruments for the discursive control of the individual inmate. Michel Foucault's 1975 classic *Discipline and Punish* most paradigmatically represents this interpretation of the modern prison as, in Jonathan Simon's words, part of a 'society obsessed with the deep truths of the individual, exemplified by delinquents.'[5] For Foucault, the penitentiary targets the criminal's soul rather than his/her body through 'punishment that acts in depth on the heart, the thoughts, the will, the inclinations.'[6] The strategy exercised for this end is what he calls 'disciplinary power,' a form of power that rather than 'bending all its subjects into a single uniform mass, ... "trains" the moving, confused, useless multitudes of bodies and forces into a multiplicity of individual elements – small, separate cells, organic autonomies.'[7] In short, Foucault claims that the individual is 'a reality fabricated by this specific technology of power' and that '[d]iscipline "makes" individuals'[8] – a view that finds its precursor in Max Horkheimer and Theodor W. Adorno's contention that the modern penitentiary is informed by the self-centred individuality of bourgeois 'monadism' in the sense of Leibniz's *La Monadologie*.[9] Others echo this sentiment, but such assessments do little more than 'embod[y] an unconvincingly gloomy photographic negative image of Whiggism.'[10]

In contrast to these – positive or negative – appraisals of imprisonment (as a penal instrument) in relation to the inmates it targets, the first-hand memoirs by Balfour and 'No. 7' seem to suggest a curiously different notion of the prison. Both writers employ it as a cultural emblem that derives its meaning from the identificatory potential it has for specific social groups. Thus, my reading of late Victorian convict literature will be less concerned with the effects caused by the prison's actual operation than with such acts of signification as may arise out of its intersubjective perception. This is by no means to deny that the carceral institution's influence on the prisoner did, indeed, become an important preoccupation in penological discourse from the late eighteenth century on. Yet, to write a history of imprisonment (or its literary depiction, for that matter) chiefly from the vantage point of its relationship to the individual tends to obscure the larger cultural connotations and uses of the prison. It privileges the process of subjection (in the double sense of the word) *through* the prison over how the prison *itself* has been subjected to processes of signification. These depend on collective perceptions, on meanings always already established in a particular social environment, and, therefore, involve the prison as an object or institution in a series of culturally significant interpretative moves. Imprisonment (whether actual or textually represented) can, consequently, be understood as an enactment of such interpretations, i.e., as a social event – more precisely as a socially meaningful event – rather than a 'set of social practices.'[11]

Though Marxist interpretations of penal history do acknowledge the social contexts of imprisonment by correlating penal practices with various modes of economic production, they do not exploit the larger cultural meanings of the prison but retain a conception of it as primarily the locus of punishing offenders. The early study by Georg Rusche and Otto Kirchheimer along the lines of the Frankfurt School, for instance, centres on an investigation of penal *practices* even when their examination of 'the causal relationship between methods of punishment and the organization of society' links the effects of imprisonment (and punitive measures at large) to wider economic interests.[12] More recently, Dario Melossi and Massimo Pavarini, building on Rusche and Kirchheimer's argument, have identified prisons, next to a variety of other institutions, as 'essential' bourgeois 'instruments of social policy' ('strumenti essenziali della politica sociale') for the 'formation, production, and reproduction of the factory proletariat' ('formazione, produzione e riproduzione del proletariato di fabbrica').[13] Whereas this approach does emphasize the social significance of the prison, it remains monodirectional in that it concentrates on the prison's controlling and repressive effects – albeit those effects that concern a whole social class rather than merely individuals. What remains obscure in this picture are both the gestures of perceiving the prison *per se* (from the inside as well as the outside) and the matrix of collective (self-)classifications framed by such perceptions.

Therefore, I propose that whatever personal or class subjections prisons entail, they can always also be turned into emblems that, within a given culture, provide the means of social identification. Hence, they may obtain social meanings and become part of a wider circle of cultural semiotics, which can be charted in recourse to the analysis of bourgeois totems (that is, the totemic categories of the *pensée bourgeoise*) advanced by the cultural anthropologist Marshall Sahlins. Sahlins's observation that the 'object stands as a human concept outside itself, as man speaking to man through the medium of things' allows for assigning (non-natural) objects 'the power of making even the demarcation of their individual owners a procedure of social classification.'[14] What makes this totemist conception of Western society relevant for my reading of imprisonment is Sahlins's move from the materiality of objects to their being collectively perceived as culturally constitutive. If by means of 'the systematic arrangement of meaningful differences assigned the concrete, the cultural order is realized also as an order of goods,' the distinct intrinsic qualities of such goods, which serve as the 'totems' of industrial societies, can be seen as reflective of social differentiations.[15] Even though, with regard to imprisonment, neither the juxtaposition of *intrinsic* qualities (of, let's say, different types of penal institutions) nor the concept of 'owning' a prison can serve as a viable analytical category, I, nevertheless, suggest following Sahlins's totemist move towards relating the conceptualization of objects to procedures of social classification. In this sense, prisons *per se* can be considered to generate differentiations by serving as a line of demarcation between two or more qualities or entities. They can function as material reproductions of class (and other) relations by virtue of becoming the visible projection for and conceptual objectification of a boundary that distinguishes between what belongs to them and what does not. And, *qua* representing this boundary, they evoke such meaningful differences as allow for what Sahlins has called procedures of social classification, constitutive of the cultural order. Consequently then, instead of referring to some sort of 'ownership' of a totemic object, it seems more useful to talk about an *association* with the totem (as an inevitable result of the imprisonment) – or, more precisely, with one of the classificatory categories it delimits.[16]

Thus, two basic questions emerge for an analysis of prison narratives. What types and forms of differentiatory relationships does the prison perpetuate as an emblem or totem of the *pensée bourgeoise* of Victorian society? And, how do such differentiations serve processes of identification for those standing on opposite sides of the boundary? To repeat, both queries focus on the symbolic function of the prison within the process of cultural signification, on the social meanings (and ironies) encoded in convict autobiographies – rather than on the prison's immediate effect on (or power over) an individual or a social class.[17] As such, they move beyond the analytical categories put forth by Ioan Davies in what amounts to the most comprehensive (and erratic) monograph in English on writing from prison. Though Davies, too, highlights the delimiting nature of the prison when he views imprisonment as the 'recognition of being in another culture,'[18] this recognition seems to lead less to social significations of (cultural) otherness than to textual responses to the new experience. Hence, the prison becomes 'a centre of intellectual activity' or 'a school for writers' nurturing an 'incarcerated imagination.'[19] (Considering the still comparatively low percentage of prisoners actually writing, Davies' faith in the self-reflective effects of imprisonment sounds suspiciously close to that of radical nineteenth-century proponents of reformatory prisons.) The writing produced in prison is, first and foremost, seen in relation to its redemptive function – with Davies' assessment that through it prisoners 'try to rescue themselves and us' moving in a rather grandiose manner from the prison cell to humanity at large.[20] Yet, even those critics who (unlike Davies) are less concerned with autobiographical responses to the prison experience than with (more or less) fictional representations of captivity also stress the liberating effect of being in jail. Hence, W.B. Carnochan sees confinement as an 'invitation to reflection,' commonly leading to 'a hope of transcendence,'[21] and other writers have approached this possibility of transcendence in recourse to various literary modes: Victor Brombert, for instance, traces a Romantic tradition which portrays the cell not only as a 'place of suffering' but as a 'place of protection, of reverie, of freedom' as well.[22] This almost dialectical link between 'enclosure and spirituality'[23] is also at the heart of Christa Karpenstein-Eßbach's more idealist argument that the situation of imprisonment 'belongs to and structures the inventory of forms of literary imagination.'[24] Finally, Mary Ann Frese Witt takes existentialist literature as a starting point to perceive prisons as potentially 'voluntary, beneficial enclosures,' so that 'the deprivation of physical liberty opens the way to a spiritual freedom.'[25] What these interpretations have in common is an attempt to causally link imprisonment to forms of transcendence, imagination, or inner freedom – a link that centres subjectivity and selfhood on the individual experience of space but that fails to address how the jail partakes of the larger, collective production of meaning and, thus, provides the means of social identification so central to many jail narratives. It is this wider cultural semiotics that I will now turn to in my reading of some late Victorian prison autobiographies.

II

A fine example of the use of the prison as a socially delimiting marker is *Five Years' Penal Servitude* (1877), a best-selling book whose 'restrained intelligence ... makes it the classic account of later Victorian prison life.'[26] It was published anonymously as the memoir of 'One Who Has Endured It,' who has been identified as Edward Callow.[27] However, for reasons I will return to later, I shall refer to its author as 'One Who Has Endured It.' His initial detention in Newgate for an unspecified business crime was followed by his conviction and a mandatory nine-month period of separate confinement in Millbank. He was subsequently moved to Dartmoor for penal servitude and was released after a remission of his sentence to four (instead of five) years. Like nearly all writers of Victorian prison narratives, 'One Who Has Endured It' is an exceptional convict in that he belongs to the educated middle class. While most inmates actually had a poor (rural or urban) working-class background, the majority of those who left an account of their experiences were either political detainees (such as Fenians, suffragettes, etc.) or well-educated 'gentleman prisoners' (mostly businessmen charged with commercial crimes like fraud or embezzlement).[28] It is this latter group of writers (of which 'One Who Has Endured It' is the first major representative and which also includes Jabez Spencer Balfour) on which I will focus in order to show how the prison was emblematically used to underscore the cultural value system of the late Victorian bourgeoisie.[29]

Like most other writers, 'One Who Has Endured It' does not reveal any close identification between himself and the space of the prison. Instead of conveying a sense of 'endurance' (as one might assume, given his alias), he eagerly distances himself from the carceral reality in general and his fellow inmates in particular. A notion of respectability is retained that follows repeated claims of innocence (3 et passim).[30] Not a criminal in his self-perception, 'One Who Has Endured It' writes that he was supposedly indicted in the place of someone he refers to as 'my Mephistopheles' (8). This unspecified other person is, thus, subtly portrayed as the real criminal – as an adversary associated with hell, sin, and deception – which, in turn, means that 'One Who Has Endured It' himself should not be associated with criminals. Consequently, he reports that his eminent lawyer, having known him from boyhood on, was surprised to even see him imprisoned (8). While I, by no means, wish to doubt his innocence, this insistence on his integrity is quite unnecessary in a text whose self-proclaimed intention is to correct previous accounts of penal practices through a 'plain unvarnished tale' (2). Yet, for virtually every middle-class prisoner who published his own experiences, affirmations of innocence seem to have been essential.[31] However, as early as 1881 a writer for *Blackwood's* mocked those ex-convicts (including 'One Who Has Endured It') who 'lapse from external respectability into crime' and 'have generally something like an apology to state.'[32] These apologies include Balfour blaming a succession of mishaps and complaining that his 'side of the case has never been made public'[33] (an omission his own narrative does not care to correct either), 'No. 7' insisting that it was minor trifles and the false testimony of others that got him into a criminal career (9–10; 20–1), and the 'Ticket-of-Leave Man' asserting that he had lived 'in the character of a gentleman, and with the reputation of an honourable man.'[34] Attempting to be more honest, Jorgen Jorgenson refers to his desire for gambling – slyly personified as an abstract Other, that is, the 'grip of the gambling fiend' – as getting him into trouble over and over again.[35] Finally, 'One Who Has Tried Them' simply dismisses the matter altogether: 'Why, where, or for what I was arrested, matters not to the reader.'[36]

Such assertions imply that the writers remain respectable despite having been arrested. Under no circumstances do they want to be associated with the average criminal who constantly moves in and out of jail. On the contrary, when, in Jorgenson's words, their 'sensibilities of the heart are drawn forth by the early culture of the mind,' they feel severely out of place.[37] 'One Who Has Endured It' is particularly insistent on his not belonging to the mass of convicts. He proudly points out that (in Millbank) he was in the ward of 'the quietest and best behaved men in the prison' (103) and, as to his character, he quotes the testimony of various authorities: to a warder at Millbank he 'seemed a respectable man' (73); a Metropolitan detective declared that 'you're not one of our birds' (361); and the Newgate chaplain 'presumed he need not ask me the usual questions, could I read and write' (27). As being able to read a book associates him with 'the better class' of society (109), even little incidents like that chaplain's compliment – as well as the familiarity he suggests between the two of them (27–8) – are inserted as a sign of his difference and to show that their values are alike, that 'One Who Has Endured It' is an upright man. In fact, what he most enjoys about his discharge is not the reunion with his family (which he does not even mention though it had concerned him during his imprisonment) but to get 'once more into the habits of civilisation' (362) and to move 'in what is known as a respectable life' (23). To dispel any doubt, he furthermore alludes to his respectable business-life at the time of his writing the book (20–1). The prison experience is represented as temporary, as a trip of four years, with the before and after clearly set off (22–3). This entails both that death in jail has to be considered a particularly 'sorry end for a man who has once lived respected and beloved' (118) and that he express his content over the fact that he did not meet any of his former fellow inmates after his release – with the exception of two 'men, like myself, who had been in good positions' (24), one of whom, at least, 'stood greatly on his dignity' (25; see also 130–1).

While the notion of respectability thus serves the self-assurance of 'One Who Has Endured It,' it is even more significantly employed as a dissociative marker from other convicts. These he refers to as 'brutes in mind and demons in heart' (208), 'coarse foul-mouthed brute[s]' (179), 'great scoundrels, with but few redeeming qualities' (124), 'a different species to ordinary men' (208), and 'irreclaimable item[s] of humanity' (135), whose presence is 'too horrible to think of' (137). Others talk of 'wild beasts,'[38] of 'miscreants' who have 'no higher aspiration than to gratify [their] animal nature,'[39] or of how 'the atmosphere is ... a little hell' in their presence.[40] Epithets like these are designed to represent the prison as the place of the ethically least acceptable stratum of society and, hence, as the very opposite of respectability.[41] Signifying, as it does, crime and degradation, the prison differentiates middle-class writers like 'One Who Has Endured It' from moral and social otherness alike. When he remarks, with respect to a repeatedly convicted receiver of goods, that '[t]hose are the men to catch, and who richly deserve the punishment they get' (53), he emphatically reinforces the view that the really guilty criminals truly belong to the prison and yet, by virtue of having claimed his innocence and superior position, he can still dissociate himself from this social function of imprisonment. While in Dartmoor, he moves even further. For the '*London roughs*,' who are 'almost irreclaimable, and not at all amenable to any ordinary moral influence' and whose 'animal instincts and propensities predominate to the almost total exclusion of any intellectual or human feeling' (208), he can conceive of only one treatment: the lash (209; see also 331 and 377–9). Though he sometimes has to converse with the most brutal of criminals by necessity, 'One Who Has Endured It' makes sure that the reader never views his interest in them as genuine (67). In fact, he prefers solitary confinement because it prevents him from 'being herded and brought into daily, hourly contact with ... ruffians and blackguards' (133). Similarly, the anonymous convict writing about his 'Twenty Years' Penal Servitude' claims that separation would prevent him, 'a gentleman, with refined and honourable feelings,' from 'associating with thieves and pickpockets,' from having 'to herd with the scum of society' that can only speak its own, different slang language anyway.[42] Tellingly, both writers dread being *herded* with other convicts, thus signalling through the very choice of words that they perceive these fellow inmates more as cattle than as men.[43]

The use of the prison in the above examples as an emblematic, totemic boundary between respectability and 'savage' forms of criminality is time and again expressed through the notion of *class*. For instance, 'One Who Has Endured It' describes himself (even after years in Dartmoor) as 'a different class of man from the usual run' (249), and the anonymous author of 'A Convict's View of Penal Discipline' likewise distinguishes the 'respectable class' from the 'dangerous class' of prisoners[44] – the latter of which others see as 'men, chiefly from the lowest ranks.'[45] Most consequential, however, is the application of the class concept in the suggestions for penal reform put forth by the 'Ticket-of-Leave Man.' He denies any 'tenderness for that ruffian class, who ... exist from childhood to old age' and he, therefore, shows no 'sympathy with crime or with the criminal class.'[46] Hence, his proposal – made in favour of those prisoners who, like himself, 'do not belong to the absolutely criminal class'[47] – is to delimit people of his own background from those irrevocably criminal. In contrast to other writers, he is, however, not satisfied with establishing such delimitations on a rhetorical level. Instead, he wants to send the criminal 'class' off to an island colony where they would have to obtain their own subsistence under the strict enforcement of a military law. The advantage of this scheme is supposed to be that if 'they determined still to be birds of prey [that is, thieves] they could only prey upon each other, and would cease to be a curse and a nuisance to honest men.'[48]

This strategy of associating (implicitly at least) the criminal Other with exotic places serves differentiating purposes yet more forcefully when social and even ethnic categories are introduced to characterize members of the criminal 'ranks.' Of the two 'grades of society' 'One Who Has Endured It' watches in the exercise yard at Newgate, namely the 'City merchant' and 'the wretched little street Arab,' it is the latter (and definitely not the former) 'whose destination in all probability ... would be a reformatory' (30). Two things are remarkable in this assessment. First, vagrants are automatically and immediately the social group which is seen to need the reformatory and which is, thus, associated with crime. Second, these vagrants are not only a moral or a social Other but are further differentiated through racialist clichés (here borrowed from such writers as Henry Mayhew) that 'One Who Has Endured It' could safely assume would be shared by his readers.[49] The ordinary criminal portrayed as an Arab living in the streets is clearly from a different world, is definitely alien. Likewise, 'One Who Has Endured It' points out the distance between himself and a Jewish receiver of goods (a kind of more realistic and 'civil' Fagin), who 'knew at once I was not one of his "children"' (257). And, when 'No. 7' meets 'the first of a long series of remarkable prisoners with whom it is not, thank heaven! given to every man to rub shoulders' (11), he immediately differentiates himself from a man who turns out to have 'a more than sentimental leaning towards the ways of the African savages' (11). This person's proclamation of allegiance to 'that dusky [Zulu] potentate Chetawayo' (12) leads 'No. 7' to a series of denouncements: he compares him to Nero (14), detects 'a taint of the salamander in his composition' (15), and associates him with the inferno (15).[50] Thus, this character, who supposedly 'richly deserved [his] punishment' (12), is not only of a different social class but is, as such, likened to 'savages,' animals, a tyrant, and the devil. The delimitating function of the prison can hardly be employed in a more sweeping manner. Yet, 'No. 7' has another metaphorical likening of criminals to a different ethnic group in stock. He, who, it should be noted, claims rather absurdly that he is writing not in *English* but 'in plain Anglo-Saxon' (202), uses the following simile to consider the difficulties of released convicts in becoming law-abiding. Citing the example of his fellow prisoner 'B 2, 14,' described as 'an Ethiopian in the social sense' (49), he writes: 'No one nowadays cares to undertake the task of whitewashing an Ethiopian. It is an ungrateful job, and never has been done with complete satisfaction, either to the Ethiopian or to the white-washer' (48).

Such metaphorical differentiation from the criminal Other not only adds ethnic to social categories of classification but, furthermore, evokes perceptions inscribed in the Victorian imperial project, in particular the hierarchical juxtaposition of 'white' Europeanness and colonial 'darkness.' 'No. 7' gives this larger project even more immediate visibility when he points out that the governor of Chatham Prison had previously been in charge of 'the serfs on the banks of the Ganges' and that running a colony or a prison does not seem to make much of a difference to him (57). He suggests that structures of colonial rule are easily reproduced within the prison administration. 'No. 7' does not only apply an imperial centre-periphery dichotomy; his ludicrous pronouncement to be using pre-Conquest language additionally involves a mythical sense of Anglo-Saxonness that subtly follows the then-current silencing of Norman-French roots in favour of a pseudo-historical veneration of Germanic ancestry.[51] Thus, the delimitation of criminals through ethnic metaphors implicitly partakes in the larger Victorian celebration of the 'racial' difference – understood as superiority – of Anglo-Germanic culture, a celebration that is itself indispensable (if highly tenuous) for the legitimization of colonial interests.[52]

British Victorian writers who employ the prison as a totem of social and ethnic difference in order to distance themselves from those associated with it apply, then, a racialist discourse similar to that which H. Bruce Franklin sees at the heart of the US-American penitentiary system. Franklin, in his seminal study of writings largely by African-American captives (both slaves on nineteenth-century plantations and black convicts in twentieth-century penitentiaries), argues that a state-sanctioned form of alienating racism underlies the incarceration of minorities in the United States. He analyses what groups of people are created by a 'system of "corrections"' that is dominated by a 'white' establishment and concludes that the prison produces for African-Americans 'an experience different from that of the white convicts,' namely a collective sense of marginalization.[53] Thus, the uses the prison is put to by local and federal authorities in the United States help to delimit ethnic identities – an effect similar to that of the rhetorical construction of imprisonment in those British accounts written from an established middle-class perspective. This is not to deny that the British and US-American systems developed separately in many significant ways, but to emphasize that the transatlantic dissemination of penal ideas ensured a certain degree of ideological similarity (apart from congruences in more practical matters of prison management),[54] despite the differences in origin between a nineteenth-century British prison ethos that was derived out of a mission to deal with domestic crime and which developed as a substitute for transportation, and the incarceration of minorities in the United States, which Franklin views largely as a continuation of the slavery system.[55]

III

Considered in their entirety, late Victorian convicts writing about their experiences generally employ the prison as a totem, as a reproduction of class (and 'race') relations, in order to underscore the value system of the middle class. Their memoirs associate it with otherness and, thus, rhetorically turn a material object into an emblematic boundary or, more precisely, into a culturally significant marker of moral and social delimitation on any of three levels: the prison becomes (a) the place for ethically unacceptable criminals (seen as the degenerate antipodes of respectable society), who are (b) defined (often by means of metaphorical stigmatization) as a socially different *class*, and who can (c) be discursively related to animals or exotic regions (frequently through racialist clichés). What is central to the jail narratives is not so much a concern with the abuses by warders or governors or the harsh reality of the punishment (such as bad food, hard labour, etc.) – abuses and discomforts which are, of course, recounted but which do not *per se* seem to define the prison experience[56] – but the indignation of potentially being associated with a criminal subculture. For the 'gentleman writers' here discussed, the prison is not primarily an institution of personal subjection but the means of social identification through an act of dissociation from its alleged meaning as the place for 'real' criminals. This dissociation is both immediately physical (in that the convict-writers distance themselves from the carceral reality and their fellow inmates alike) and of larger symbolic significance (in its delineation of 'ordinary' criminals as alien members of a different world). The prison, as a medium of cultural communication, becomes meaningful for both collective (self-) classifications and the *pensée bourgeoise* of Victorian society at large. Middle-class group identity is upheld by an insistence on respectability – reflective of moral, class, and ethnic status – that is rhetorically opposed to the space of the criminal Other supposedly circumscribed by the penal establishment. Thus, when 'No. 7' is strangely at odds with the happiness of a young convict about his imprisonment (25–6), this does not only corroborate his theory that for most prisoners being incarcerated is just another form of the 'slum' they live in outside of the jail – a slum where 'No. 7' himself feels no sense of belonging – but also points to what he considers the prison's primary significance: it becomes an almost 'natural' place for the very criminal class that is not only customarily associated with it but which he, furthermore, sees as itself reproducing this association.

Such acts of self-delimitation imply two distinct, yet simultaneously operating conceptions of otherness. First, the fellow inmates are portrayed as unfamiliar, and in fact incomprehensible. They are defined as a fixed entity that the Self neither can nor should relate to – a fixation which both represses and enhances their otherness: it becomes repressed as a value itself and enhanced as decidedly different. As such, it is discursively controlled in a way that, following Emmanuel Levinas, can be seen as reflective of Western thought's colonizing mission.[57] Secondly, however, this colonization of the Other appears as a way not only to contain the perceived outward difference of the majority of prison inmates, but also to come to terms with one's own otherness in relation to generally accepted and perpetuated social values. The idea of being imprisoned as a criminal needs to be transformed into appearing 'strange' to the 'gentlemen convicts' themselves in order for them to maintain their sense of identity. Therefore, difference becomes an issue of the inner self, and the Other to be delimited is, in Julia Kristeva's sense, the unacceptable part of ourselves seemingly in need of repression.[58] Hence, the Victorian prison accounts here analysed conceive otherness both as an external difference to be colonized (vis-à-vis Levinas) and an internal difference to be repressed (vis-à-vis Kristeva). Both moves together reinsure the Self its socially as well as psychologically acceptable status.[59]

In order to achieve this reinsuring goal and, thereby, correlate the opposition between respectable society and the prison with the opposition between themselves and the prison, most writers delimit the Self from the Other in a way that relegates each to an entirely different system – most forcefully when the criminal belongs to a foreign, almost alien (such as animalistic, 'Arab,' or 'Ethiopian') realm emblematically defined by the jail. In order to emphasize the prison's ontological status as allegedly 'alien,' I will introduce Horst Turk's term *alienity* for this strategy of textualizing difference by fully marking the Other off, by (dis)placing it into a distinct systemic category (as opposed to a strategy that would construct otherness as *alterity*, where Self and Other seem merely different shades within the same system, that is, where the Other can serve as an 'alter ego').[60] Alienity, then, describes a conception of otherness that categorizes external differences as utterly unrecognizable, while it simultaneously contains personal anxieties through extreme forms of repressing internal differences. It is through this strategy of alienity that the authors of the convict memoirs can dissociate themselves from the prison – representative of the majority of the other, 'truly criminal' inmates – and emerge as 'paragons of all that is honourable and respectable,'[61] as belonging to a very different value system. If it is not the prison, however, that can serve as an arbiter of an identity based upon those values, then the desired association with respectable society needs to be validated through the narratives themselves. For this end, many of the works both employ a variety of textual strategies (such as suggestions for penal reform, rejections of liminality, the adaptation of an outside perspective, or an identification with the official point of view) and place themselves as integral parts within the bourgeois public sphere (e.g., through the use of aliases, intense claims of veracity, or editorial mediation). I will, therefore, conclude with a sketch of how the narratives support strategies of alienity that make the prison operational for processes of collective identity-formation. It is this insistence on the collective rather than on the individualization of prisoners that I will, finally, also trace in some works by non-convicts.

As a writer who is particularly concerned with retaining his distance from all negative associations of the prison, 'One Who Has Endured It' reasons that for a gentleman like him it is not so much his 'sin' itself – and here he consciously avoids the term 'crime' – but his 'being detected, *convicted*, and punished' (and, hence, his being identified by society with ordinary criminals) that would mean his 'moral death, accompanied with ruin and disgrace to his family and relatives' (365).[62] Therefore, in order to escape such identifications, he (like other writers) advocates penal reforms that would implement a system of classification for exceptional categories of prisoners and isolate the 'large number of criminals' from 'the man in a good position' (365)[63] or that would, in the words of 'No. 7,' 'separate the sheep from the goats' (213; see also 203–6). Overtly the system of classification, as suggested by 'One Who Has Endured It,' aims at a legal separation between those first-time offenders who have only committed 'commercial lapses' (374) and are still 'comparatively innocent men' (364) and inmates repeatedly convicted, that is, 'hardened and confirmed rogues' (375) who 'simply complete their education in vice' (364–5). Yet, covertly it seeks to establish a more general relationship of alienity, a clear point of reference to distinguish between 'gentleman prisoners,' keen on re-establishing their social status, and those seen as ordinary criminals. The decisive impulse to actually implement classification did, however, come from a substantial attack on the prison system by Irish political prisoners who considered themselves serving a higher cause and, therefore, did not wish to be considered criminal at all.[64] Even the Fenians, therefore, often revert to a rhetoric of alienity resembling that of the other writers here analysed, as when, for instance, they refer to the mass of the other prisoners as 'the garrotters and Sodomites of England' or 'those leprous outcasts of society.'[65]

If classification is meant to codify a relationship perceived and expressed through forms of alienity, then entering a prison is not *per se* a liminal experience, not an unconditional rite of passage leading to a new identity.[66] Quite the contrary: the middle-class prisoners continue narrating from the position of their unquestioned identity and the penal institution itself remains as different in their view as it is in the eyes of society at large. Even though the prison is clearly established as a boundary, this boundary is not supposed to be transgressed through some sort of rite of passage if the notion of respectability is to be maintained. Those other convicts, however, who do fully transgress the boundary, are not seen to enter a world much different from the one they are leaving behind either – at least, if the maxim of 'No. 7' is accepted that they are simply moving '[f]rom the slums *to* the slums' (129). The almost detached matter-of-fact description by 'One Who Has Endured It' of his being first brought to jail indicates that he is merely perceiving outward changes that do not affect either his sense of self or his previous attitude towards the prison and its inmates (see 3–8). He does not see being placed in jail as liminal but refers to it instead as a 'visit' (5), which points at his feeling of not belonging, of being different from the rest of the prisoners. Though physically and legally part of the prison, most writers continue to represent it as a boundary separating themselves from a clearly foreign system and they can, consequently, emerge unchanged from their incarceration (at least according to their own claims).

This representation is further underlined through the narrative point of view as the authors of the prison accounts adopt an outside perspective, often even that of the penal authorities. 'No. 7,' for example, styles himself as an 'explorer' describing 'the countries through which he has passed' (201). Thus, he does not even appear like a convicted *in*mate at all but more like a social traveller interested in but not part of the places he describes. This interest is manifested in his conscious efforts to 'search after remarkable criminals' in order to interview them and use the notes of such interviews for printing a book and according the prisoners 'a niche in the criminal Walhalla of the country' (23–4).[67] He assumes the position of a participant-observer taking an outside look even at himself as the future author of his own book. Likewise eager to write from an external perspective, 'One Who Has Endured It,' however, adopts a different strategy: he begins with building a bridge to his readers by insinuating that his insecurity about prison terminology resembles theirs. When talking about the chaplain at Newgate, he adds in parentheses – as if he were not sure about the claim – that 'Ordinary I believe is the proper term for his reverence' (19). Tellingly, he afterwards never even uses the inside term 'ordinary' but instead sticks to that of 'chaplain.' More significantly, though, 'One Who Has Endured It' throughout takes the view of the prison officials. He approves of giving a bath to newly received inmates as 'a very requisite institution' (7), is introduced by a warder to the tricks of detectives (32–3), is concerned with the warders' efficiency in upholding discipline (94–6), collaborates, in his superior position in the tailor's shop, with the authorities rather than his fellow inmates (323–4), and considers as 'good in every way' the power of the governor to censor the prisoners' correspondence with the outside world (332).[68] Whatever their claims, writers such as 'One Who Has Endured It' and 'No. 7' do not depict the reality of late Victorian convict establishments disinterestedly but adopt their particular point of view with the primary intention of marking their position within (or rather outside of) the penal system – especially in relation to their readers, administrators, and fellow inmates. Alienity, therefore, not only describes the legal relationship between the prison administration and those administered but is also reproduced, as a textual strategy, in the relationship between the narrator and the narrated object.

This reproduction works upon the tacit assumption that the authors of the late Victorian prison accounts can identify with the very society that is legally and rhetorically controlling the functions and meanings of imprisonment. And, as Martin Wiener points out, even if and when those functions and meanings are critically scrutinized, such complaints are 'essentially with the administration of the system rather than with the system itself, let alone with the moral universe behind it.'[69] Hence, the complaints become in themselves part of a socially differentiating gesture: for 'gentleman prisoners' who do not wish to associate with the 'roughs' by whom 'many of the evils of the system are hardly perceived,'[70] any criticism of penal practices helps to distinguish them from those ignorant of (or indifferent towards) administrative faults. Indeed, the extensive suggestions for prison reform by 'One Who Has Endured It' not only show a rhetorical distancing from the 'troublesome and criminal portion of the population' (363–4) but were also to some degree endorsed by the Royal Commission on Penal Servitude of 1879, the so-called Kimberley Commission.[71] The narrative by 'One Who Has Endured It,' while being a product of its author's imprisonment, can, consequently, also be read – in retrospect at least – as participating in an official discourse on penal methods. My final section will show how this reading – which displaces the text's experiential origin in an actual prison and turns the writer's internal perceptions into external ideas – is generated by the convict accounts themselves.

IV

In order to become part of an official discourse, prison memoirs first had to enter a dialogue with public opinion – more precisely, they had to circulate through what Jürgen Habermas has analysed as the *bourgeois public sphere*, that is the 'world of a reasoning reading public' where 'commentary and criticism of the crown's acts, of parliament's decisions' could be expressed.[72] In addition to textual strategies of alienity that enable not only a dissociation of the writers from other inmates but, in turn, an association with middle-class values, paratextual and editorial means are employed to allow for an easy participation of the prison accounts in the late Victorian public sphere. Almost all texts contain some sort of editorial comment on their truthfulness, comments designed to testify to the authenticity of what is related. Even the author's 'name' can be used for this end. It is essentially important to identify 'One Who Has Endured It,' not Edward Callow, as the author of *Five Years' Penal Servitude* – not because we cannot be absolutely sure about his 'real' identity, or because it might have been a way to protect anonymity (which could, of course, also have been achieved by picking an entirely fictitious name), or because the name does not mean much anyway, but because the narrative gesture behind the pseudonym is revealing: the idea that we are reading the account of someone who has actually gone through the prison system himself is, in many ways, the book's main attraction for its potential readership. 'One Who Has Endured It' can surely give a much more 'truthful' testimony of the prison's 'reality' than 'Edward Callow' or 'E.C.' (or 'XYZ' for that matter). 'One Who Has Endured It' guarantees the illusion that reality and its representation can be collapsed into one,[73] an illusion repeated at the very beginning of the publisher's prefatory note: 'The Publishers, before offering this work to the public, have satisfied themselves that the following narrative is what it purports to be – the genuine record of five years' penal servitude by one who endured it' (iii). In the ensuing text, the author himself reiterates this claim as he both denounces the veracity of previous publications on the topic and promises a 'plain unvarnished tale' of what he 'actually suffered, saw, and experienced' (2), an 'authentic narrative of the convict service from a point of view not often offered to the world' (40). Other writers make similar pronouncements. 'One Who Has Tried Them' – again, a telling pseudonym – puts all personal considerations on the side in order to relate 'the simple and *exact* truth,'[74] while the 'Ticket-of-Leave Man' seems to be even more self-scrutinizing when he admits his 'feelings of shame, horror, and disgust' about himself and yet continues that he has primarily made these acknowledgments so that 'my readers may be assured that I know something of the subject upon which I am writing.'[75] Authenticity can, thus, surface as a consequence of self-accusation. But it is not only the writers themselves who insist on the accuracy of their writing. Francis Scougal, who was permitted to interview prison inmates, claims that 'the facts themselves speak with the voice of truth.'[76] And the editor of the *Hibbert Journal* who reprinted the account of 'One Who Has Suffered It' assures his readers that he is 'personally satisfied' after having himself ascertained 'the *bona fides* of the writer of this article,' a statement that gains additional credibility when we learn that 'the writer expressed himself willing to receive no remuneration whatsoever.'[77] Even the authors of *Convict 99*, a sensational novel of an innocent gentleman being sentenced to lifelong penal servitude (which often reads like an unskilful fictionalization of the account of 'One Who Has Endured It'), assert it to be 'a true story of penal servitude' (according to the book's subtitle) written 'on behalf of those ground down beyond redemption under the iron rigour of a merciless convict system.'[78]

What is meant to guarantee the authenticity of the prison narratives is the authority of their authors. In turn, this authority is based on the assumption that those authors are trustworthy. Considering that they are or were convicts, trusting their integrity is by no means a matter of course. It is rather an editorial gesture designed to underline, once more, their difference from the large majority of ordinary criminals – a difference that is crucial for sanctioning the circulation of the texts within the public sphere as credible and acceptable documents. The note of the *Cornhill Magazine's* editor about 'A Letter from a Convict in Australia to a Brother in England' neatly mirrors this process: 'It may be unnecessary to state that this Letter is really the production of a convict, now in Australia.'[79] If this seems unnecessary information, why state it at all? To begin with, it is necessary to testify to the authenticity of the account. Yet, the statement also emphasizes the difference between the editor and the author, especially after the former's comment that '[w]e, of course, hold ourselves responsible neither for its statements nor its sentiments.'[80] The moment the account enters the public sphere as a publication in one of the major Victorian magazines, it is both consecrated through the editor's reassurance of his own integrity and turned into a credible document following the editorial insistence on its authenticity. In addition, the subsequent account itself stresses its credibility as well as earnestness by means of a strangely distant tone full of technical detail and the fact that it is addressed to the writer's brother, both of which give it the authority of a schoolmaster lecturing not only the addressee but the larger, respectable public. In fact, the appeals to the brother gradually diminish and the whole reads like a reformist tract eager to enter a communication with its readership.

While verisimilitude often becomes the vehicle for entering the forum of the bourgeois public sphere, it can also mask a more creative side. James Francis Hogan's introduction to Jorgen Jorgenson's convict narrative is a case in point. Though Hogan insists on the text being an 'authoritative history,' 'adhering strictly to the recorded facts,' he does, nonetheless, defend his 'presenting [it] in what I trust will be found to be a readable and consecutive narrative.' What he claims to be authoritative is, thus, a text brushed over and made more familiar and attractive to the 'ordinary reader.'[81] Even in the account of 'One Who Has Endured It' the avowed truthfulness partially disguises narrative liberties. On the one hand, he wants the reader to picture 'to himself exactly what [convict life] really is, stripped of all romance' (224). This rejection of romance (as the very opposite of realism) is complemented by his dislike of sensation fiction 'of the "Jack Sheppard" and "Claude Duval" style of literature in the penny dreadfuls' (31), treating of 'gentlemen pirates, highwaymen, and bandit captains' (67). On the other hand, though, this dislike influences what he excludes from his own account: for all his claims to realism, he refuses to give any description of those prisoners he calls 'brutes in mind and demons in heart' because 'the reader would cast aside the book with horror and disgust' (208). 'One Who Has Endured It' here reveals that even he is writing not so much for the truth but for the reader. The writer and the editor appear as mediators between the narrated 'facts' and the public sphere where these facts obtain their significance for an evaluation of both the author and the prison system in general.

If the prison narratives thus participate in the public sphere and official penological discourses, they can, indeed, express not only the inside views of a convict but the outside opinions of middle-class society. As such, their rhetoric of alienity, of employing the prison as a totemic boundary in order to represent those associated with it as a social Other, resembles the metaphorical stigmatization and delimitation of criminals in works by prison officials and other eminent Victorian intellectuals. The notion of criminals forming a morally different and potentially dangerous class was particularly current among those involved with the administration of penal institutions. Edmund Du Cane, the infamous first head of the newly nationalized prison system, approves of considering criminals a 'class of fools' with a 'natural proneness to evil,'[82] while George Laval Chesterton, a long-time governor of Cold Bath Fields House of Correction, calls them 'the degraded classes' which form 'the pests and outcasts which infest society,'[83] and the chaplain of Pentonville Prison, Joseph Kingsmill, refers to 'the lowest and vilest class of criminals.'[84] But it is not only the concept of class that is equally applied by those striving to present themselves as respectable convicts and those writing from an outside perspective. Demonic and animalistic perceptions reappear as well. The journalist William Hepworth Dixon, upon visiting Cold Bath Fields prison, notices 'only demons' with 'such animal and sensual mouths and jaws; such cunning, reckless, or stupid looks' that they can hardly be called human.[85] And the arch-Victorian intellectual Thomas Carlyle is most explicit when he denominates prisoners as 'degraded underfoot perverse creatures,' as hopeless 'abject, ape, wolf, ox, imp and other diabolic-animal specimens of humanity,' or as 'rotten material.'[86] He can only see in them 'the Genius of Darkness (called Satan, Devil, and other names).'[87] Finally, even ethnic categories are applied not only in some of the convict narratives but also in Henry Mayhew and John Binny's classic sociological study of the London prisons. They consider the 'dangerous classes' 'little higher than Hottentots in the scale of civilization' and, thus, predict 'a criminal epidemic ... that diffuses itself among the people with as much fatality to society as even the putrid fever or black vomit.'[88]

The inside accounts and various outside views share not only numerous concepts and metaphors to describe criminals, but also their very approach of delimiting *collective* identities through such descriptions. The prisoners do not emerge as a 'multiplicity of individual elements,' as Foucault has it (see above),[89] but as a coherent, if highly disreputable group which can serve as the Other of a social respectability that, in turn, frames the middle-class identity of both convict writers and other

Victorians commenting on imprisonment. Furthermore, even the conception as well as construction of nineteenth-century penal institutions ideologically or materially supports the discursive production of collective, not of individual identities (as most prison historians, including Foucault, have suggested). In lieu of a conclusion, I will, therefore, briefly discuss Jeremy Bentham's Panopticon, the influential (though highly impractical) emblem of British prison reform. Designed to be applicable 'without exception, to all establishments whatsoever, in which ... a number of persons are meant to be kept under inspection,' the Panopticon is supposed to serve as a model to treat all kinds of prisoners alike, '[n]o matter how different, or even opposite the purpose.'[90] While the architectural set-up of Bentham's model prison includes partitions to 'cut off from each prisoner the view of every other,'[91] the uniform management of every inmate contradicts this feature's possible effect of individualizing an incarcerated person. Instead, the separation of the inmates into individual cells operates on the assumption that there are other prisoners the self is being separated from and, more importantly, that all of these are treated in a similar fashion. Thus, it creates an awareness, among the convicts, of being part of a group – even at the moment of complete physical separation from that group.[92] As individual inmates are subjected to the prison, their own perceptions can turn it into an object of collective signification. Rather than visibly representing Leibnizian monadism, the structure of the modern penitentiary, therefore, seems to resemble the *modus operandi* of the nation state as what Benedict Anderson has famously called an 'imagined community.'[93] (In fact, as the present volume argues as a whole, the prison's development appears to go hand in hand with the formation of modern nations and, hence, their subjects as interrelated citizens.) In the prison, then, is the 'crowd, a compact mass, a locus of multiple exchanges, individualities merging together, a collective effect, ... abolished and replaced by a collection of separated individualities,' as Foucault argues,[94] or is it merely reinvented in the inmates' imagination, conscious of a common fate shared by all other prisoners? Whatever its alleged intention, the very structure of Bentham's Panopticon (and of later Victorian penal experiments) furnishes a sense of collective rather than individual destiny and, thus, undermines individualization the very moment it seems to establish it. To argue that in 'the "reformed" prison, the inmate collectivity ... had been broken up and silenced'[95] and to take the concept of the individual as the defining element of the modern penitentiary ignores this underlying ambivalence. Like the act of reading printed documents in the modern nation, the imprisonment in a reformed penal institution generates less a sense of individualization than of being placed into a larger crowd. Consequently, the subjection of prisoners through various forms of 'disciplinary power'[96] does not abolish group identities but furthers them by strictly separating the collective Self (of the inmates) from the Other (of the prison authorities) through processes of alienity. What is important about Victorian penal institutions is not so much their normalizing impetus *per se*, but their evocation of alienity and social differences. Hence, the prison's organization mirrors perceptions inscribed into the first-hand accounts of late nineteenth-century 'gentlemen convicts' (as well as into studies by those writing about imprisonment from the outside). Both disrupt the institution's alleged intention to target the individual by turning it into a totem of collective identification. While this is not the place to enter into an extensive critique of the modern penal system, it seems, nonetheless, worth asking whether it is not this disruptive ambivalence – inscribed into the organizational structure as well as discursive representation of imprisonment – that can be seen as a decisive reason for its essential failure.

Whatever the case, the strong emphasis on collective differentiation in the various forms of nineteenth-century prison discourse clearly defies David Brion Davis's contention that Victorians had no 'sense of a pluralistic society ... where conflicting subcultures might flourish side by side.'[97] First-hand narratives, outside perspectives, and, indeed, the very structure of the penal system itself are all based on the assumption that there *is* a criminal 'subculture' that is markedly different from the Victorian bourgeoisie which controls the public sphere as well as the legal system and with which respectable gentlemen, even if they are in jail themselves, need to associate. Thus, the prison could emblematically be used both to accept the existence of this subculture and to displace it: criminals were literally and rhetorically contained in prisons in a way that allowed them to serve, to be colonized, and to be repressed as a social and moral Other. By urging that the portal of every English jail ought to display the words 'From the slums *to* the slums,' 'No. 7' merely suggests an overt public sanctioning of this general process of othering the perceived criminal subculture, of associating it with a very different world, which may almost interchangeably be represented as a slum or as a prison.

NOTES

1 No. 7, *Twenty-Five Years in Seventeen Prisons: The Life-Story of an Ex-Convict: With His Impressions of Our Prison System: By 'No. 7'* (London: F.E. Robinson, 1903), 129. Subsequent quotations from this text will be cited parenthetically.
2 Jabez Spencer Balfour, *My Prison Life* (London: Chapman and Hall, 1907), 14. For a discussion of Balfour, see 'The Story of the Liberator Crash: With Some Account of the Career and Character of Jabez Spencer Balfour,' special issue of *'Westminster Gazette' Popular* 5 (November 1893): esp. 9–15.
3 The only notable exception, Philip Priestley's *Victorian Prison Lives*, a narrative compilation of inside views of nineteenth-century British jails, marvellously recreates the atmosphere of Victorian imprisonment with much attention to material details. However, while this makes his book an indispensable guide to contemporary sources, Priestley hardly reaches a level of critical analysis; see Philip Priestley, *Victorian Prison Lives: English Prison Biography, 1830–1914*, new ed. (London: Pimlico, 1999).
4 Torsten Eriksson, *The Reformers: An Historical Survey of Pioneer Experiments in the Treatment of Criminals*, trans. Catherine Djurklou (New York: Elsevier, 1976), ix; Christopher Hibbert, *The Roots of Evil: A Social History of Crime and Punishment* (London: Weidenfeld and Nicolson, 1963), 461. Further, Anthony Babington speaks of 'the slowly awakening instincts of compassion and humanity' (Anthony Babington, *The Power to Silence: A History of Punishment in Britain* [London: Robert Maxwell, 1968], 86) and Ursula Henriques argues that the 'pressure for reform was a product of the growing humanitarianism of the later eighteenth century' (U.R.Q. Henriques, 'The Rise and Decline of the Separate System of Prison Discipline,' *Past and Present* 54 [February 1972]: 63) – both essentially following Leon Radzinowicz's seminal (and most explicitly Whiggish) claim that 'Lord Macaulay's generalization that the history of England is the history of progress is as true of the criminal law of this country as of the other social institutions of which it is a part.' Leon Radzinowicz, *A History of English Criminal Law and Its Administration from 1750*, vol. 1, *The Movement for Reform* (London: Stevens and Sons, 1948), ix.
5 Jonathan Simon, 'Discipline and Punish: The Birth of a Postmodern Middle-Range,' in *Required Reading: Sociology's Most Influential Books*, ed. Dan Clawson (Amherst: University of Massachusetts Press, 1998), 51.
6 Michel Foucault, *Discipline and Punish: The Birth of the Prison*, trans. Alan Sheridan (New York: Vintage, 1979), 16.
7 Ibid., 170.
8 Ibid., 194, 170.

9 Max Horkheimer and Theodor W. Adorno, *Dialektik der Aufklärung: Philosophische Fragmente* (Frankfurt am Main: S. Fischer, 1969), 202.
10 Martin J. Wiener, *Reconstructing the Criminal: Culture, Law, and Policy in England, 1830–1914* (Cambridge: Cambridge University Press, 1990), 8. To reference a few other examples, Michael Ignatieff maintains that in the case of British penal history 'carceral discipline "directed at the mind" replaced a cluster of punishments "directed at the body"' and that such techniques fostered the 'vulnerability of inmates to victimization.' Michael Ignatieff, *A Just Measure of Pain: The Penitentiary in the Industrial Revolution, 1750–1850* (New York: Columbia University Press, 1978), xiii, 209. And Robin Evans, though less concerned with the administration of modern penitentiaries, similarly argues that their architecture 'would, for the first time, take full advantage of its latent powers ... as a vessel of conscience and as pattern giver to society' in order to 'fabricat[e] normality.' Robin Evans, *The Fabrication of Virtue: English Prison Architecture, 1750–1840* (Cambridge: Cambridge University Press, 1982), 6, 8.
11 David Garland, *Punishment and Modern Society: A Study in Social Theory* (Oxford: Clarendon Press, 1990), 282. In other words, my essay shares the approach of this volume as a whole, which is less concerned 'with the material practices of captivity than with the assumptions on which those practices rest' (see above, 9).
12 See Georg Rusche and Otto Kirchheimer, *Punishment and Social Structure* (New York: Columbia University Press, 1939), 4.
13 Dario Melossi and Massimo Pavarini, *Carcere e fabbrica: Alle origini del sistema penitenziario (XVI–XIX secolo)* (Bologna: Società editrice il Mulino, 1977), 70. In a more erratic and less systematically materialist manner, the early radical work of Sidney and Beatrice Webb comes to similar conclusions about the abusive, oppressive nature of imprisonment. However, their judgment that 'it is probably quite impossible to make a good job of the deliberate incarceration of a human being in the most enlightened of dungeons' leads them to discard the need for prisons altogether; see Sidney Webb and Beatrice Webb, *English Prisons under Local Government* (London: Longmans, Green and Co., 1922), 247.
14 Marshall Sahlins, *Culture and Practical Reason* (Chicago: University of Chicago Press, 1976), 178, 176.
15 Ibid., 178.
16 For a more extensive discussion of the theoretical premises informing my reading of Victorian prison autobiographies see Frank Lauterbach, 'Textual Errands into the Carceral Wilderness: Prison Autobiographies and the Construction of Cultural Hegemony,' in *In the Grip of the Law: Trials, Prisons, and*

the Space Between, ed. Monika Fludernik and Greta Olson (Frankfurt am Main: Peter Lang, 2004), 135–40.
17 This is, however, not to say that these two approaches are necessarily mutually exclusive. They can, in fact, be combined, in reference to specific historical situations, in quite a productive manner, as indicated by the example of H. Bruce Franklin's *Prison Literature in America: The Victim as Criminal and Artist*, expanded ed. (New York: Oxford University Press, 1989).
18 Ioan Davies, *Writers in Prison* (Oxford: Basil Blackwell, 1990), 16.
19 Ibid., 3, 7.
20 Ibid., 7.
21 W.B. Carnochan, 'The Literature of Confinement,' in *The Oxford History of the Prison: The Practice of Punishment in Western Society*, ed. Norval Morris and David J. Rothman (New York: Oxford University Press, 1995), 445, 428.
22 'Lieu de souffrance, la cellule est également envisagée comme lieu de protection, de rêverie, de liberté.' Victor Brombert, *La prison romantique: Essai sur l'imaginaire* (Paris: José Corti, 1975), 13.
23 'Clôture et spiritualité' (ibid., 12).
24 'Die Gefängnissituation ... gehört zum Inventarium der Ausformungen literarischer Imaginationen und strukturiert sie.' Christa Karpenstein-Eßbach, *Einschluß und Imagination: Über den literarischen Umgang mit Gefangenen* (Tübingen: Edition Diskord, 1985), 15–16.
25 Mary Ann Frese Witt, *Existential Prisons: Captivity in Mid-Twentieth-Century French Literature* (Durham, NC: Duke University Press, 1985), 4.
26 Priestley, *Victorian Prison Lives*, 9.
27 Ibid.
28 This further questions Ioan Davies' perception of the prison as 'a centre of intellectual activity' (Davies, *Writers in Prison*, 3; see above), since it, at best, stimulates those inmates who are better educated and more used to 'intellectual' communication to begin with.
29 On the historical significance of the 'gentleman prisoners' see Wiener, *Reconstructing the Criminal*, 310–13. It should be noted that even those accounts of 'ordinary' criminals that do exist generally reflect a similar value system, since they went through an editorial process that adapted the texts for its own purposes (as I discuss below).
30 Quotations from the account of 'One Who Has Endured It' are cited in the text from *Five Years' Penal Servitude: By One Who Has Endured It* (London: Richard Bentley and Son, 1877).
31 See Priestley, *Victorian Prison Lives*, 53–5.
32 'Reminiscences of Prison Life,' *Blackwood's Edinburgh Magazine* 130.1 [=789] (July 1881): 25–6.
33 Balfour, *My Prison Life*, xii.

34 Ticket-of-Leave Man, *Convict Life: Or, Revelations concerning Convicts and Convict Prisons: By a Ticket-of-Leave Man*, 2nd ed. (London: Wyman and Sons, 1879), 1.
35 James Francis Hogan, ed., *The Convict King: Being the Life and Adventures of Jorgen Jorgenson, Monarch of Iceland, Naval Captain, Revolutionist, British Diplomatic Agent, Author, Dramatist, Preacher, Political Prisoner, Gambler, Hospital Dispenser, Continental Traveller, Explorer, Editor, Expatriated Exile, and Colonial Constable* (London: Ward and Downey, 1891), 137.
36 One Who Has Tried Them, *Her Majesty's Prisons: Their Effects and Defects: By One Who Has Tried Them* (London: Sampson Low, Marston, Searle, and Rivington, 1881), 1:1.
37 Hogan, *Convict King*, 126.
38 D[onald] S[haw], *Eighteen Months' Imprisonment* (London: Routledge and Sons, 1883).
39 Ticket-of-Leave Man, *Convict Life*, 5, 6.
40 'A Letter from a Convict in Australia to a Brother in England,' *Cornhill Magazine* 13.5 (May 1866): 500.
41 Similar images can, curiously enough, even be found in the account of Mark Jeffrey, one of the few convict narratives written by a habitual, lower-class criminal. Jeffrey, a violent, unruly burglar completely opposing social authority, depicts himself as a 'caged beast' and as 'some unnamed wild beast of the field, having no feelings or desires'; see [Mark Jeffrey], *A Burglar's Life: Or, The Stirring Adventures of the Great English Burglar, Mark Jeffrey: A Thrilling History of the Dark Days of Convictism in Australia*, ed. W. Hiener and J.E. Hiener (Sydney: Angus and Robertson, 1968), 48, 180.
42 'Twenty Years' Penal Servitude,' *Chambers's Journal of Popular Literature, Science, and Art*, 4th series 200 (26 October 1867): 673, 676.
43 Upon his discharge, 'One Who Has Endured It' more explicitly refers to them as deer (see 361).
44 'A Convict's Views of Penal Discipline,' *Cornhill Magazine* 10.6 (December 1864): 722.
45 'A Letter from a Convict,' 491.
46 Ticket-of-Leave Man, *Convict Life*, 3, 238.
47 Ibid., 238.
48 Ibid., 245.
49 I use the term 'race' and its grammatical derivations only when referring to the specifically derogatory Victorian notions of ethnicity – thus following Werner Sollors, 'Ethnicity,' in *Critical Terms for Literary Study*, ed. Frank Lentricchia and Thomas McLaughlin, 2nd ed. (Chicago: University of Chicago Press, 1995), 289.
50 The association of criminals with hell and, thus, utter sinfulness is a common

strategy – as in the above-cited example of 'One Who Has Endured It' denominating his adversary, who is supposedly at fault for his conviction, as 'my Mephistopheles' (8).

51 For a summary of racial Anglo-Saxonism in nineteenth-century England, see Reginald Horsman, *Race and Manifest Destiny: The Origins of American Racial Anglo-Saxonism* (Cambridge: Harvard University Press, 1981), 62–77.

52 Considering the long-standing link between the punishment of crime and colonial expansion (the shipping of certain convicted offenders, first, to the transatlantic staple colonies and, later, to Australia), the proposal by 'One Who Has Endured It' to resume transportation, this time to New Guinea, for the really 'troublesome and criminal population of the country' (379) further illustrates the nexus between colonial interests in alien lands and the othering of convicts. (For a more general assessment of the relationship between transportation as a penal practice and British imperial interests see also Jason Haslam and Julia M. Wright's introduction to this volume.)

53 See H. Bruce Franklin, *Prison Literature in America*, xiii, xv. The path from plantation slavery to the convict lease system and the dissemination of the penitentiary idea is, then, only a microcosmic mirror-image of the development of the European criminal code from the late Middle Ages on, a development which J. Thorsten Sellin (following a thesis first presented by Gustav Radbruch) outlines as follows: '[P]unishments, which in the past offending [chattel] slaves alone had suffered, had been enshrined in law and would become fixtures in the criminal laws of all Western nations'; see J. Thorsten Sellin, *Slavery and the Penal System* (New York: Elsevier, 1976), 178.

54 The prison reform movement was at its core international, largely due to the influence of the two rival forms of punishment developed in the United States, the Silent System at Auburn State Prison in New York and the Separate System at the Eastern State Penitentiary in Philadelphia. Both were visited extensively by foreign penologists in the 1830s (and were written about by many more who had never even visited them at all), an exchange that culminated in the first international prison congress at Frankfurt (Main) in 1846. Among those visitors were Gustave de Beaumont and Alexis de Tocqueville for France in 1831, William Crawford for the United Kingdom from 1832 to 1833, Dominique Mondelet and John Neilson for Canada in 1834, and Nicolaus Heinrich Julius for Prussia in 1835. (On the cross-national spread of penal theories and practices see Orlando F. Lewis, *The Development of American Prisons and Prison Customs, 1776–1845: With Special Reference to Early Institutions in the State of New York* [Albany: Prison Association of New York, 1922], 228–36.)

55 See H. Bruce Franklin, *Prison Literature in America*, xv et passim.

56 While moments of outrage against a prison official are rare in the account of 'One Who Has Endured It,' two of the incidents he relates do show uncharacteristic reactions that momentarily undermine his carefully constructed difference from other inmates: when being harassed by the apothecary, he notices that his 'monkey was up' and feels 'savage' (229). And the 'petty tyranny' of one of the warders is his example for what 'bring[s] up the devil in men's hearts and brains' (291).
57 See Emmanuel Levinas, *Totalité et infini: Essai sur l'exteriorité* (La Haye: M. Nijhoff, 1961).
58 See Julia Kristeva, *Etrangers à nous-mêmes* (Paris: Fayard, 1988).
59 On the psychological need to retain a sense of decency in the face of one's very real situation of being imprisoned and stigmatized as criminal, see also Monika Fludernik's illuminating elaborations in her contribution to this volume.
60 For this use of the conceptional pair *alienity* and *alterity* see Horst Turk, 'Alienität und Alterität als Schlüsselbegriffe einer Kultursemantik,' *Jahrbuch für Internationale Germanistik* 22.1 (1990): 10–12. Turk also provides a detailed etymological derivation from the Latin terms *alienus* and *alter.* Following this outline, I do not mean to link the notion of alienity to the Marxist idea of alienation, but rather to stress, in a metaphorical sense, the implication of 'belonging to something foreign (to somebody else, to some other)': '*[A]lienus* drückt ... die fremde Zugehörigkeit aus (einem anderen gehörig)' (Turk, 'Alienität und Alterität,' 10–11).
61 One Who Has Endured It, *Five Years' Penal Servitude*, 367.
62 Once out of prison, 'One Who Has Endured It' is uneasy about the possibility that society might 'regard him as a leper ever after' (366). In order to avoid this stigma, he advocates that all care should be taken for first-time convicts not to be recognized as such upon their discharge (e.g., by their clothes). Their past ought to be obliterated and the values of their newly resumed life be asserted (see 352–4, 357–8). Repeat offenders who show no sign of reform should, however, be permanently excluded from society (see 369).
63 Here even the grammatical use of number – that is, the distinction between plural and singular forms – implies that 'One Who Has Endured It' considers himself an exceptional (i.e., singular) prisoner.
64 See Wiener, *Reconstructing the Criminal*, 326–8.
65 Quoted in ibid., 312.
66 The interpretation of imprisonment as an initiation through a rite of passage from the outside to the inside world was introduced by John Bender, who applied Victor Turner's anthropological concept of liminality to the study of

early eighteenth-century prison literature; see Bender, *Imagining the Penitentiary: Fiction and the Architecture of Mind in Eighteenth-Century England* (Chicago: University of Chicago Press, 1987), 26–35. As Monika Fludernik has pointed out, Bender's use of the concept is, however, problematic, as rites of passage in Turner's sense 'are utterly *different* from the situation of his initiates either *before* or *after* their liminal experience,' whereas being 'initiated' into the prison environment is a transitional stage already resembling the ensuing experience of imprisonment (and sometimes even the life before); see Fludernik, 'Carceral Topography: Spatiality, Liminality and Corporality in the Literary Prison,' *Textual Practice* 13.1 (Spring 1999): 66.

67 His book does, indeed, abound in little anecdotes and biographical sketches of other inmates.
68 In addition, the very idea of classification implicitly endorses the prison's administrative authority as being in charge of separating the inmates.
69 Wiener, *Reconstructing the Criminal*, 323.
70 'A Letter from a Convict,' 499.
71 See Wiener, *Reconstructing the Criminal*, 325–6, 309–10.
72 'Welt [d]es räsonierenden Lesepublikums'; 'Kommentierung und Kritik von Maßnahmen der Krone, von Beschlüssen des Parlaments.' Jürgen Habermas, *Strukturwandel der Öffentlichkeit: Untersuchungen zu einer Kategorie der bürgerlichen Gesellschaft*, new ed. (Frankfurt am Main: Suhrkamp, 1990), 183, 126.
73 Hence, even the use of the present perfect instead of the past tense (as in 'One Who Endured It') implies the continuing mental presence of the time in prison at the moment of narrating it.
74 One Who Has Tried Them, *Her Majesty's Prisons*, iii.
75 Ticket-of-Leave Man, *Convict Life*, 2.
76 Francis Scougal, *Scenes from a Silent World: Or, Prisons and Their Inmates* (Edinburgh: William Blackwood and Sons, 1889), ix.
77 One Who Has Suffered It, 'Concerning Imprisonment,' *Hibbert Journal* 8.3 (April 1910): 582.
78 Marie C. Leighton and Robert Leighton, *Convict 99: A True Story of Penal Servitude* (London: Grant Richards, 1898), ii. Only the writer of 'Reminiscences of Prison Life' marks an exception when he explicitly refrains from giving any authenticity to what he is representing and, instead, satisfies himself with 'afford[ing] a few morsels of amusement to the casual reader' ('Reminiscences of Prison Life,' 23).
79 'A Letter from a Convict,' 489.
80 Ibid.
81 Hogan, *Convict King*, 3.

82 Edmund F. Du Cane, *The Punishment and Prevention of Crime* (London: Macmillan, 1885), 3.
83 George Laval Chesterton, *Revelations of Prison Life: With an Enquiry into Prison Discipline and Secondary Punishments*, rev. ed. (London: Hurst and Blackett, 1856), 1:iii, 7.
84 Joseph Kingsmill, *Chapters on Prisons and Prisoners, and the Prevention of Crime*, 3rd ed. (London: Longman, Brown, Green, and Longmans, 1854), 116.
85 W. Hepworth Dixon, *The London Prisons: With an Account of the More Distinguished Persons Who Have Been Confined in Them: To Which Is Added a Description of the Chief Provincial Prisons* (London: Jackson and Walford, 1850), 244, 245.
86 Thomas Carlyle, *Thomas Carlyle's Collected Works*, vol. 19, *Latter-Day Pamphlets* (London: Chapman and Hall, 1870), 67, 68, 74.
87 Ibid., 67.
88 Henry Mayhew and John Binny, *The Criminal Prisons of London and Scenes of Prison Life* (London: Griffin, Bohn, 1862), iii, 80.
89 Foucault, *Discipline and Punish*, 170.
90 Jeremy Bentham, *The Works of Jeremy Bentham, Now First Collected*, ed. John Bowring (Edinburgh: William Tait, 1838), 3:40.
91 Ibid., 41.
92 Even the two rival plans that were eventually imported from the United States to Britain after the failure of Bentham's panoptical idea supported a sense of collectivity: the Separate System, though resistant to any form of actual association, does also imply the presence of other prisoners in a very similar situation, and the Silent System foregrounds this presence through its permission of joint work with fellow inmates (if in a subdued manner).
93 Hence, Anderson's exposition of the nation both as imagined and as a community can easily be applied to the experience of the penitentiary as well: 'It is *imagined* because [its members] will never know most of their fellow-members, meet them, or even hear of them, yet in the minds of each lives the image of their communion' and 'it is imagined as a *community,* because ... the nation is always conceived as a deep, horizontal comradeship'; see Benedict Anderson, *Imagined Communities: Reflections on the Origin and Spread of Nationalism*, rev. ed. (London: Verso, 1991), 6, 7.
94 Foucault, *Discipline and Punish*, 201.
95 Ignatieff, *A Just Measure of Pain*, 208.
96 See Foucault, *Discipline and Punish*, 170–94.
97 'Nineteenth-Century Reformism: A Discussion,' in *Humanitarianism or Control? A Symposium on Aspects of Nineteenth-Century Social Reform in Britain and America*, ed. Martin J. Wiener, special issue of *Rice University Studies* 67.1 (Winter 1981): 76.

CHAPTER 5

'Stone Walls Do (Not) a Prison Make': Rhetorical Strategies and Sentimentalism in the Representation of the Victorian Prison Experience

Monika Fludernik

Placing the 'Romantic Prison'

Best known in the line from Richard Lovelace's poem 'To Althea, from Prison,' the topos of mental freedom in prison is one that has a long history reaching back to the Greek Stoics and featuring as some of its most famous examples Boethius's *De consolatione philosophiae*, Sir Thomas More's *A Dialogue of Comfort against Tribulation*, and the poetry of Charles d'Orléans in the fifteenth century.[1] This literary topos also emerges in the central argument of Victor Brombert's study *The Romantic Prison*, in which he discusses several literary prisoners who use the time of their confinement to meditate or to engage in creative writing.[2] Prison, for these fictional protagonists, becomes a place of refuge from the outside world, a haven of peace and quiet that is optimally conducive to creative productivity. Frequently, the topos combines with another literary constellation – that of the lover as prisoner of his beloved dame, a theme of great popularity in the fifteenth to seventeenth centuries, and still latent, for instance, in Fabrice del Dongo's imprisonment in the Farnese tower in Stendhal's *The Charterhouse of Parma*.[3]

Two features are prominent in Brombert's figuration: the prisoner's individuality on the one hand, and the benign conditions of imprisonment on the other. Unlike the medieval and early modern instances of the 'freedom of the mind' trope, nineteenth-century occurrences of this literary topos refer to prisoners who are kept in fairly comfortable circumstances, are allowed some movement (for instance, a walk on the battlements of the castle in which they are kept), can chat with their guards, receive good food (frequently from outside), and are supplied with books and writing materials. Such luxuries historically only applied to imprisoned nobility, such as Sir Walter Raleigh (who was able to engage in scientific study and compose a history of the world during his years of incarceration in the Tower). The literary topos as outlined by Brombert contradicts nineteenth-century penal practices in two major respects. Firstly, the subjects that figure as literary protagonists are frequently prisoners of a special kind; not common thieves, highwaymen, or larcenists, but educated people of some cultural and intellectual refinement who have been victimized for political reasons. Secondly, the type of imprisonment to which they are subjected belongs to neither the 'old' nor the 'new' prison regime in the terminology of Foucault and Bender.[4]

The second point requires some elaboration. As the reader will remember, the old (pre-nineteenth-century) prison served on the whole to detain suspects before trial or execution rather than to inflict punishment on them as a form of legal sentencing. Except for extremely dangerous, very famous, or comparatively rich prisoners – who were kept in cells to themselves – most detainees shared prison space and usually also had the privilege of roaming the yards of the prison. The literary protagonists that we have been talking about therefore live in carceral conditions that correspond to those of the earlier privileged prisoners rather than to those of the mass of prison subjects. The privacy allowed to them prefigures an important feature of the new prison regime, that of the penitentiary, namely solitude. As Bender and Ignatieff have demonstrated, the rationale for keeping convicts in separation was to preserve them from the bad influence of hardened fellow prisoners and to encourage them to meditate on their crimes, producing contrition and a penitential attitude.[5] It is precisely this central feature of the new prison model, discipline, that is also missing from the 'freedom of the mind' topos, and to this extent the literary representations that Brombert analyses do not conform to contemporary nineteenth-century theory and practice. However, since the literary prisoners are not 'ordinary' criminals, contemporary nineteenth-century prison conditions would not in any case have applied to them, as one can see in the treatment of male political prisoners, many of whom were indeed spared the humiliations of the hard labour that constituted the disciplinary regime of the penitentiary.[6] In fact, the customary punishment for political prisoners in Germany was honourable incarceration in a fort or military prison, *Festungshaft*, which was specifically designed to exempt these prisoners from the dishonourable subjection to hard labour and from the taint of association with ordinary criminals. On the other hand, in some cases this supposedly more humane treatment left the prisoner at the disposal of a vengeful and tyrannical regime, and in a few cases incarceration in a fort turned into a real-life dungeon scenario.[7] One will therefore have to conclude that the literary representation of happy prisoners in Romantic literature, such as discussed by Brombert, constitutes a very special case in terms of the realities of nineteenth-century conditions of imprisonment. However, this leaves us with the question why literary authors should have turned to this exceptional and therefore unrealistic prototype rather than depicting the 'real thing.'

One answer to this question can certainly be provided by referring to the continuing relevance of the literary tradition in which the originally Stoic and then religious topos of mental freedom played an important role. However, persuasive as this argument is, it receives some dampening from the fact that the literary tradition, though on its less respected level, does include the semi-literary genre of the criminal (auto)biography and the Newgate Calendar – a body of texts that concentrates on 'ordinary' crime and, at least at first blush, might appear to be a much more appropriate frame for the representation of crime, criminality, and imprisonment. In fact, the Newgate Calendar and the popular criminal (auto)biographies can fruitfully be compared to nineteenth-century prison memoirs, although here, too, the fictional model and historical accounts differ in interesting ways. I will come back to this subject later in the paper, but would like to mention another highly interesting aspect that might help explain nineteenth-century literature's gradual turning away from the available model of criminal (auto)biography.[8] This aspect is illustrated with great clarity and persuasiveness by Frank Lauterbach in his stimulating essay in this volume. Lauterbach, using a sociological framework, argues that Victorian prison memoirs served to endorse the boundaries between respectability and criminality and therefore concentrated on gentlemen prisoners with whom the reader could partially sympathize and identify socially. By reproducing society's exclusionary discourse against criminals in their own characterization of fellow convicts, these writers corroborate society's customary demonization and animalization of common criminals but exempt themselves from their class, protesting that the justly harsh treatment given their fellow convicts should not be extended to respectable subjects like themselves.

I would like to contend that the prevalence of the 'mental liberty' topos in Romantic literature may be serving similar ends. It allows the reader to sympathize with the (non-criminal) victim of oppression, presenting the prisoner as 'one of us'; and it deliberately represses the contemporary disciplinary realities, thereby invoking prison as an exotic scenario that has escapist potential. In addition, the topos emphasizes the individualistic *Bildungsroman*-related schema of personal moral development that is so common in the nineteenth-century novel and can be regarded as a secularization of a religious prototype, the spiritual autobiography. In this essay I wish to discuss some alternative or complementary strategies of stigma-management in Victorian prison literature.[9] On the one hand, writers of autobiographical texts completely avoid romantic associations by discussing their experience as rationally and unemotionally as possible (though they may describe the sufferings of *others* in very emotional tones). On the other hand, much newspaper reporting on individual tragedies occurring in Victorian prisons resorts to alternative literary models, not that of the happy prison but the model of eighteenth-century sentimental literature.

This latter point requires some elaboration. In the eighteenth-century sentimental novel, said to start with Sarah Fielding's *David Simple* (1744) and including Oliver Goldsmith's *The Vicar of Wakefield* (1762), Henry Mackenzie's *The Man of Feeling* (1771), and Sterne's *A Sentimental Journey* (1768) as its major representatives, imprisoned subjects (usually confined in dungeon-like prisons) occur alongside the poor, the mad, and the bereaved as proper objects of the sentimental gaze.[10] Although ostensibly designed to provoke the reader into charitable acts, these texts have frequently been criticized for their tendency to indulge in tear-jerking melodrama in which the readers' inclinations towards pity are exhausted in the emotional turmoil produced by the description of misery and do not result in good deeds that would help to relieve the victims of oppression and deprivation.[11] As we will see, Victorian prison literature has recourse to the models of the sentimental novel by stressing the victimhood of the prison subject and by emphasizing a highly charged emotional reaction to his or her plight that implicitly transforms the scene into a spectacle and caters to the reader's taste for emotional involvement. This strategy of sentimentalizing the prison experience frequently correlates with what I see as the fictionalizing of the situation. I will return to this point at the end of the paper.

In this essay, the experience of imprisonment is analysed both from an external viewpoint in journalism and penal theory – this perspective correlates with an emphasis on social sanction and the stigmatization of the criminal subject – and from the subjective viewpoint of the inmate which highlights the victim role of the prisoner and makes his/her experience accessible through a variety of rhetorical strategies. Empathy for the incarcerated is produced by argumentative means in the discourse of 'us' versus 'them' and through the emphasis on the exaggerated cruelties of prison life. This exoticization of the prison scenario and the emphasis on the inhumane treatment endured in the silent world of the Victorian penitentiary connect my analyses with the two key issues of this volume, namely the historical continuity between the system of slavery and that of the modern prison on the one hand, and the connection between enslavement by forced labour and colonial expansion on the other.

My corpus consists of Victorian prison narratives. I will concentrate on a number of prison memoirs, newspaper stories, and literary texts. On the basis of this analysis, I propose to sketch how the literary representation of imprisonment develops in the nineteenth century. As I will argue, both autobiographical and journalistic reports supplement their rhetorical strategies of rational persuasion by trying to involve the reader's feelings. Sympathy for the prisoner is produced through a variety of literary topoi and by resorting to the framework of sentimental fiction and melodrama. In fact, the distinction between fact and fiction is a moot point in this material. What can be discussed much more fruitfully is how the presentation of information about the prison world combines with the discourses of social control, and how, on the other hand, exculpatory arguments tie in with the projection of an implicit or explicit victim role for the convict. In addition, these texts rely on their entertainment value by supplying the public with supposedly secret information, using sensationalist images of the inaccessible prison world and well-proven schemata from the sentimental novel and drama. The image of the prisoner as monster and outcast in the discourse of social control therefore competes with the counter-image of the prisoner in the reformers' discourse in which the role of the convict as victim is exaggerated and amplified in the generic framework of the sentimental novel. This ambivalence and the contestatory dialogics in the representation of the Victorian prison experience echo similar ambivalences in the Victorians' views about the lower classes and poverty. There, too, the discourse of social control directed against the undeserving poor is significantly countered and undermined by sentimentalist depictions of innocent and pitiable poverty – by the destitution of the deserving poor. The situation emerges as typical of the basic Victorian episteme that is linked to a bourgeois class consciousness imbrued with a punitive ethic, in which the discourses of morality and social control serve to repress the economic and class-related causes of the social symptomatic.

'Real' Prisons: The Rhetoric of Memoirs

We have extensive documentation about the way in which prisons were run in the nineteenth century, and we have reams of papers on prison reform and the public's opinions about how they *should* be run. What is lacking is the inside view of the ordinary criminal. Most convicts in the Victorian period were poor, semi-literate, and without access to the public ear. Prison memoirs written by real ex-convicts therefore tend to have been composed by the few who were middle-class subjects. As Lauterbach has demonstrated so convincingly, these accounts are unreliable for a number of reasons. They tend to project the views of an outsider on the system, of somebody who is really on the side of the warders rather than his fellow convicts, and they usually corroborate general middle-class attitudes towards crime, criminals, punishment, and penal institutions.

It is a historical fact that the penitentiary was designed by politicians and penologists who, despite an avowed concern for the moral improvement of their charges, ultimately ordered prison life in a way that neglected to consider the long-term effects on human subjects exposed to the penitentiary regime. In the wake of the political drive for deterrence, punishment, and social disciplining, the experience of inmates, their feelings and sufferings, disappeared into oblivion. The prisoner became an object of scientific study, and his supposed needs and required productivity were measured in implacably mechanical fashion to yield proposals for so many ounces of bread a day and so many hours on the treadmill or so many revolutions of the crank.[12] Prison reforms, recurrent throughout the century, were heavily influenced by public opinion and tended to vacillate between benevolence and reformation on the one hand and rigorous punishment and inhuman severity on the other. A great number of debates were conducted on the amount of food that should be given to prisoners, with the public claiming that the insufficient fare was too generous by far in comparison with the poorest honest labourer, who had even less and was subjected to the vagaries of the market and threatened with starvation.[13] Similarly, the excessive and indiscriminate use of the treadmill and the crank was partly aided by the press, where correspondents such as Charles Dickens lobbied for humiliating and demeaning punishment through forced labour of the toughest and most useless and monotonous kind: 'I think it right and necessary that there should be in jails some degraded kind of hard and irksome work, belonging only to jails. ... I have not the least hesitation in avowing ... that it is a satisfaction to me to see that determined thief, swindler, or vagrant, sweating profusely at the treadmill or the crank, and extremely galled to know that he is doing nothing all the time but undergoing *punishment*.'[14]

It is disheartening to see better-educated prisoners, who composed their prison memoirs on their release, condoning this cruelty in Victorian prisons as, after all, appropriate to the hardened criminals whom they, like the educated public, saw as little better than beasts. Gentlemen convicts, those that composed these memoirs, regarded themselves as *different* from the generality of their fellow inmates, and their trustworthy status as narrators is directly dependent on that class identification. Readers trust these narrators because they share similar, negative views of criminals. Lauterbach illustrates how these prison memoirs participate in a public debate on prison reform since they can lay claim to an inside view. By inserting the respectable middle-class external perspective on criminality into the prison itself, they serve to reproduce those processes of collective identity formation that fortify middle-class community against the threats of lower-class and criminal others. The rejection of community with the other convicts can, moreover, be explained, psychologically, as a face-saving strategy, and, narratively, as a rhetorical ploy designed to capture the benevolence of one's audience. At the same time these memoirs participate in a literary structure familiar from travelogues, that of the journey into unknown, exotic regions and of the traveller's safe return from these parts.

This dissociation from fellow convicts in the memoirs of Victorian gentlemen convicts can also be explained as a useful psychological survival strategy under difficult external conditions. It is almost a cliché of prison literature that new arrivals insist on their innocence, react with shock and disbelief at finding themselves in prison, and asseverate that they are victims of intrigue, judicial error, or sheer bad luck. Such arguments help to preserve self-esteem in circumstances carefully designed to erode pride, confidence, or self-assurance in the prisoner. Going to prison is hell, even more so in Victorian times than now in the West. The accumulation of degrading rituals of initiation into the penitentiary then and now constitutes a trauma in its own right. Following closely on the shock of sentencing, first-time prisoners are just emerging from the horror and disbelief that overwhelmed them in court when they are treated to a series of humiliations that tend to deeply unbalance their personal identity: handcuffing, being dragged to a prison van, thrust into it in close association with a mass of perspiring humanity, dragged out of the van and marched into forbidding prison architecture, deprived of all possessions including handkerchiefs, wedding rings, pencils, tobacco, or nowadays even contact lenses, ordered to undress, strip-searched, measured, deloused, given dirty and ill-fitting prison wear, and finally herded into cells. Such treatment forcefully impresses on the prisoner that from now on he (or she) is one among many and completely at the mercy of the prison guards.[15] The convict is stripped of all former distinctions and transformed into an ugly sample of the standard convict subject. He has lost all rights, especially the right to decent and friendly human intercourse to which he has been used outside. The first-time prisoner therefore receives a major psychological shock, losing his hold on his former self which was carefully crafted on self-esteem, self-presentation and 'face' (as the linguists call it). Prison discipline, especially moralistic Victorian prison discipline, conveys to the prisoner that he is of no worth at all, and should accept his punishment with humility and in a penitential mood. In order to achieve this, the prisoner's previous record needs to be erased and the morality of society inscribed on his heart and conscience.

There are two strategies through which prisoners manage to survive this attack on their self-esteem and identity. They either adopt a new collective identity as prisoners who develop their own counter-world in opposition to the prison regime; or they deny their commonality with the other prisoners, adopting the perspective of the warders and trying to become model prisoners or at least exceptions to the general rule. The first reaction results in gaining a new social status within the prison community and allows the recuperation of self-esteem but at the price of adopting the morality and norms of behaviour that persist in penal institutions. By contrast, gentlemen prisoners survive the impact of de-individualization by going into a process of denial and by reconstructing their self-esteem on the basis of their difference from the other prisoners, laying claim to their socially based distinction. Such attitudes will make gentlemen prisoners outsiders among their fellow inmates, although in Victorian times the cellular system and the severe restrictions placed on communication between prisoners made it less dangerous to adopt this course than in, say, present-day Californian institutions. The adoption of a role of (moral and social) superiority in relation to the rest of the prison community additionally enabled gentlemen prisoners to insist on their relative innocence or victimization.

The role of the gentleman convict, therefore, fulfils a useful psychological function as a survival strategy. It boosts the prisoner's self-esteem (though at the expense of sociability) and allows him to preserve his customary socially conditioned world view and opinions. Much as this attitude smacks of a betrayal of these authors' status as prisoners, it made good psychological sense, since they did not have any experience of a 'criminal world view' before their exposure to it in prison, strongly resented being identified with individuals whom they utterly despised, and were able to counteract the degradation of their prison status by aspiring to the esteem of the guards, becoming industrious and non-violent model prisoners. In this they were aided by the prison regime that privileged the middle-class virtues of industry and obedience. That the expectations of a social norm of industry and humility could be met by prisoners who were only play-acting, thus ridiculing the idea of the penitentiary, is illustrated quite forcefully by Dickens in *David Copperfield* in the scene where David encounters Uriah Heep in prison: 'I am shown two interesting penitents.'[16]

The majority of Victorian inmates were vagrants and thieves, people who had little stake in society and held 'anti-social' views already outside prison. For them, joining the community of the prison anti-world came as a matter of course, and this confrontational outlook was further strengthened by clashes with the requirements of the prison regime. The monotonous and mechanical work forced on inmates was chafing to all prisoners, but especially so for those unused to any regular sort of work. As a consequence, the common prisoner frequently fell foul of the authorities, received corporal punishment, and ended up even more rebellious. The social disciplining through hard labour which went on in Victorian prisons can certainly be regarded as part of class warfare, in which the middle class was trying to remodel the underclasses in its own image.

While the mass of regular prisoners were being maimed in the Procrustean bed of social disciplining, gentlemen prisoners suffered mostly from the unaccustomed physical exercise involved in hard labour and from the unwonted discomforts and punishments of the Victorian prison regime: hunger and cold, lack of light and bedding, and so on. Especially the treadmill tended to destroy the health of those with weak constitutions, as did the practice of punishing prisoners unable to perform the set tasks by starvation diets, dousing with cold water, and sleep deprivation, all leading to even worse performance and more punishments.[17]

The discourse of gentlemen prisoners' memoirs can additionally be explained in terms of narratological strategies of persuasion and especially the necessary creation of sympathy on the part of the reader. Victorian prison memoirs did not merely or exclusively serve to reinforce class boundaries but, paradoxically, *by doing so*, they started to create a receptive attitude towards proposals for improving and humanizing prison conditions and were then able to decry prison abuses with greater success. In other words, writers of prison memoirs adopted the mask of the 'gentleman prisoner' in order to win the confidence of the middle-class reader and to establish a relationship of trust between them. Only when the reader sees the author as, basically (despite his crimes), 'one of us' will he be willing to listen to critical arguments about the prison regime, or to accusations of grave violations of the rights of prisoners. One need only imagine a prison memoir written by an unrepentant thief or murderer whose every moral statement offends the middle-class reader's sense of propriety. Such a memoir – especially if it purports to be a historical document and not a piece of fiction – will be put down with disgust, and any complaints about the cruel treatment of prisoners shoved aside; after all, in such a reader's opinion, such a person well deserves what he is complaining about.

The fiction of the prisoner's respectability or even innocence therefore serves as an important tactic of ingratiation which, by playing on the audience's negative attitudes towards criminals, manages to achieve their sympathy for the author and, in the wake of this sympathy, can lead to an understanding of the injustices and cruelties of the prison regime which any Christian and right-minded person must condemn. Thus, Jabez Spencer Balfour throughout the first part of his prison memoir *My Prison Life* (1907) never even hints at dissatisfaction with the prison food, even though the description he provides clearly exposes it as insufficient. Only in the second part of his memoir does he discuss possible reforms, pleading for a more variegated prison fare and belatedly mentioning that many prisoners went hungry and became ill through lack of nutritious meals.[18] The entire memoir serves less the purpose of describing a private experience than the aim of initiating prison reform on the basis of the author's practical experience of it. In fact, many of the memoirs by gentlemen prisoners read like tracts in disguise or like sensational novels, and may have been produced solely for the purpose of intervening in debates about prison reform.

This brings me to a third question, that of the literary prototypes operating in these texts. I have noted the relevance of the travelogue as a model and wish to extend my discussion to the topic of exoticism. Since the introduction of the penitentiary, prisons have become closed territories into which the public rarely intrudes. (This is arguably even truer today than it was in Victorian times.) Prisons were viewed as mysterious worlds, unknown, forbidden, and therefore exciting places that, because they were sealed off from the public eye, started to exert a strange fascination on the ordinary citizen. The fact that the number and duration of prison visits began to be more severely restricted and the public was not admitted to the actual living quarters of the inmates meant that what went on behind prison walls became a political concern and resulted in a mass of press reports, parliamentary inquiries, and inspections. It also sparked fantasies about the hidden world of the penitentiary, which either tended to be of the utopian Benthamite order (a well-regulated, perfectly controlled society of warders and their charges) or veered towards lurid tales of cruelty and unchecked tyranny (terms strangely similar to contemporary orientalist speculations about the sexual secrets of the Turkish harem).

One can observe here the makings of an exoticist vision of the penitentiary. The less that is known, the more the readers' projections and fantasies are stimulated, and exaggerated accounts start to flourish. It is in this light that one needs to appreciate the sensationalist success of Charles Reade's *It Is Never Too Late to Mend* (1856).[19] Reade used the scandal of a suicide case in Birmingham jail, reported in *The Times*, as the basis for his novel.[20] The article in the *Times* revealed unheard-of excesses of cruelty by the warders which drove prisoners to madness and suicide. These excesses included punishment by food and sleep withdrawal, dousing in cold water, and the regular application of the straitjacket for prisoners' sheer physical inability to achieve the desired number of revolutions on the crank. The article in the *Times* not only disclosed the unsavoury practices that had been going on in Birmingham Borough jail, but it also described them largely within a literary framework of sentimentalism. Consider the following passage:

> Maiden, a young man about 19 years of age, was imprisoned for the heinous crime of running away from his employment. He was treated by the surgeon for fever, but, notwithstanding this, was put to the crank and failed to perform the task. He was immediately placed in the jacket and collar (the day being Saturday) and kept in it from 9 in the morning until 8 at night. He was deprived of food from breakfast time on Saturday till dinner

time on Sunday and then regaled with 6oz of bread and a can of water. On one occasion he was nearly strangled in the collar, having fainted, and recovered when a warder found him so and revived him with cold water. Consider the lad's crime, the venial offence of neglecting his work, his illness, his inability to perform such a task when under treatment for fever, the visit of the governor to increase the weight of the crank when he found the lad unable to do the work, and the horrible accumulation of punishment that followed the unperformed task, we shudder when we read of the comparably humane treatment of political offenders in the Neapolitan prisons. It is a mild despotism compared with this revolting cruelty.[21]

The reference to despotism and to Neapolitan prisons is instructive, since it invokes both an exoticist scenario, with echoes of orientalist discourse, and the horrors of the Inquisition as conventionally depicted in Gothic novels. This rhetorical strategy serves to undermine the current British view that England had a humane legal system whereas the continent housed tyrannical regimes that subjected their citizens to despotic cruelty. This claim, current since Elizabethan times, came under attack during the late eighteenth century when writers such as William Godwin and Mary Wollstonecraft argued that England had as tyrannical institutions as France:

> Thank God, exclaims the Englishman, we have no Bastille! ... Unthinking wretch! Is that a country of liberty where thousands languish in chains and fetters? Go, go, ignorant fool! and visit the scenes of our prisons! Witness their unwholesomeness, their filth, the tyranny of their governors, the misery of their inmates! After that show me the man shameless enough to triumph, and say, England has no Bastille![22]

The report in the *Times* clearly picks up on this same rhetorical strategy of inversion. The charge that British institutions are more barbaric than continental prisons noted for their inhumanity is especially embarrassing in the light of Victorian pride in a carefully supervised, sanitary, and well-ordered penitentiary system which now turns out to have been a myth.

Many prison memoirs take their authoritative stand on the side of the well-ordered though harsh prison system and deny or mitigate the prevalence of tyrannical regimes in the institutions that they experienced at first hand. The ex-convict therefore comes to represent the reliable and authoritative witness who has made the journey to the secret country behind prison walls and has now returned to tell of his adventures. Although the attributions of savagery to the other inmates do indeed reinforce the boundaries between respectability and unalloyed criminality, the animal metaphors additionally invoke the discourse of the travelogue, since they underline the ethnographic framework of going into strange lands and encountering savage tribes ruled by savage kings. However, unlike the ordinary traveller, who can often assume an uninvolved perspective (as can the readers of such memoirs), the prisoner enters the gates of hell and is absorbed into the mass of 'dogs' and 'scum.' Thus F. Brocklehurst, who was sent to prison for a month because he refused to pay a fine for speaking in public (not at Hyde Park Corner, where it would have been legal), complained, 'As I have before suggested, I might have been a dog, so imperatively and abruptly did he call me to him.'[23]

Despite the fact that many writers of memoirs indicate that they kept to themselves and believe they are distinct from their fellow sufferers, what makes their reports memorable are, however, precisely their sufferings and how they endured and survived the ordeal. Thus, Jabez Spencer Balfour, who took a fall from member of Parliament to a sentence of twenty years' penal servitude as a consequence of being involved in a major investment scandal, characterizes Portsmouth prison as a 'heartbreaking, soul-enslaving, brain-destroying hell' and criticizes a great number of humiliating prison rituals (handcuffing, strip search) and abuses (cold cells, hammocks that collapse, cell searches, warders who tyrannize their charges).[24] He also expresses his belief that the punishment is sufficiently deterring for those committing crimes out of levity (a group in which he included the Fenians) but useless for the really hardened criminals.[25] Even more negative are the views of the anonymous Manchester merchant who was sent to prison for twelve months as a consequence of his arrest for being drunk and disorderly. He vociferously accuses the authorities of unwarranted cruelty, noting the terrible punishment of the treadwheel, the insufficient quantity of food, the suffering from cold in the winter, and the frequent application of the lash, accusing them of 'inflicting brutalities upon innocent people.'[26]

For many texts, therefore, the thrill of the exotic setting and the emotional involvement with the suffering gentleman prisoner provide sufficient interest for the reading public, who can then be influenced to agree with the author's evaluations of the quality of the prison service. That the indignities of convict life and the inhumanity of some of the prison rules figure so largely in these accounts certainly betrays a

'Stone Walls Do (Not) a Prison Make' 157

middle-class bias, since these are the things most irksome to 'respectable' folk; they are also the aspects most likely to appeal to a middle-class readership. Thus, Spencer Balfour's remarks about the unnecessary humiliations of handcuffing and strip-searching are likely to strike seasoned inmates as ridiculous in comparison with their experience of hunger, cold, and the lash. Moreover, such texts do not and cannot denounce what most Victorian prisoners found particularly difficult to adjust to, namely the regular and heavy work load, the required cleanliness, and above all, the rule of silence. Although experts on prison conditions such as Dickens acknowledged (and indeed endorsed) the impact of these circumstances as especially punishing, the gentlemen convict memoirs only touch on them. With their own background in mind, and focusing on their readership, their one chance of creating sufficient sympathy and a willingness to believe in their report was to create a common moral ground with their audience. And that common moral ground clearly consisted in the values of industry and cleanliness, virtues that the lower orders were thought to signally lack. However rigorous the work routine in prison, the authors of these memoirs, barring abuses, treat prison discipline as salutary and just. They also nearly all turn out to be good and diligent workers. Nor do gentlemen prisoners often complain about the food. With the public clamouring that prisoners should not receive more and better food than honest folk starving for lack of occupation, the writers imply that the nastiness of prison fare must be part of a just punishment: alimentation needs to be adequate to keep body and soul together, but it should make no concession to taste or pleasure in consumption. Thus, one finds many remarks about the good quality of the dark bread or soup, although some prisoners obviously receive no meat and no vegetables or other vitamin-rich foods.[27] Even Balfour hints that some delicate prisoners like himself become ill because of the prison food and need fattening in hospital.[28]

The most important strategy employed to create sympathy with the reader is the projection of victimization. Only if the prisoner has been able to establish a common ground with the audience and has won their sympathy for being, basically, a decent and respectable person can he attempt to elicit pity for unjust treatment. In this attempt, the author resorts to the patterns of the sentimental novel in which weak and innocent creatures (mostly the proverbial virtue in distress) are in the clutches of evil and cruel villains. Abuses of the system are, moreover, systematically demonstrated in the experience of *other* prisoners, in order to evade any suspicion that the writer is trying to curry favour with

158 Monika Fludernik

the reader or is indulging in complaint. Moreover, dwelling on one's own sufferings smacks of the maudlin and implies weakness; the gentlemen prisoners considered here want to suggest that their treatment was just and that they were able to endure it. The sentimental schema of the innocent victim of villainous abuse is clearly present in these autobiographical texts, but it remains subdued in comparison with fictional texts that emphasize the sentimental effect. It is to such texts that we will now turn.

So far we have analysed nineteenth-century British prison memoirs as rhetorically elaborated autobiographical accounts of the prison experience, mostly by so-called gentlemen prisoners who use a variety of rhetorical strategies to influence their readership. By reproducing stereotypical views against 'criminals' current among the Victorian middle classes, they try to achieve understanding, sympathy, and a willingness to listen to their proposals for reform. In particular, they argue that rogues should be punished severely, that prisoners must be disciplined, and that industry and cleanliness are the primary virtues to be inculcated in prison inmates. Since most prison memoirs deal with penal servitude, this emphasis on punishment corresponds with the type of hardened criminal thought to deserve rough treatment. As we will see, the emphasis in Victorian fictionalized texts is quite different, and also less focused on penal servitude.

The Fictionalization of the Prison Experience in the Magazine Literature and the Novel

Besides autobiographies, there are a number of additional genres of documentary literature that purport to be true accounts of the Victorian prison world but frequently lapse into fictionalizing. True-to-life reports of the situation inside prisons, or of the history of an individual prisoner, could be gained at first hand not only from the prisoners themselves, in their memoirs, but also from prison chaplains, from warders, and from regular prison visitors. In addition to this, newspaper reporters gained access to prisons and published their findings. Like the memoirs, these texts purport to tell the truth, to present to the public a firsthand account, and to intervene in current political debates about penal policy by supplying confirmation or falsification of popular opinion and prejudice. The most famous accounts of trips to Newgate are Charles Dickens's articles in *Sketches by Boz* (1833–6).[29] In these he presents himself as an observer on the scene whose emotions are stirred by his vicarious experience of imprisonment in Newgate. Dickens as reporter empathizes with the wretches in the condemned cells and depicts their despair by fictionally transporting himself into their situation and representing to the reader what they must be suffering:

> We entered the first cell. It was a stone dungeon, eight feet long by six wide, with a bench at the upper end, under which were a common rug, a bible, and a prayer book. An iron candlestick was fixed into the wall at the side; and a small high window in the back admitted as much air and light as could struggle in between a double row of heavy crossed iron bars. It contained no other furniture of any description.
> Conceive the situation of a man, spending his last night on earth in this cell. Buoyed up with some vague and undefined hope of reprieve, he knew not why – indulging in some wild and visionary idea of escaping, he knew not how – hour after hour of the three preceding days allowed him for preparation, has fled with a speed which no man living would deem possible, for none but this dying man can know. He has wearied his friends with entreaties, exhausted the attendants with importunities, neglected in his feverish restlessness the timely warnings of his spiritual consoler; and, now that the illusion is at last dispelled, now that eternity is before him and guilt behind, now that his fears of death amount almost to madness, and an overwhelming sense of his helpless, hopeless state rushes upon him, he is lost and stupefied, and has neither thoughts to turn to, nor power to call upon, the Almighty Being from whom alone he can seek mercy and forgiveness, and before whom his repentance can alone avail.[30]

> The girl belonged to a class – unhappily but too extensive – the very existence of which should make men's hearts bleed. Barely past her childhood, it required but a glance to discover that she was one of those children, born and bred in neglect and vice, who have never known what childhood is: who have never been taught to love and court a parent's smile, or to dread a parent's frown. The thousand nameless endearments of childhood, its gaiety and its innocence, are alike unknown to them. They have entered at once upon the stern realities and miseries of life, and to their better nature it is almost hopeless to appeal in after-times, by any of the references which will awaken, if it be only for a moment, some good feeling in ordinary bosoms, however corrupt they may have become. Talk to *them* of parental solicitude, the happy days of childhood, and the merry games of infancy! Tell them of hunger and the streets, beggary and stripes, the gin-shop, the station-house, and the pawn-broker's, and they will understand you.[31]

The first scene creates a spectacle of the prison cell in the condemned hold. Dickens addresses readers and asks them to imagine themselves in this virtual scenario. This creation of an imaginary spectacle clearly invokes Sterne's prisoner in the Bastille. Yorick in *A Sentimental Journey* imagines a scene in which he watches through the spyhole a prisoner who is lying on straw, chained to the dungeon wall.[32] Here, too, the observer, the reader, is supposed to recoil at the horror of the situation. In the second passage, by contrast, no spectacle is created, but the sentimental parameters are put in place by the phrase 'make men's hearts bleed.' Despite the clear intention to create a tear-jerking scene, the reporter in this passage is much more analytical in alluding to the social misery of the orphan child. The virtual scenario of a family home serves as the paradise that this girl has never experienced. Here the poignancy of the scene lies in forcing the reader to imagine what it would be like not to have had a childhood. In other contexts, Dickens *qua* Boz is much less taken by some of the women prisoners. His observation of a hardened criminal mother in conference with her bewildered daughter provides a glimpse of habitual criminals in action that resonates with echoes from Daniel Defoe's *Moll Flanders*:

> A little farther on, a squalid-looking woman in a slovenly, thick-bordered cap, with her arms muffled in a large red shawl, the fringed ends of which straggled nearly to the bottom of a dirty white apron, was communicating some instructions to *her* visitor – her daughter evidently. The girl was thinly clad, and shaking with cold. Some ordinary word of recognition passed between her and her mother when she appeared at the grating, but neither hope, condolence, regret, nor affection was expressed on either side. The mother whispered her instructions, and the girl received them with her pinched-up, half-starved features twisted into an expression of careful cunning. It was some scheme for the woman's defence that she was disclosing, perhaps; and a sullen smile came over the girl's face for an instant, as if she were pleased: not so much at the probability of her mother's liberation, as at the chance of her 'getting off' in spite of her prosecutors. The dialogue was soon concluded; and with the same careless indifference with which they had approached each other, the mother turned towards the inner end of the yard, and the girl to the gate at which she had entered.[33]

This type of presentation obviously deploys fictional techniques, since the narrator freely speculates about the feelings and morals of his subjects, and dramatizes his own emotional involvement. Especially in reference to the condemned cells, he adheres to the frame of the sentimental novel. Dickens also commiserates with an Italian prisoner and the inmates of the Eastern penitentiary in Philadelphia.[34] The narrator, like Yorick in his fantasies, watches the sufferings of another human being, expatiating on the pains he experiences in empathizing with the despair and misery of the prisoners, and ends up doing nothing about it. Yorick represses the vision – it is too painful to continue contemplating – and Dickens leaves the prison. By writing about these terrible experiences, the reporter and the witness both psychologically master the shock which they have received and try to induce a second-hand sympathy in the reader, who is even less able to help directly, though able to shed tears of pity.[35] Yet, Dickens is also very clear-minded about those who can no longer be rescued and reintegrated into society: in the third passage quoted above he wastes no sympathy on the two female figures. His lack of emotional involvement correlates with the hardheartedness and indifference observed in mother and daughter. It is the implied absence of a sentimental scene that gives this passage its poignancy.

Although, at least in his *American Notes*, Dickens manages to draw a clear lesson about the silent system and condemns it without qualification, the exercise in sentimentalism frequently serves its own sensational and melodramatic purposes without benefiting the object of compassion. The reader of sentimental fiction and sentimentalizing journalism cannot directly change the situation even if the reporter is trying to do some consciousness-raising on particularly unjust laws or prison regulations. It is only by flooding the market with such accounts on a specific topic that the public can be moved out of its lethargy, as was the case with the campaigns against slavery and their climax with the publication of Harriet Beecher Stowe's *Uncle Tom's Cabin*. By comparison, imprisonment for debt, although deplored in text after text from the Renaissance to the Victorian novel, was abolished only in 1869.

In drawing on fictional and rhetorical devices, Dickens's reports were not unusual for journalism of the day on this subject. Two series of articles are especially relevant: 'The Gaol Chaplain' in *Bentley's Miscellany* (1839–44) and 'The Condemned Cells' in *Fraser's Magazine* (1840–1). The series 'The Condemned Cells. From the notebook of the ordinary of Newgate' by Charles Wall has a very specific didactic purpose:

> In giving publicity to these papers, the object is to present our readers with a view of criminal characters, as they have been seen in the condemned

cells while awaiting the execution of the judgment of the court. We record facts, together with an occasional reference to the effects of the then existing criminal laws, omitting a description of many harrowing scenes which the rigid execution of those laws brought under our view – scenes that have moved and beguiled tears from the eye of the oldest janitor in the prison, such as the valedictory interviews between the doomed and their parents, wives, children, or other near and dear relatives.[36]

Despite the journalist's disclaimer, he does indeed go on to depict a heart-rending scene between a repentant forger and his wife, who 'was lying senseless on the floor. The children, aged six, eight, and ten, were crying over her.'[37]

Similarly pathetic scenes are frequent in the series. In the second 'chapter' of October 1840 the condemned man called Charles is a good-looking young clerk of a noble family who protests his innocence of forging bank notes. A good three columns of the article are devoted to the mother and beautiful sister arriving at Newgate to have an interview with their beloved Charles: 'Even this iron-hearted man [the keeper] was touched with the appearance of so much beauty in distress.'[38] The courage and despondent submission to Fate displayed by Charles, who is sentenced to death despite his innocence, are rendered in detail, with the ordinary trying to succour the prisoner by conversation about religious subjects.[39]

Another example concerns the case of two brothers who had been tricked into robbery without realizing it. The elder brother turns grey during the first night in prison, succumbing to the horrors of imprisonment and the worry for their future:

> He trembled as does a kid when thrust into the cage of a boa-constrictor for food. The fear of the future was then present to him; and in his excited imagination, the executioner was busy about his person. In the next instant the demon of rage triumphed and rendered him furious for revenge. He gnashed his teeth, his hands were clenched, every nerve was braced, each muscle was tensely constringed, and his whole frame was gathered up like a *tiger* prepared to spring on his prey. A pause, and the futility of his efforts was apparent to his mind; his head dropped on his chest, when tears of conscious weakness came to his relief. ... The elder of the two brothers had passed a night of horrors; he appeared in the yard as haggard as if the work of years under an accumulated weight of woes. A patch of hair on the right side of the head, as large as the palm of the

hand, but perfectly circular in its form, which the previous evening had been of a dark brown colour, had now become white. His eyes, also, had lost several shades, in depth of colouring, while their action indicated excessive shyness and cunning. They had, also, sunk deeper into the sockets, and appeared to be constantly peering round for a place where he might escape from his keepers, or he might hide from those who proffered him words of consolation.

His case was, however, past cure. The night in the cells had done its work on the mind, its possessor no longer spoke of injury inflicted upon him, or talked of revenge. He was like a plant cut down in one night by a frost; the stalk or stem, indeed, remained; but the blossom and beauty had departed, and the symbols of decay only remained.[40]

The passage dwells on the victimhood of the older brother by describing him as a sacrificial kid presented to merciless justice in the images of a boa constrictor and a frost that can kill a delicate plant. It moreover indicates that the effect of imprisonment is twofold: premature death but also transformation into a wild beast inaccessible to human reason. The writer notes that the severity of the particular law was modified three years after the brothers' death. The text continues with extensive pathetic scenes describing the family's visits to the brothers in prison. In typically sentimentalist fashion, these encounters are first described as unrepresentable: 'The several interviews that were granted to the brothers with their mother and sister were of too painful a nature to be detailed at length, they may be more readily imagined than described.'[41] By involving the reader emotionally with the plight of their protagonists, Wall's ordinary and the narrator both convey a criticism of capital punishment and attack some of the abuses of pre-trial detention.

The series entitled 'The Gaol Chaplain' published by Erskine Neale in *Bentley's Miscellany* has an argumentative narrator, the chaplain, who first did not want to take this job. The chaplain's account encloses stories about individual cases that came to his attention. Sometimes these are related in the first person, as is the case of the poacher in chapter 2 who is accused of highway robbery and sentenced to transportation. He has been in prison several times, but quakes at seeing the treadmill.[42] Earlier he had been imprisoned for poaching and was sentenced to hard labour: '"Put him on the treadmill," was the order of the visiting justice: "nothing finer than the treadmill! brings a fellow at once to his senses: works a thorough cure: he rarely pays us a second visit who has been once on the treadmill!"'[43] The poacher continues,

I was placed on the mill! Its punishment was to reform me. Reform me! It made me irritable, quarrelsome, sullen, savage! Reform me! It merged my thoughts in bodily fatigue and exhaustion. Instead of encouraging me by cheerful employment in prison to seek labour as the means of honest subsistence when I left it, it confirmed me in my hatred to labour by compelling me to submit to it in its most painful, irksome, and exhausting form. And yet there are those who have greater cause to complain of it than myself. If men, young and strong men, sink under its infliction, how can it be expected that women, weak and wretched women, can bear up against it? There are very few of them who can undergo such labour: there is the greatest difficulty in teaching them to be upon the wheel, and escape accident: and frequently I have known women bleed at the nose when first put to the wheel. How many have been caught at the wheel and maimed by it for life! and yet there are humane and benevolent individuals who contend for it as a proper punishment for women upon a prison diet! And the judges wonder, and gaolers complain, that prisoners – their period of confinement completed – leave prison more sullen, callous, hardened, desperate characters than when they entered them! The wonder would be if they were otherwise![44]

Here the chaplain puts his own views about the iniquities of the game laws and the undue severities of the prison regime into the mouth of a prisoner. Since that prisoner has just been shown to be innocent of the charge of highway robbery (for which he is to be transported), though guilty of poaching (for which his story provides extenuating circumstances), the readers' sympathies are nudged towards a criticism of the legal and penal institutions, but in a manner that saves the chaplain from directly involving himself with such criticism.

In chapter 5, a story is told 'in the third person' and, as one notes already in the first paragraph, is strongly dependent on literary models:

It was a bright laughing morning in spring, the sun shone cheerily, and a gentle breeze, as it swept softly and wooingly over the beautiful bay of Naples, broke the deep blue waves into innumerable sapphires. Light skiffs flitted gaily over its bosom, the rude chorus of the fishermen rose lazily from the shore; while ever and anon the measured beat of the wave upon the sand fell upon the ear with a soothing and delicious murmur.

Fair and gladdening as was the scene, some there were who viewed it apparently blind to its beauty, and insensible to its influence. In a window commanding the bay sat that morning a youthful, but unsociable party, loitering over a late breakfast.[45]

The text continues with dialogues in the manner of novels and other typically novelistic devices for creating suspense, ending chapter 6 with 'But whoever was he upon whom was passed this lavish encomium?' and including such statements as, 'Louis Lennard, however clear and well-defined his own plans might appear to himself, was, at the age of four-and-twenty, a mystery to all around him.'[46] The story goes on to dabble with mysterious affairs as yet kept secret from the reader. Whereas Wall, like Dickens, abided by the reporter's duties of closely following the observer's standpoint, using his impressions of the protagonists' harrowing experiences as a touchstone for the readers' reactions, Neale uses a more direct strategy of involving his readers. He supplies pseudo-authenticity by inserting supposedly autobiographical extracts into the text; and he transgresses the boundaries of journalism into the inevitably fictional representation of the minds of his story's participants. By additionally employing typically literary narrative openings, he leaves the genre of reportage behind and starts to write fiction that pretends to historical truth.

Later in the series, 'The Gaol Chaplain' continues as a succession of ever more sensationalist cases that do not even have a direct bearing on the chaplain (some are mere hearsay accounts). Thus we have the case of a woman servant executed for poisoning dumplings, who is innocent of that particular charge but guilty of an earlier heinous murder nevertheless. In revenge for being tricked into a fake marriage, she has killed the son of her betrayer. In the next story, Dr Meddlycott plays the detective to find out whether a former patient of his killed her new-born infant.[47] These texts are narrated in the shape of fictional tales with the framing authentication by the chaplain-narrator a mere front.

The same can be said of the anonymous *Memoirs of Jane Cameron* (1864), which are supposedly written by a prison matron. Although this two-volume text is less novelistic in texture and reminds one of the episodic narratives of criminal autobiography, the occurrences and general shape of the story suggest that it is in part fictional, too. The descriptions of prison life, the relationship of Jane with her female warders, and the problems that she experiences with the prison regime are quite convincingly represented; where the text starts to move off into fiction is in relation to Jane's love affair with Black Barney, and the story of Marie, her friend, who marries and becomes respectable. This part of the plot teems with coincidences, and the degree to which the text draws on literary motifs raises the suspicion of fictionality. Later memoirs of wardens and prison visitors are much less sensational and quite authentic in their drabness.[48] There is only a short step from sentimentalized magazine articles to the novels and plays of prison life. Edward Stirling's *Margaret Catchpole*, a play in three acts from 1855, for instance, shares some of the sensational melodrama with *Jane Cameron*.[49] Margaret is a typical instance of the fallen woman whose naïvety and love for her criminal seducer result in getting her involved in crime herself. Margaret could be regarded as the female equivalent of Lillo's George Barnwell (except that she does not commit murder). Unlike Barnwell, however, Stirling's Margaret throughout remains a virtuous victim of others' villainous manipulations.[50]

Apart from Dickens's novels, Victorian fiction does not include many prison texts, particularly novels set in realistic contemporary prison settings. (I exclude the work of Stevenson and other medieval or continental dungeon settings.) Charles Reade's *It Is Never Too Late to Mend* and the Leightons' *Convict 99* (1898) are two prominent examples of the genre.[51] They discuss prison abuses at great length, but also participate in the sensational and the sentimental element. Thus, both novels have villains interfering between the heroine and her betrothed, who is in prison; both novels abound in coincidental encounters (in Australia, in Reade's case), in acts of courage and heroism (Lawrence Gray's rescue of the warder's daughter in *Convict 99*); and both dwell on the unsavoury element in prison discipline – Reade for political reasons, the Leightons less clearly so. Whereas Reade is explicitly fictionalizing the events of Birmingham Borough Jail, the Leightons do not pretend to recast authentic material. Yet the facts in each case are similar: the portrayal of the cruelties of prison life and the circumstances of food deprivation, gruelling prison work, and warder tyranny correspond in the two versions.

Charlotte M. Yonge's *The Trial; or, More Links of the Daisy Chain* (1864) is perhaps the most realistic and least sensational of prison novels, at least in its portrayal of prison conditions.[52] The novel's sensational focus concerns the search for the real murderer and the possibility of proving Leonard Ward's innocence. Like *Martin Chuzzlewit* (1843–4), *The Trial* additionally criticizes American land speculation and discusses American mores.[53] As far as the legal strand of the novel is concerned, Leonard's trial for murder, conviction, expectation of execution, and the commutation of his sentence to penal servitude for life are presented as symbols of his moral and religious ordeal and prepare him for his career as a missionary. Throughout, Leonard, like a saint, suffers patiently and tries to see his unmerited punishment as a trial imposed from heaven. Where the novel becomes really interesting is in the depiction of the psychological toll taken by exposure to the convict establishment. Solitary confinement drives Leonard to doubt his innocence, and when his little sister dies in America, he starts to blame himself for having driven his family abroad. (His brother Henry Ward emigrated in order to avoid the bad reputation of a convict brother.) When Tom May finally acquires the proof of Leonard's innocence and rescues him from Portland, Leonard has wasted away physically and mentally. He would presumably have fallen irreparably ill and died before long unless rescued from prison.

Although the novel does not explicitly criticize the prison service and indeed insists on praising all the prison officials, the text clearly impugns the humanity of Victorian penal policy from a medical and humanitarian perspective. The novel never suggests that the penal system is *unjust*; on the contrary, even Leonard himself submits to his ordeal as the just punishment of the law; yet the implication seems to be that this justice takes a toll much in excess of humane correctional practice. The implicit argument is underlined by the reactions of the novel's central figure, Dr May, the medical man in Stoneborough, whose concern for Leonard's mental and physical health provides a moral touchstone for the reader; it is underlined by the tragedy to which Leonard's family, especially the gifted Averil, are exposed as a consequence of the conviction. When Dr May goes to visit Leonard at Portland, his reaction to the 'excellence of the arrangements' there provides a clear guideline to the reader. His friend Hector demonstrates the outline of the cells: '"Just twice as wide as a coffin," said Hector, doing the honours of one,' and the doctor 'almost gasped at the thought of the young enterprising spirit thus caged for nine weary months, and to whom this bare confined space was still the only resting-place.'[54] The text continues:

> He had yet to see the court, where the prisoners were mustered at half-past five in the morning, thence to be marched off in their various companies to work. He stood on the terrace from which the officials marshalled them, and he was called on to look at the wide and magnificent view of sea and land; but all he would observe to Hector was, 'That boy's throat has always been tender since the fever.' He was next conducted to the great court, the quarry of the stones of the present St. Paul's, and where the depression of the surface since work began there, was marked by the present height of what had become a steep conical edifice, surmounted by a sort of watchtower. There he grew quite restive, and hearing a proposal of taking him to

the Verne Hill works half a mile off, he declared that Hector was welcome to go; he should wait for his boy.[55]

This scene's realism bears comparison with the strategies of creating sympathy that we have observed earlier. Yonge does not resort to pathos. Instead, she has a trustworthy protagonist take the position of an observer of the penal law in action. It is his reaction to the cruelties of Victorian prison life that teaches the reader the relevant message. Although Dr May is clearly affected by what he sees, the novel eschews downright sentimentalist scenarios and emotional effects. Yonge can therefore be argued to have transformed the fictional representation of the Victorian prison and to have evolved a more realistic representation of the iniquities and abuses of the system.

In this section we have looked at journalistic and literary depictions of Victorian prison lives. I have attempted to show how the supposedly authentic reports frequently deploy a variety of fictionalizing strategies, creating spectacles typical of sentimental fiction, involving the readers emotionally by appealing to their sympathy, using literary motifs and genre elements (such as the chapter opening with reference to the weather), and providing access to the interiority of the key characters. This suggests that the authors I have discussed realized that fiction might be better at creating the effects they sought to achieve.

Conclusion

> Light and whitewash, abundant fare, garments sufficient but eminently unbecoming, were less impressive than dungeons, rags and bread and water.[56]

The representation of penitentiary realities labours under an inherent disadvantage; it is in principle less gripping, less sensational than the trial and execution story, or the traditional depiction of cruel imprisonment in castles and dungeons. Modern imprisonment fails to catch one's imagination; its description is as tedious as actual imprisonment would be to the sufferer. Given this inherent disadvantage of the subject, the Victorian fictional prison texts that I have discussed arguably counteract this threat of boredom by a number of strategies that emphasize the sensational and emotional aspects of the situation. In contrast to the rational and largely non-emotive discourse of the prison memoirs, the semi-fictional and fictional texts discussed in the second half of this paper try to capture the reader's interest and sympathy by employing a number of literary strategies.

The above discussion has demonstrated that nineteenth-century representations of imprisonment in novels and non-fictional prose texts – in so far as they relate to contemporary conditions – are heavily modelled on what, by twentieth-century standards, would be called fictional parameters. One of these parameters is persuasiveness. The rhetoric of non-fictional memoirs is geared towards creating a common evaluative ground between audience and writer and towards engaging the reader's sympathies. Other non-fictional texts in newspapers introduce the neutral figure of the chaplain or prison visitor from whose trustworthy perspective the institution can be criticized and sympathy may be created for those usually falling outside the readers' concerns. Purely fictional texts, finally, take this process merely a step further. They either introduce a positive neutral participant on the scene (the chaplain in Reade's *It Is Never Too Late to Mend*), or allow the innocent protagonist to become the hero of the story, providing the reader with extensive inside views of the imprisoned subject and his trials and miseries.

The emphasis on ordeals and miseries is important. All texts are critical of contemporary prison realities. Unlike the romantic representations of imprisonment discussed by Victor Brombert and unlike the Dickensian canon, Victorian prison memoirs, magazine literature, and novels never use the topos of carceral freedom. On the contrary, in their texts even those convicts who by reading are able to alleviate the hardship of prison discipline never move to a higher plane of mental creativity, since they remain caught in the restrictions of the prison system. Indeed, as in the case of Oscar Wilde, the disciplinary routines of convict prisons do not lend themselves to mental freedom but, on the contrary, have a deadening effect on all inmates.

Moreover, despite the mention of religious services and the humanity of prison chaplains, these documents prove to be signally bare of religious inspiration, penitence, or contrition. (Yonge is a signal exception to this.) The major states of mind produced by the Victorian prison system are callous indifference, despair, and anger. The required humility and consciousness of guilt that the penitentiary was designed to inculcate are clearly lacking in the texts that I have discussed. Even in Dickens's *David Copperfield*, Uriah Heep merely fakes the desired behaviour of ''umbleness.' Canonical Romantic and pre-Romantic poets may have believed in the human ability to be free in mind and soul while incarcerated or chained in physical reality, but Victorian prison texts no longer reiterate the slogan that 'Stone walls do not a prison make.' Instead, they keep recurring to the walls' deadening effect on the prisoners' psyche and morale. Francis Scougal, a prison visitor, contrasts the 'world in general [that goes] on its way amid fair sights and engrossing interests, without one thought of those who are lying pent up in the perpetual gloom and silence of the prison walls' with the 'denizens of the silent world [who] are left to pine out their dreary lives unheeded and unaided.'[57] Prisoners do not feel free in spite of their confinement; on the contrary, their one abiding obsession is to be liberated. He talks of one prisoner's 'burning desire of liberty – the almost frantic craving to be free – to escape from these stone walls which held him captive, from that closely barred window where the light of day was only granted in such niggard fashion to his longing eyes.'[58] Tragically, this prisoner dies from over-excitement at his impending liberation. Victorian prison worlds in fact and fiction no longer paint the hopeful and self-contented image of the artist at play in peace and quiet, but demonstrate how the penitentiary walls end up crushing the human spirit, how the iron of the prison bars eats into the human soul.

NOTES

1 Sir Richard Lovelace, 'To Althea from Prison' (1649), in *The Poems of Richard Lovelace*, ed. C.H. Wilkinson (Oxford: Clarendon Press, 1953), 78–9; Boethius, *Tractates: The Consolation of Philosophy* (AD 523), trans. H.F. Stewart et al., Loeb Classical Library, 74 (Cambridge, Mass.: Harvard University Press, 1973); Sir Thomas More, *A Dialogue of Comfort against Tribulation* (1534), vol. 12 of *The Yale Edition of the Complete Works of St. Thomas More*, ed. Louis L. Martz and Frank Manley (New Haven: Yale University Press, 1976); Charles d'Orléans, *The English Poems of Charles d'Orléans*, ed. Robert Steele, EETS o.s. 215 (Oxford: Oxford University Press, 1941).

2 Victor Brombert, *La prison romantique: Essai sur l'imaginaire* (Paris: José, Corti, 1975); *The Romantic Prison: The French Tradition* (Princeton: Princeton University Press, 1978).

3 See Karl Heinz Göller, 'The Metaphorical Prison as an Exceptional Image of Man,' *Fifteenth-Century Studies* 17 (1990): 121–45; Henri [Beyle] Stendhal, *The Charterhouse of Parma* (1839), trans. Margaret R.B. Shaw (London: Penguin, 1958).

4 Michel Foucault, *Discipline and Punish: The Birth of the Prison* (1975; New York: Vintage, 1979); John Bender, *Imagining the Penitentiary: Fiction and Architecture of Mind in Eighteenth-Century England* (Chicago: University of Chicago Press, 1987).

5 Michael Ignatieff, *A Just Measure of Pain: The Penitentiary in the Industrial Revolution, 1750–1850* (London: Macmillan, 1978). Bender, unlike Foucault and Ignatieff, does not focus on the disciplinary aspects of the penitentiary in hailing Henry Fielding's *Amelia* or Laurence Sterne's *A Sentimental Journey* as prototypes of the new episteme.
6 Consider, for instance, the treatment of Wilhelm Weitling; see Wilhelm Weitling, *Gerechtigkeit. Ein Studium in 500 Tagen* (Kiel: Mühlan, 1929). However, note the ordeal of Silvio Pellico in the Spielberg: his conviction for treason subjected him to the full rigour of the Hapsburgian penal discipline designed for hardened and irredeemable criminals. See Silvio Pellico, *My Prisons* (1868; Boston: Roberts Brothers, 1970).
7 See especially the case of Friedrich von der Trenck, who was kept incarcerated in Magdeburg in a dark, damp dungeon hole for over ten years, manacled and with his neck and feet encased in irons. Trenck's life ended under Robespierre's guillotine on suspicion of being a Prussian spy. See Sigrid Weigel, *Und selbst im Kerker frei ... ! Schreiben im Gefängnis* (Marburg/Lahn: Guttandin and Hoppe, 1982), 20–3.
8 The locution 'gradual turning away' indicates that early in the nineteenth century one prominent genre was that of the Newgate novel, which still harked back to the criminal (auto)biography, but this model had disappeared by the time of Dickens.
9 See Erving Goffman, *Stigma: Notes on the Management of Spoiled Identity* (Englewood Cliffs, NJ: Prentice-Hall, 1963).
10 On the sentimental novel and sentimentalism, see, for instance, Janet Todd, *Sensibility: An Introduction* (London: Methuen, 1986); Wolfgang Herrlinger, *Sentimentalismus und Postsentimentalismus: Studien zum englischen Roman bis zur Mitte des 19. Jahrhunderts* (Tübingen: Niemeyer, 1987); John Mullan, *Sentiment and Sociability: The Language of Feeling in the Eighteenth Century* (Oxford: Clarendon Press, 1988); G.J. Barker-Benfield, *The Culture of Sensibility: Sex and Society in Eighteenth-Century Britain* (Chicago: University of Chicago Press, 1992); Ann Jessie van Sant, *Eighteenth-Century Sensibility and the Novel: The Senses in Social Context* (Cambridge: Cambridge University Press, 1993); Michael Bell, *Sentimentalism, Ethics and the Culture of Feeling* (London: Palgrave, 2000). For a study that presents sentimentalism positively see Philip Davis, 'Victorian Realist Prose and Sentimentality,' in *Rereading Victorian Fiction*, ed. Alice Jenkins and Juliet John (London: Palgrave, 2002), 13–28.
11 See especially Robert Markley, 'Sentimentality as Performance: Shaftesbury, Sterne, and the Theatrics of Virtue,' in *The New Eighteenth Century: Theory, Politics, English Literature*, ed. Felicity Nussbaum and Laura Brown (London: Methuen, 1987), 210–30.

12 See the chilling accounts in Henry Mayhew and John Binny, *The Criminal Prisons of London and Scenes of Prison Life* (1862; London: Frank Cass, 1971) and in Philip Priestley, *Victorian Prison Lives: English Prison Bibliography, 1830–1914* (London: Methuen, 1985).

13 See accounts of prisoners eating candles in *Five Years' Penal Servitude: By One Who Has Endured It* (1877; New York: Garland, 1984), 299–301.

14 Charles Dickens, 'In and Out of Jail,' *Household Words* 7.164 (14 May 1853), 244–5.

15 Since the vast majority of prisoners treated in my corpus are male, I will continue with the male pronoun for the generic prison subject.

16 Charles Dickens, *David Copperfield* (1849–50; London: Penguin, 1997), 823–36.

17 Cf. *The Times*, 12 September 1853, 9–10.

18 Jabez Spencer Balfour, *My Prison Life* (London: Chapman and Hall, 1907), 262–3.

19 Charles Reade, *It Is Never Too Late To Mend* (London: Collins, 1856).

20 See *The Times*, 12 September 1853.

21 *The Times*, 12 September 1853, 10.

22 William Godwin, *Caleb Williams* (1794), ed. David McCracken (Oxford: Oxford University Press, 1991), 181.

23 F. Brocklehurst, *I Was in Prison* (London, Unwin, 1898), 131. The schema somewhat resembles that of the American captivity narrative in which white prisoners are forced to conform to Indian mores and convert into Indians. There is a wealth of literature on the captivity narrative. See, among much else, Carroll Smith-Rosenberg, 'Captured Subjects/Savage Others: Violently Engendering the New American,' *Gender and History* 5 (1993): 177–95; and Richard VanDerBeets, 'A Surfeit of Style: The Indian Captivity Narrative as Penny Dreadful,' *Research Studies* 39 (1971): 297–306.

24 Balfour, *My Prison Life*, 67–8.

25 Ibid., 71–2.

26 *Twelve Months Imprisonment of a Manchester Merchant in a Kirkdale Gaol: His Experience of Prison and Prisoners. With Suggestions of Improvement in Prison Discipline* (Manchester: Abel Heywood, 1880), 101.

27 See also *Memoirs of Jane Cameron, Female Convict*, by a Prison Matron, Author of 'Female Life in Prison,' 2 vols. (London: Hurst and Blackett, 1864), 125.

28 Balfour, *My Prison Life*, 189–90 et passim.

29 See Charles Dickens, 'Chapter 25: A Visit to Newgate,' in *Sketches by Boz: Illustrative of Every-Day Life and Every-Day People* (1833–6), illustrations by George Cruikshank and 'Phiz' (London: Oxford University Press, 1957), 201–11.

30 Dickens, *Sketches by Boz*, 212.

31 Ibid., 205.
32 Laurence Sterne, *A Sentimental Journey through France and Italy by Mr. Yorick* (1768), ed. Ian Jack (Oxford: Oxford University Press, 1984), 73.
33 Dickens, *Sketches by Boz*, 204–5.
34 Charles Dickens, 'The Italian Prisoner,' chapter 17 in *The Uncommercial Traveller and Reprinted Pieces* (1860), ed. Leslie C. Staples (London: Oxford University Press, 1968), 169–78; Charles Dickens, *American Notes and Pictures from Italy* (London: Oxford University Press, 1957), 99–111.
35 The shedding of tears is of course a well-documented reaction of the sentimental narrator or traveller. See Fred Kaplan, *Sacred Tears: Sentimentality in Victorian Literature* (Princeton: Princeton University Press, 1987).
36 Charles Wall, 'The Condemned Cells,' *Fraser's Magazine* 24 (July 1841): 46.
37 Ibid., 47.
38 Charles Wall, 'The Condemned Cells,' *Fraser's Magazine* 22 (October 1840): 488.
39 Ibid., 492.
40 Charles Wall, 'The Condemned Cells,' *Fraser's Magazine* 23 (February 1841): 227.
41 Ibid., 234.
42 Erskine Neale, 'The Gaol Chaplain,' *Bentley's Miscellany* 13 (May 1843): 515.
43 Ibid., 516.
44 Ibid., 517.
45 Erskine Neale, 'The Gaol Chaplain,' *Bentley's Miscellany* 13 (June 1843): 569–70.
46 Ibid., 572.
47 Erskine Neale, 'The Goal Chaplain,' *Bentley's Miscellany* 14 (September 1843): 250–9.
48 See, for instance, Francis Scougal, *Scenes from a Silent World* (1889) (New York: Garland, 1984); Arthur Griffiths, *Secrets of the Prison-House: or, Gaol Studies and Sketches* (1894: New York: Garland, 1984); Gordon Gardiner, *Notes of a Prison Visitor* (London: Oxford University Press, 1938).
49 Edward Stirling, *Margaret Catchpole, the Heroine of Suffolk: or, The Vicissitudes of Gaol Life* (1848; London: Duncombey, 1885).
50 The reference is to one of the key texts of the eighteenth-century sentimental drama: George Lillo, *The London Merchant; or, The History of George Barnwell* (1731), in *The Beggar's Opera and Other Eighteenth-Century Plays*, ed. David W. Lindsay (London: Dent, 1993), 259–326.
51 Reade, *It Is Never Too Late To Mend*; Marie C. Leighton and Robert Leighton, *Convict 99: A True Story of Penal Servitude* (London: Grant Richards, 1898).

52 Charlotte M. Yonge, *The Trial; or, More Links of the Daisy Chain* (1864; London: Macmillan, 1902).
53 Charles Dickens, *Martin Chuzzlewit* (1843–4), ed. Margaret Cardwell (Oxford: Clarendon Press, 1982).
54 Yonge, *The Trial*, 256, 257.
55 Ibid., 257.
56 Ibid., 260.
57 Scougal, *Scenes from a Silent World*, xiii.
58 Ibid., 95.

CHAPTER 6

'National Feeling' and the Colonial Prison: Teeling's *Personal Narrative*

Julia M. Wright

The storming of the notorious Bastille prison in July 1789 inaugurated the French Revolution and revitalized the use of the prison as a central metaphor in critiques of the oppressive state.[1] Because of escalating prosecutions against political radicals in the British Isles – members of the London Corresponding Society, the Society of United Irishmen, publishers and purveyors of literature deemed seditious – the prison of the 1790s was both the actual site of what Iain McCalman has termed a 'counterculture' and the discursive site through which radical authors could articulate the varied impact of an oppressive state on its citizens.[2] In radical culture throughout the first decades of the nineteenth century, the prison served this double purpose. The imprisonment of writers and editors who worked for radical periodicals led to the specific construction of the prison as the site for the dissemination of radical discourse: as Kevin Gilmartin has noted, 'Writers and editors prominently subscribed articles from prison and from exile,' and one 'introduced the ironic claim that his prison cell had become the perfect classroom for a radical autodidact.'[3] Imprisoned for political libel from 1813 to 1815 because of statements he made about the Prince Regent, Leigh Hunt taunted the authorities by elaborately decorating his prison cell and holding alternative court in it, welcoming such notable visitors as Lord Byron, Thomas Moore, and dozens of other prominent radicals and liberals – offering a 'gleeful, luxurious insolence toward Power projected from margins.'[4] Dealing with events of the 1790s but from the perspective of the 1820s, across this period of intensive prison writing from a specifically radical and countervailing perspective, Charles

Hamilton Teeling's *Personal Narrative of the Irish Rebellion of 1798*, and to a lesser extent its *Sequel*, engage this British rendering of the prison but amend it to address the specifics of Irish nationalism as a reaction to British colonial hegemony in Ireland.

Teeling's accounts have traditionally been dismissed as inaccurate histories of the 1798 United Irishmen uprising, but they are clearly designed to serve a polemical rather than a documentary purpose.[5] In 1828, when the first *Narrative* was published, agitation for Catholic Emancipation had again reached fever pitch, and the act would be passed, despite much public opposition in Britain, in the following year. In 1832, the year Teeling's *Sequel to Personal Narrative* was published, the controversial Reform Bill and the companion Irish Reform Bill were before the British parliament, dealing particularly with expanding the franchise and regional representation. Both of these pieces of legislation spoke directly to the political platform of the United Irishmen. Perhaps in part because of escalating tensions over voting reform and Catholic Emancipation, there was also a renewed interest in the Uprising. Novels broadly sympathetic to the United Irishmen, such as Alicia Lefanu's *Tales of a Tourist* (1823), Sydney Morgan's *The O'Briens and the O'Flahertys* (1827), and Michael Banim's *The Croppy, A Tale of '98* (1828), began to appear, in addition to various other memoirs, including *The Autobiography of Archibald Hamilton Rowan* (1826; 1840), Thomas Moore's *Memoirs of Captain Rock* (1824) and *Life and Death of Lord Edward Fitzgerald* (1831), and Jonah Barrington's *Rise and Fall of the Irish Nation* (1833), a number of which were advertised in the first edition of the *Personal Narrative*.[6] Teeling's memoirs first appeared in this context, tacitly contributing to these discussions of the uprising, the politics of religion, and Irish political rights, as well as, more indirectly, the contemporary prison reform movement.[7] The basis for the efficacy of Teeling's polemics lies in theories of the sentimental, as both *Personal Narratives* represent and elicit emotional responses implicated in Enlightenment moral theory. Teeling, for instance, offers letters that his father wrote during his own imprisonment because 'They may afford subject for reflection and improvement to the youthful mind, and will imprint on the hearts of my children an affectionate remembrance of his worth' (*Sequel*, 324).

Ireland and the Invocation of National Sentiment in the 1790s

Before proceeding to the prison sections of Teeling's *Personal Narrative*, I wish to further situate both the *Personal Narrative* and the *Sequel* in terms of late eighteenth-century politics and the philosophy of sensibility which informed contemporary political discourse. In 1798, there was a popular uprising against British colonial rule in Ireland, led and named for the United Irishmen but including other nationalist groups. Tensions had risen throughout the 1790s, in large part because of the erosion of the Irish parliament's powers and the continued refusal to grant Catholic Emancipation (that is, allow Catholics to vote, hold political office, and enjoy other political rights on the same terms as Anglicans).[8] Founded in 1791, the Society of United Irishmen was predominantly urban and Protestant at first. But, after much heated debate, its leaders reached out to rural Catholic nationalist organizations, published newspapers directed towards the lower classes, and promoted the idea that all Irish people, regardless of language, religion, or class, were equally citizens of the nation and so had inalienable political rights.[9] This, of course, made the British authorities nervous; already fearful that French Revolutionary principles would be imported to Britain, a fear heightened by the post-Revolution growth of radical societies in Britain, they deemed such language treasonous. In 1796, they arrested a number of the United Irishmen leaders in Belfast. In March 1798, they arrested those leaders' colleagues in Dublin, including the very popular Lord Edward Fitzgerald, and imposed martial law. The Uprising began within weeks, with significant conflicts in both the south and the north of Ireland. It took government forces months to suppress the Uprising and thousands were killed; then followed months of trials, many of them irregular even by the 1790s' standards, and then exiles and executions.[10]

Teeling and his family were in the thick of the conflict. As one of the United Irishmen's 'social radicals,' Teeling was instrumental in the 'merger' of the predominantly Protestant United Irishmen with the predominantly Catholic Defenders.[11] Shortly thereafter, in September 1796, he was one of the first arrested and charged with treason in a sweep of the area for political dissidents.[12] According to his own account, he was arrested by Lord Castlereagh, a family friend and a highly controversial figure closely allied with reactionary British politics.[13] In August 1798, a French force, under the command of General Humbert, landed in Ireland to assist the Uprising, and Charles's brother Bartholomew Teeling was among them. According to Charles's account, Bartholomew was captured, in a clear breach of military protocol, while 'bearing proposals to the commander of the British troops' from the French general (*Sequel*, 305). But Charles does not mention that his brother had gone to France as an agent of the United Irishmen. Bartholomew's participation in the French landing was part of the plan: the

French were supposed to link up with nationalist forces in Ireland, and United Irishmen leaders were distributed among the French forces to facilitate that end.[14] Bartholomew was charged, convicted, and executed within months of his return. Their father, Luke Teeling, was arrested and incarcerated in the hold of a prison-ship for four years. In the *Sequel*, Teeling includes a letter his father wrote from prison, in which Luke Teeling declares that his 'great and only crime lies in being considered the head of the Catholics in this county, and active in their cause at the time of our Convention' (328).[15]

The terms of the conflicts in which the Teelings were involved were shaped by the emergent discourse of modern nationalism. It is almost a commonplace in recent writings on nationalism that while its roots can be traced to earlier, similar ideologies, various forces in the late eighteenth century, among them the French Revolution and its aftermath, acted as a catalyst to produce a distinctive ideology.[16] In this context, the term 'nationalism' is generally used to refer to a sense of communal identity that includes a shared history, culture, and belief system, and often a particular language, as well as a concern for the collective good and sometimes claims to a particular territory.[17] But the basis for this communal identity lies in another Enlightenment model at work in much of the political discourse of the period, namely eighteenth-century moral theory and its attendant notions of sympathy, sentiment, and sensibility. During the Romantic period, in the early years of nationalist ideology and the ascendancy of sentimental literature, sensibility as a concept was deployed to authorize certain views of the nation. In such terms, the Irish national subject, regardless of class or religious affiliation, sympathizes with the suffering of Catholics under Penal Laws, the imprisoned nationalist, or the widows of the dead, and is also susceptible to a specifically national sentiment – a love of country that is predicated on a sympathy with other national subjects rather than a reverence for institutions, a commitment to a certain ideology, or an attachment to the land.

This form of national bonding was particularly efficacious in turn-of-the-century Ireland because of variations in heritage, language, religion, and class politics. Most of the then-current concepts of nationality assumed an almost genetic determinism in which one could speak readily of a 'national character.'[18] But the concept of 'national character' posed a problem in an Ireland rendered heterogeneous by waves of colonization, religious and linguistic differences, and various other genealogical and cultural divisions. While some United Irishmen ballads reclaimed 'Paddy' as a stock type to characterize the Irish as commonsensically radical, and post-1850 nationalism rooted identity in the soil and the Irish language (as Seamus Deane has argued),[19] the United Irishmen typically circumvented the question by focusing on legal questions of sovereignty and the public interest, as well as appeals to reason and universal human rights inspired by such writers as Thomas Paine.

But when they do address a non-legalistic cohering factor, they tend to do so on emotional terms. This is the case particularly when Unitedmen emphasize the inclusion of Catholics in their national vision, that is, when attempting to bridge the widest cultural gulf in Irish politics, that between a predominantly middle- and upper-class Protestant organization of native English speakers and a predominantly lower-class Catholic constituency in which many had Irish as their first language – and were treated differently under the law because of the Penal Statutes. In the 'Original Declaration of the United Irishmen,' they assert, 'we think it our duty, as Irishmen, to come forward and state what we feel to be our heavy grievance.'[20] In another declaration, for which United-man Dr William Drennan was charged with sedition, they define their 'beloved principle, which takes in every individual of the Irish nation, casts an equal eye over the whole island, embraces all that think, and feels for all that suffer.'[21] In his 1838 response to the 'True History of the Battle of the Diamond,' Teeling offers one of the more explicit articulations of this deployment of sentiment to supersede cultural difference. Giving the history of various rural nationalist groups, particularly the Peep-of-day Boys and the Defenders, Teeling describes the former as composed of 'Protestant Dissenters' and the latter as composed, 'in its origin, of Roman Catholics. I use the qualified term, origin, because I may have occasion, hereafter, to show, that, as a great National crisis advanced, sectarian feelings gave place to sentiments of a more expanded nature – in the Union of Irishmen, of all religious persuasions.'[22] Such appeals resonate with eighteenth-century concepts of sensibility; and, together with the legally framed appeals for justice, they are firmly situated within the context of the eighteenth-century moral theory that informed the literature of sensibility. Teeling's memoirs of the 1798 uprising follow from these United-Irishmen precepts in developing a sentimental nationalism in which the people are bound together by their shared suffering rather than by their participation in historical progress or their relationship to the land.

Repeatedly in Teeling's texts, nationalist sensibility is figured in terms of harmony, cooperation, fellow feeling, self-sacrifice, and union. Colonial activity is, in an often heavy-handed oppositional logic, described in terms of division, violence, hierarchy, and self-interest. Thus, Teeling writes,

> outstepping the line which unjust and impolitic laws had drawn between them and their less-favoured fellow citizens, they united against the common oppressors of their country, and forfeited their lives and their fortunes for the emancipation of her sons. ... We turn to the records of NINETY-EIGHT, and there trace the most distinguished characters of the day, of every Christian communion and religious creed, sinking the distinctive name of partizan or sectarian, in the proud appellation of IRISHMAN, and forming one great national bond of fraternal union. (*Sequel*, 285)

In the philosophy of sensibility, a circuit of moral recognition lies behind moral action: a virtuous person will respond sympathetically to suffering, and will thus be motivated to act in a way that will mitigate or end that suffering. Moreover, the more virtuous will be more 'sensible' to suffering, and so respond more intensely, while the virtue of the sufferer can also heighten the response. Enlightenment writers suggested, moreover, that a rational awareness of the public good informs our sympathy and that this is the basis of justice. Thus, in *An Inquiry Concerning the Principles of Morals* (1751), David Hume proposes that we 'define[] virtue to be *whatever mental action or quality gives to a spectator the pleasing sentiment of approbation;* and vice the contrary.'[23] In *The Theory of Moral Sentiments* (1759), Adam Smith writes that sympathy 'is by no means confined to the virtuous and humane, though they perhaps may feel it with the most exquisite sensibility. The greatest ruffian, the most hardened violator of the laws of society, is not altogether without it.'[24] These ideas, of course, were still current in the early nineteenth century, particularly in abolitionist literature in the United States and the British Isles. This premise that sympathy is the basis for social bonds is clearly outlined in Smith's study. Smith argues, 'By the imagination we place ourselves in his situation, we conceive ourselves enduring all the same torments, we enter as it were into his body, and become in some measure the same person'; 'this is the source of our fellow-feeling for the misery of others, that it is by changing places in fancy with the sufferer, that we come either to conceive or to be affected by what he feels.'[25]

This concept of sympathy became critical to some strands of nationalist thought. In 1774, Henry Home, Lord Kames, argued that 'patriotism is connected with every social virtue; and when it vanishes, every virtue vanishes with it'; patriotism 'triumphs over every selfish motive, and is a firm support to every virtue. In fact, where-ever it prevails, the morals of the people are found to be pure and correct.'[26] This nationalism is not patriotism as a love of country, but a moral engagement with a sympathetic community from which the nation, and its morality, derive. Moreover, it is intensified and validated when the nation is threatened: 'Patriotism is enflamed by a struggle for liberty, by a civil war, by resisting a potent invader, or by any incident that forcibly draws the members of a state into strict union for the common interest.'[27] We can find this logic throughout early nineteenth-century Irish nationalist discourse. For instance, Drennan, in his 'A Protest against an Union Between Great Britain and Ireland' (1800), suggests that national sentiment makes 'a man ... capable of every thing good and great,' and that, without a nation, the people 'become a mere number ... without any inherent principle of motive of common action, unattached to each other.'[28] Similarly, in an anonymous 1816 novel entitled *The Matron of Erin*, a character asserts, 'the common sufferings of Irishmen unite us, however differing in religious persuasion, for the general good.'[29] In *Woman; Or, Ida of Athens* (1809), Sydney Owenson (later Lady Morgan) suggests, through the novel's senior voice of moral authority,

> 'It is,' said he, 'from the harmonies and conformities of nature, that man should borrow his political and moral adaptions, and learn from the Legislature of the Universe those beneficent laws, which should form the social compact of mankind. Whenever the institutions of government shall tend to excite and develope the natural sensibility of man, the happiness of the state will be affected, for virtue itself is but composed of the affections; and the maxim of wisdom, or the exertion of art, proceeds only from that secret impulse, by which nature urges man, to enlighten and to cherish his brother man.'[30]

In his memoirs, Teeling offers a particularly clear illustration of the ways in which the discourse of sensibility and eighteenth-century moral theory could be used to argue for and define the nation in powerful ways. Teeling follows the view, articulated, for instance, by Hume, that sympathy and disgust are dispensed in accordance with a reasoned sense of the public good. Teeling thus, perhaps predictably, directs the reader to find the colonial authorities disgusting and so perceive them to be acting against the public good, and the United Irishmen the converse. But he also translates 'fellow-feeling,' to use Smith's term, into 'national feeling' and 'national sympathy.' Thus, instead of identifying a character as virtuous because others sympathize with his or her suffering or because of a capacity to sympathize with others, he identifies the United Irishmen as virtuous because of the people's sympathy with their suffering and because of their own sensibility to the people's suffering: that is, he represents the United Irishmen and the people in a sympathetic bond, each commiserating with the other's suffering, and so mutually validating the other's virtue while demonstrating their own and, in the process, constituting a nation in defiance of colonial pressures (and, as the prison sections show, carceral containment). This informs a common claim of the 1790s, namely that the people form radical societies because of oppression; in Teeling's representation, the colonial regime institutes the suffering through which the national bond is forged, and thus the Irish are not only innocent of instigation, but morally bound to rebel.[31]

John Thelwall is an important precursor in this context. A member of the London Corresponding Society and credited with provoking, through his powerful political speeches, the Two Acts of 1795 which made seditious speech treasonous and further limited the right to assembly, Thelwall was charged with treason and was held in some of the more notorious British prisons. In 'Stanzas on Hearing for Certainty that We Were to be Tried for High Treason,' published in *Poems Written in Close Confinement in the Tower and Newgate Upon a Charge of Treason* (1795), Thelwall writes,

> Short is perhaps our date of life,
>   But let us while we live be gay –
> To those be thought and anxious care
>   Who build upon the distant day.
> Though in our cup tyrannic power
>   Would dash the bitter dregs of fear,
> We'll gaily quaff the mantling draught,
>   While patriot toasts the fancy cheer.[32]

It is the invocation of patriotism that most interests me here. While Brombert suggests that the 'happy prison' in Romantic literature arises from the identification of solitude with transcendence and creativity,[33] the prison in Thelwall's writing – and later in Hunt's – is a 'happy' one in so far as it functions as the site of defiance and reveals the limits of the state's power. It offers a specifically political form of transcendence:

the prisoner, stripped of the rights sanctioned by the state, finds a core of political values and relationships that exceeds the state's control.[34] Patriotic feeling, solidarity between political and non-political prisoners, and the will to resist tyranny are almost naturalized, gathering added force from the simplifications the prison offers. This is not a contemplative, lyrical prisoner, as in Brombert's 'Happy Prison,' but a Promethean one: P.B. Shelley's Prometheus proclaims from the rock to which he has been 'nailed' by the tyrant Jupiter, 'Pity the self-despising slaves of Heaven, / Not me, within whose mind sits peace serene / As light in the sun, throned.'[35]

Moreover, in this poem by Thelwall and in Teeling's autobiographical account, this political transcendence is a specifically national one that alienates the government from a purportedly 'authentic' national polity. Teeling's account of his arrest and imprisonment, dominating the first half of the *Personal Narrative*, clarifies the distinctions between the government and the people on political and moral terms. Teeling's prison account prepares the reader to review, in the morally active terms of Enlightenment sympathy, the subsequent pages on the 1798 Irish Uprising as well as the 1832 *Sequel*, which focuses on the relationship between the United Irishmen and France.[36] Clearly polemical accounts rather than faithful 'objective' histories, Teeling's *Narratives* draw on the terms of Enlightenment sensibility in order to validate national feeling and aspirations, and represent the colonial regime as immoral and unnatural. The prison setting provides the stage on which Teeling displays scenes which seek to persuade the reader of the truth of his claims.

National Feeling and Imperial Insensibility

The opening pages of Teeling's first *Narrative* deal with the popular response to repressive government measures which escalated from the dismissal of sympathetic officials to the arrest of Teeling and others. By developing a contrast between the people and the government agents in terms of their sensibility, and specifically their 'fellow feeling' for the prisoners, Teeling tacitly defends the morality of the United Irishmen's position. After a prefatory polemic against colonial rule, Teeling offers a section entitled 'National Indignation on the Removal of Lord Fitzwilliam from the Administration of Ireland' (5); Teeling thus locates the source of 'national feeling' in the general disappointment that led to a 'day of *national mourning*' (6n). This moment of shared suffering is the origin of the national sympathy of the narrative, a sympathy that ties the soldiers, the leaders of the United Irishmen, political prisoners, and 'the people' at large in a national union from which the Anglo-Irish Ascendancy and its British allies are necessarily alienated because of their insensibility.

This construction of national sympathy, and its ability to register national morality, is a recurring point in Teeling's narrative, as each reference to prevailing political opinion is articulated in phrases which suggest 'national feeling.' The opening pages of the first *Narrative* abound in such phrasing: 'every county, city, and town in Ireland expressed ... in the undisguised language of the heart, the most poignant regret' (6); 'One feeling pervaded the whole assembly: it was a feeling of sorrow and deep indignation' (6); 'Such was the general sentiment expressed throughout Ireland' (6); 'It was impossible to resist the national impulse' (10). The United Irishmen and their sympathizers are consistently, even persistently, represented as sentimental and 'benevolent,' a key word in the discourse of sensibility.[37] Of the sister of a nationalist prisoner, Teeling writes, 'the benevolent feelings of her heart extended to every soul in distress' (47), and, of a Catholic opposed to the United Irishmen, that he was not 'insensible to the feelings of fraternal regard' (52). Lord O'Neill, similarly, is a figure of national authenticity in terms of both genealogy and sensibility: his 'ancestors swayed princely authority in the land before Britain had a title in that land to bestow' (31); 'benevolent and kind, he felt for the misfortunes which he could not relieve' (31).

The people in general also exemplify this benevolence and sympathy. While only a 'cold and distant salute passed between' Teeling (now under arrest) and the local military official, General Nugent, a crowd gathers outside. Teeling represents the crowd, and most of the soldiers, as sympathetic: 'Strong personal resentment against the author of my arrest was expressed in language too unequivocal to be mistaken, and the soldiers who formed my guard ... evinced no disposition hostile to the sentiments which my countrymen expressed. The feelings of the army, were, in fact, at that period considerably identified with those of the people' (16–17). The people exhibit '[c]onsiderable apprehensions' and 'much anxiety' (17) on Teeling's behalf. Support for Teeling in his hometown is such that he is approached by his guard: 'two grenadiers ... addressed me with a feeling and emotion which evinced their sincerity; – "*Now*, sir," said they, "*now* is your time; *our company* is on guard, our comrades are faithful; you have nothing to fear; no sentinel will stop you"' (17). Teeling declines out of chivalric concern for the guards' well-being. The guards, who Teeling notes are in communication with 'the people' (17), then hatch a plan for attacking Castlereagh, the 'apostate patriot' (14) as Teeling dubs him. Again out of noble concern for the safety of others, Teeling stops the assault. He 'had now no possible mode of direct external communication' (18) because he had been placed in the back of the building away from the crowd, so he speaks to the guards, 'exhort[ing] them [the guards], in the most forcible language, to a peaceful and orderly demeanour' – his 'sentiments were conveyed to the people' (18). Teeling represents himself, rather than Castlereagh, as controlling the situation and morally authorizes that control by suggesting that he used this power to protect the people and avoid violence. He also indicates that he derives that power not from institutional authority but from the sympathetic bond which ties together the nation's citizens, including Teeling, the soldiers, and the civilian population.

The oppressors are unable to exert such power because they are alienated from this sympathetic bond through their general insensibility. Ministers are termed 'unfeeling' (58) and Castlereagh is described as having neither 'the heart of an O'Neill, nor the feelings of a father' (30). Castlereagh specifically has the rhetoric of politeness instead of a feeling heart: when Teeling's father appeals to his former friend to be allowed to visit his son, Castlereagh 'refused, in the polite language of the courtier' (30). The only occasion on which he evinces feeling is during a confrontation with Teeling's mother during his search of the family home, and there it operates as a sign of the sensibility of Teeling's mother: 'her gentle but lofty spirit was roused, and burying maternal grief in the indignant feeling of her soul, "I was wrong," she exclaimed, "to appeal to a heart that had never felt the tie of parental affection – your Lordship is *not a father*." She pronounced this with a tone and an emphasis so feeling and so powerful, that even the mind of Castlereagh was not insensible to its force' (15–16). Castlereagh thus proves Adam Smith's rule that 'The greatest ruffian, the most hardened violator of the laws of society, is not altogether without [sympathy],'[38] but in the context of establishing the extremely sympathetic nature of Teeling's mother, and implicitly of properly Irish people in general. Similarly, by way of preface to an execution, Teeling writes, 'The calm resignation and unshaken fortitude which supported men through the severest trials, and accompanied them in the last stage of their mortal career, seemed a matter of unaccountable surprise to those who were insensible to the love of country and the innate feelings of virtue, which teach us how to die' (31–2).

As his attention to Castlereagh's merely rhetorical politeness and unsympathetic heart suggests, Teeling draws on Paine's characterization of established authority as theatrical and arbitrary in order to represent the colonial authorities as unfeeling actors.[39] He writes of Nugent, 'His visit was attended with considerable parade, and a good deal of that empty pomposity, more characteristic of the fop than the soldier' (16). The interrogation of Teeling and other political prisoners 'only tended to betray the indecision of the council, and to expose the weakness which all their assumed courage and importance could not conceal' (21), and the government makes 'some little effort to uphold a show of legislative authority' (51). Teeling frequently represents the authorities as unconvincing performers, empty shells incapable of understanding their audience, so to speak, and so unable to connect with them in any meaningful sociopolitical bond.

Throughout these early scenes, the sympathy of the people for the prisoners is well established and, more significantly, Teeling repeatedly draws attention to the power of that sympathy to cross the borders established and policed by the colonial forces. While Castlereagh and his military officials appear to be in control, it is Teeling who exercises control over Castlereagh's life through his sympathetic connection to the people and it is Teeling who commands the soldiers. An assertion such as Teeling's claim, 'public sympathy for those who suffered in the cause was general and sincere' (11), does double duty, at once uniting the nation in a sympathy for suffering, like that described by Home and later Ernest Renan, and condemning the colonial regime as immoral for instituting and being insensible to that suffering.[40] This early representation of the ineffectuality of an insensible administration in the context of Teeling's arrest is then played out in the specific space of the prison.

Colonial Incarceration and National Liberty

Teeling not only alienates the authorities from the national circuit of sympathy, but also represents their hegemony as fragile – if not doomed – because their legislative and material fortifications only further excite that sympathy. Teeling thus adds documentary weight to his declaration, 'Whilst the dark soul of despotism was employed in devising new modes of privations and restraint, the fair spirit of liberty was awake, and the sympathy of virtue, which tyrants never feel – which fetters cannot bind, nor bolts restrain, – communicated confidence, entertainment, and hope' (27–8). Teeling makes the synecdochal function of the prison nearly explicit when he writes of a repressive turn in the prison,

> By one of those acts of petty despotism, in which the governor of our prison but too often indulged, we had for some time been restricted from the usual enjoyments, if enjoyments they might be termed, which government had permitted him to extend to the state prisoners under his *paternal* care. This restriction extended to the privation of exercise and air, and even the most remote or partial communication with our friends. We had offended against the majesty of the governor, for we had presumed to converse in a language which he did not understand, and for this offence were all communication and social intercourse interdicted. Our conversation being, as he supposed, of a treasonable nature, *the safety of the prison and the safety of the state were equally in danger.* Had this occurred in an earlier stage of our imprisonment, we should have treated the matter in a more trivial light, terror and seclusion being then the order of the day; but having tasted a little of the *liberty* of a prison, we were too democratic in principle to surrender our rights at discretion. (32–3; second emphasis mine)

Teeling is careful here. He ascribes only to the governor the explicit identification of prison and state, while offering his own echoes of this claim in much more indirect terms. The governor is figuratively, but not overtly, tied to the British monarch, particularly in the reference to the 'majesty of the governor.' The reference to his 'paternal care' also furthers the reference, recalling the sovereign's claim to be a father to his people and George III's intensification of this claim by publicly foregrounding his domestic role as father to a large family. The ironic reference to the '*liberty* of a prison' – and the prisoners' 'rights' in relation to it – strongly recalls the language of Revolutionary debate, in which Britain claimed to assure liberty for its subjects (an assurance strongly identified with the Magna Carta and the post-Reformation break with the Catholic church), and the radicals called for the 'rights of man.' There is also a more subtle parallel at work here. In 1782, limited powers were restored to the Irish Parliament; in the next decade, some remaining anti-Catholic legislation was modified or repealed, allowing Catholics to practise law, gain greater access to education, and so forth. Around 1793, however, as in Britain, the government became more repressive. The Insurrection Act was passed in 1796, establishing curfews and instituting the death penalty for taking oaths; that same year, some Belfast United Irishmen leaders were arrested and habeas corpus was suspended. In other words, Teeling suggests that resistance to current repressive measures was intensified by the apparently moderate policy which prevailed in the 1780s.

In this context, Teeling's emphasis on communication is a suggestive one. By focusing on the governor's fear of communication, rather than fear of more material activity (escape, violence, bribery), Teeling draws attention to the British government's fear of ideas and speech acts rather than armed insurrection. From John Jones's *Impartial Narrative of the Most Important Engagements Which Took Place Between His Majesty's Forces and the Rebels, During the Irish Rebellion, 1798* (1799; 1834) to Maria Edgeworth's *Ennui* (1809), anti-nationalist accounts of '98 tended to treat the uprising as a largely military affair.[41] Teeling, however, represents the government's repressive measures as physical responses to communications motivated only by sympathy. Thus Teeling argues that, when the governor prohibits communication, he punishes all involved in the national circuit of sympathy: those who were expecting letters, the prisoners, and the members of the public who are generally concerned about the prisoners' welfare (33). The cooperative spirit which links together those in the prison and those in the city, further aroused by the break in communication, makes it possible for the prisoners to circumvent the governor's strictures.[42] According to Teeling, they write letters, address the packet to 'the patriotic and venerable James Dickson,' and then

> having no hand through which we could procure a direct conveyance from the prison, we trusted to fortune (confident in the sympathy of our countrymen) for a favourable issue. By the ingenuity of a fellow-prisoner, who was confined in one of the loftier cells, the package was conveyed from the lower apartments to his, and thence impelled with considerable force beyond the external walls. Fortune favoured the design; the feelings of the people were alive to our situation; the package was picked up, and by a faithful hand conveyed to its destination. (33)

When Teeling's father is finally allowed to visit the prison, he exclaims, 'Thank God! ... the tyranny of man cannot fetter the mind, nor sever the tie that unites the kindred soul' (53). To counter Castlereagh's refusal to allow his old friend, Luke Teeling, to send a letter to his son Charles, Teeling offers the story of a local woman of wealth who is granted permission to give the prisoners some food, and conceals letters and writing materials in a pie. The letters once again intensify national sympathy: 'we now felt as if a new soul breathed within us; we were assured of the attachment of our friends, the sympathy of our country, and the strength of our cause' (29). To make the larger implications of these incidents clear, Teeling peppers his narrative with sweeping statements: 'the excitement of popular feeling, roused by the widely spreading sentiments of freedom which, having successfully struggled in the new world, now burst with irresistible force upon the old, and swept like a torrent every barrier opposed to its impetuous career' (3).

Teeling's polemic depends upon repeated but varied demonstrations of the power of sympathetic bonds to break or supersede institutionally imposed fetters. As Teeling and other political prisoners are being conveyed to Dublin, they stop at a garrison. They are denied food and water there, and local women who want to offer them refreshment are stopped by the guard. However, Teeling writes, the 'generous feelings of our fair countrywomen' prevailed: 'Two ... approached my carriage; this they could only effect through the hazardous expedient of passing under the cavalry horses, which evinced more gentleness than their riders. They extended their arms with difficulty, and pressed me to partake of the refreshments which they presented' (20). This transgression of borders continues in the Dublin prison. For instance, there is a 'brave veteran' with a 'benevolent heart' who recognizes the innocence of the prisoners and offers them some snuff (22). But they do not always need assistance from outside the carceral space. Though they are at first in 'Solitary imprisonment,' they learn how to 'detach the locks from our doors' so that they can socialize with each other (24). They later undermine prison forms of punishment by asking that all be punished when one is put in irons for admitting to possessing a cap with a green ribbon (a nationalist symbol):

> Letters and the dungeon presented no terrors to the manly breast, while a virtuous sympathy bespoke the generous feeling which animated every soul, and all eagerly demanded to participate in the perilous distinction of their intrepid associate. 'Let them be indulged,' exclaimed the humane commander of His Majesty's forces. His lordship viewed the operation of ironing the prisoners with a cold and malignant composure, while they, with cheerful heart and animated voice, sung aloud a popular air of the day, and again and again rejoined in the chorus –

'Though we to the dungeon go,
  Where patriots dwelt before,
Yet in the cell, or on the sod,
  We're Paddies evermore.' (38)

In the more provocative moments of the *Personal Narrative,* Teeling compares the prisoners' information network to the state's. In a passage excoriating the notorious informers used by the state throughout the 1790s, Teeling deals with the particular case of an informer named Kerr. Teeling sympathetically represents Kerr as a basically good man who was terrorized into informing on four others (44); Kerr is held, in isolation, in the same prison as Teeling and his friends. While 'he was represented by the authorities as a prisoner of state deeply involved in political crime,' rather than an informer, 'the secret was soon discovered which the wary governor was so anxious to conceal' (44, 45). In a scene now clichéd, one of the prisoners disguises himself as 'the consoling minister of religion' and manages to gain access to Kerr's cell: 'The moment proved favourable – the mind of the unfortunate man, lowered by the painful restrictions of his confinement, and perhaps touched with remorse, was in a condition to receive the impression of pious admonition and advice – neither was spared. Happily the feelings of virtue were not yet extinct in his soul' (45). In Teeling's account, it is strongly implied that the disguise is maintained to increase the pressure on the informer as well as deceive the guards. The informer is a changed man, does not give the requisite evidence at trial, and the four accused are acquitted.

Later, in a more general reference to court proceedings, Teeling writes of state informers, 'Their informations were considered secret as the inquisitorial tribunal, and yet these informations were often communicated to confidential individuals; which enabled the committee entrusted with the prisoner's defence to defeat the informer's treachery, and rescue the intended victim from the snare of death' (71). This information network operates not through the sensibility of repentant informers, like Kerr, but the sensibility of the population at large, including many who worked in government offices:

> Such was the sympathy of the public, such the intensity of interest which the cause of union excited, that neither in the civil nor military departments did that cause want a confiding and communicating friend, when confidence or communication could present any prospect of safety or jus-

tice to the accused in his defence ... and all the influence and ingenuity of the government could not guard against it. (71–2)

As in the prison, the people's drive to communicate with each other for their common interest supersedes, and undermines, government attempts to 'guard against it.' In both instances, the prisoners use sympathy to communicate on materially effective terms, winning cases that would otherwise be lost, while the governor of the prison and other government authorities use walls, guards, informers, and other repressive mechanisms to little or no effect. Or rather, there is only one effect: they so arouse the nation's moral outrage that the people rise up against the repressive regime. By proceeding from Fitzwilliam's removal to political arrests and then the prison itself, and then turning to the actual Uprising, Teeling reinforces his claim that the escalation of government repression was the proximate cause of the Uprising.

But representing the people's suffering on these sentimental terms does more than seek to elicit a sympathetic response from the reader. Through the interest of eighteenth-century moral theory in justice, it solicits a reevaluation of the criminalization of nationalist discourse and activity. Alicia Lefanu recognizes the traumatic silences created by the Uprising and sets the terms on which the wounds can be healed without legitimizing rebellion. Her pro-government hero suggests, 'Will you not allow ... the merit of good intentions to those unhappy men who suffered death or exile in consequence of their share in the rebellion of 1798 ... ? Might they not have been guided by a sincere, though mistaken zeal for the redress of injuries?'[43] This sets the stage for the eventual pardon of a repentant United-man, and it is sentiment – the sympathetic recognition of 'good intentions,' 'sincer[ity],' and 'injuries' – that allows it. Teeling and other United-man authors, however, go further.

In his 'Speech' during the trial of Archibald Hamilton Rowan, the important United-man lawyer, John Philpot Curran, declares,

> [the victim's] sufferings must ever remain before our eyes, a continual call upon your shame and your remorse. But those sufferings will do more; they will not rest satisfied with your unavailing contrition – they will challenge the great and paramount inquest of society – the man will be weighed against the charge, the witness, and the sentence – and impartial justice will demand, why has an Irish jury done this deed? The moment he ceases to be regarded as a criminal, he becomes of necessity an accuser.[44]

This passage follows directly from Hume's theory, particularly as outlined in his section on justice in *An Inquiry Concerning the Principles of Morals*. In that section, Hume argues that crime 'renders' a person 'obnoxious to the public,' and that justice is a virtue involved in the 'determin[ation of] what degree of esteem or moral approbation may result from reflections on public interest and utility.'[45] Curran is appealing to the jury, and Teeling to his reader, to cease to regard the United Irishmen as criminals – and thus, 'of necessity,' to regard them as the colonial regime's accusers. And the catalyst which will effect this change in moral evaluation, for Curran and Teeling, is a sympathetic response not only to the suffering of the prisoners, but also to the suffering which led them to act in ways that the corrupt and insensible state termed criminal.

The prison thus becomes not only a synecdoche for the state's repressive mechanisms and the location for the emergence of a transcendental polity, but also the means by which the true characters of officials and prisoners are made manifest: Teeling writes, 'There is no situation in life where the true character of a man is sooner developed than within the walls of a prison' (43). Teeling imagines a prison in which carceral authority displays its power only to reveal its moral emptiness, and the ties between the people (imprisoned and otherwise) are intensified by, and so facilitate the circumvention of, carceral controls. In Jeremy Bentham's model of the panopticon, surveillance is configured along tacitly moral lines: to be watched is to be in need of watching, and to watch is to have the authority to judge. But, in Teeling's *Narratives*, the panopticonic circuit is reversed: moral authority lies with the prisoners and so they are both capable of judging their captors and incapable of erring in their own behaviour. Moreover, through national sympathy within the *Narratives* and the readerly sympathy to be aroused by their publication, this inverted model of surveillance is extended to the people as a whole during what Lady Morgan terms the 'dawning reign of public opinion.'[46] Teeling's dramatized and often overwrought account of political imprisonments during the Uprising makes visible the state's errors, and the people's virtues, on sentimental terms in order to decriminalize the insurgents and lay instead charges at the government's door in the new court of public opinion.

NOTES

1 On 'The Myth of the Bastille' in French culture, see Victor Brombert, *The Romantic Prison: The French Tradition* (Princeton: Princeton University Press,

'National Feeling' and the Colonial Prison 193

   1978), 30–45. All quotations from Teeling's accounts of the Uprising, unless otherwise noted, are taken from Charles Hamilton Teeling, '*History of the Irish Rebellion of 1798*' *and 'Sequel to the History of the Irish Rebellion of 1798,'* intro. Richard Grenfell Morton (Shannon: Irish University Press, 1972), and are cited parenthetically. The first editions, however, were extensively consulted: *Personal Narrative of the Irish Rebellion of 1798* (London: Henry Colburn, 1828); *Sequel to Personal Narrative of the Irish Rebellion of 1798* (Belfast: John Hodgson, 1832).
2 Iain McCalman, 'Newgate in Revolution: Radical Enthusiasm and Romantic Counterculture,' *Eighteenth-Century Life* 22 (1998): 95–110.
3 Kevin Gilmartin, 'Radical Print Culture in Periodical Form,' in *Romanticism, History, and the Possibilities of Genre: Re-Forming Literature, 1789–1837*, ed. Tilottama Rajan and Julia M. Wright (Cambridge: Cambridge University Press, 1998), 55.
4 Greg Kucich, '"The Wit in the Dungeon": Leigh Hunt and the Insolent Politics of Cockney Coteries,' *European Romantic Review* 10 (1999): 245.
5 Mary Helen Thuente terms the first memoir 'a romanticized account' in her important study, *The Harp Re-Strung: The United Irishmen and the Rise of Irish Literary Nationalism* (Syracuse: Syracuse University Press, 1994), 194. Historians have also noted a bias in Teeling's elisions; see, for instance, Louis M. Cullen, 'The Internal Politics of the United Irishmen,' in *The United Irishmen: Republicanism, Radicalism and Rebellion*, ed. David Dickson, Dáire Keough, and Kevin Whelan (Dublin: Lilliput Press, 1993), 194 (hereafter *United Irishmen*). This understanding of the memoirs as history was reinforced, if not invited, by a Victorian-era change in their titles. Originally entitled *Personal Narrative of the Irish Rebellion of 1798*, the work was retitled by the Victorian publisher on the title page as *History of the Irish Rebellion of 1798* while retaining the first title for the running heads. The *Sequel* was similarly retitled.
6 Rowan's memoir was completed around 1826 and published in 1840 after being edited by William Hamilton Drummond. The advertisement in the first edition of the *Personal Narrative* offers 'popular works just published by Henry Colburn' and mentions *Memoirs of Theobald Wolfe Tone, Sir Jonah Barrington's Personal Sketches of His Own Times, Sir Jonah Barrington's Historic Anecdotes of Ireland, during His Own Time, with Secret Memoirs of the Union, The Correspondence and Diaries of Henry Hyde, Earl of Clarendon, and Lawrence Hyde, Earl of Rochester* ('comprising minute particulars of the events attending the Revolution'), Lady Morgan's novel about the uprising, *The O'Briens and the O'Flahertys*, and *The Nowlans*, one of the novels by the O'Hara Family (the pseudonym of the Banim brothers). Colburn was also the publisher of other works by Morgan, as well as the relatively liberal *New Monthly Magazine*.

7 Elizabeth Fry's calls for reform were well known a decade before Teeling's first *Narrative* was published; she published the important *Observations on the Visiting, Superintendence, and Government, of Female Prisoners* in 1827.
8 There were, of course, restrictions of gender and class as well as religion in force in the early nineteenth century. Emancipation only directly affected men of a certain class.
9 This is the rhetoric of the United Irishmen leadership but it was not always realized in practice. Sectarianism, and its particularly violent history in the seventeenth and eighteenth centuries, were powerful forces in late eighteenth-century Ireland, and so inevitably influenced members of the United Irishmen and organizations with which it cooperated.
10 Some trial proceedings were held in secret, and paid informers were regularly used, sometimes as the sole source of evidence against the accused. In 1798, Rev. James Porter was hanged in front of his parishioners after being convicted solely on the evidence of a paid informer. United-man lawyer John Philpot Curran argued against the use of such informers as early as 1794, in the trial of United-man physician Dr William Drennan, but that did nothing to moderate their use (I discuss this matter at greater length in my essay 'Courting Public Opinion: Handling Informers in the 1790s,' *Éire-Ireland* 33 [1997–8]: 144–69). There is a large body of historical work on the Irish uprising. Among the more useful studies are Nancy J. Curtin, *The United Irishmen: Popular Politics in Ulster and Dublin, 1791–1798* (Oxford: Clarendon Press, 1994); Marianne Elliott, 'Defenders in Ulster,' in *United Irishmen*; Marianne Elliott, *Partners in Revolution: The United Irishmen and France* (New Haven: Yale University Press, 1982); Marianne Elliott, *Wolfe Tone: Prophet of Irish Independence* (New Haven: Yale University Press, 1989); R.F. Foster, *Modern Ireland, 1600–1972* (Markham, Ont.: Penguin, 1989); and such collections of essays as *United Irishmen* and Jim Smyth, ed., *Revolution, Counter-Revolution, and Union: Ireland in the 1790s* (Cambridge: Cambridge University Press, 2001).
11 Kevin Whelan, 'The United Irishmen,' in *United Irishmen*, 285.
12 Elliott, *Partners in Revolution*, 107.
13 His participation in the suppression of the 1798 uprising and his involvement in the 1819 'Peterloo Massacre' made Castlereagh infamous.
14 Elliott, *Partners in Revolution*, 220.
15 Here Teeling is closer to contemporary historians' views. Elliott writes that 'His role in the Convention of December 1792 and in subsequent months was pivotal. ... [Luke] Teeling was widely recognised as one of the leaders of Catholic society in the North' ('Defenders in Ulster,' 228).

16 Ernest Gellner usefully focuses the Industrial rather than the French Revolution, stressing socioeconomic rather than geopolitical factors – an emphasis taken up by E.J. Hobsbawm and others. See Ernest Gellner, *Nations and Nationalism* (Ithaca: Cornell University Press, 1983); and E.J. Hobsbawm, *Nations and Nationalism since 1780: Programme, Myth, Reality* (Cambridge: Cambridge University Press, 1990).
17 See, e.g., Anthony D. Smith, 'Neo-Classicist and Romantic Elements in the Emergence of Nationalist Conceptions,' in *Nationalist Movements*, ed. Anthony D. Smith (London: Macmillan, 1976), 74–5, 81. Homi K. Bhabha complicates this concept of nationalism by pointing out the ruptures within nationalist discourse, but still suggests that it is the goal of the nationalist enterprise to produce such a '"totalization" of national culture.' Introduction to *Nation and Narration*, ed. Homi K. Bhabha (New York: Routledge, 1990), 3. Benedict Anderson's definition is much broader: 'it is an imagined political community – and imagined as both inherently limited and sovereign.' *Imagined Communities: Reflections on the Origin and Spread of Nationalism*, rev. ed. (London and New York: Verso, 1991), 6.
18 See works from David Hume's 'Of National Characters' (1742), in *Essays: Moral, Political, and Literary*, ed. Eugene F. Miller (Indianapolis: Liberty Classics, 1985), 197–215, to 'Of a National Character in Literature,' *Blackwood's Edinburgh Magazine* 3 (September 1818): 707–9.
19 See Seamus Deane, 'The Production of Cultural Space in Irish Writing,' *boundary 2* 21.3 (1994): 117–44.
20 The Declaration is reprinted in Teeling's first *Narrative*, 141.
21 *A Full Report of the Trial at Bar in the Court of King's Bench, of William Drennan, MD Upon an Indictment Charging Him with Having Written and Published a Seditious Libel with the Speeches of Counsel, and the Opinions of the Court at Large* (Dublin: Rea and Johnson, 1794), rpt. in *The Trial of William Drennan*, ed. John Francis Larkin (Dublin: Irish Academic Press, 1991), 41.
22 Charles Hamilton Teeling, *Observations on the History and Consequences of the 'Battle of the Diamond'* (Belfast: John Hodgson, 1838), 6.
23 David Hume, *An Inquiry Concerning the Principles of Morals* (1751), ed. Charles W. Hendel (New York: Bobbs-Merrill, 1957), 107.
24 Adam Smith, *The Theory of Moral Sentiments* (1759; London: Bohn, 1853; rpt. New York: Kelley, 1966), 3.
25 Ibid., 4.
26 Henry Home (Lord Kames), *Sketches of the History of Man*, 4 vols. (1774; Hildesheim: Georg Olms Verlagsbuchhandlung, 1968), 2:246, 314–15.
27 Ibid., 2:317–18.

28 William Drennan, 'Protest against an Union with Great Britain,' *Fugitive Pieces in Verse and Prose* (Belfast: F.D. Finlay, 1815), 212.
29 Anonymous, *The Matron of Erin: A National Tale* (London: Simpkin and Marshall, 1816), 1:21.
30 Sydney Owenson, *Woman; Or, Ida of Athens*, 4 vols. (London: Longman, Hurst, Rees, and Orme, 1809), 2:14–15.
31 Katie Trumpener notes Teeling's emphasis on emotion to argue that 'A new nationalism may be called into being in several parts of Britain, but only where a firm sense of national identification, pride and anger, has long preceded it.' *Bardic Nationalism: The Romantic Novel and the British Empire* (Princeton: Princeton University Press, 1997), 25. It is important, however, that the 'pride and anger' is validated in much United Irishmen discourse as moral outrage through the lexicon of sensibility and the moral theory with which it was connected. United-man William Drennan, for instance, suggests that national feeling focuses colonial frustration into active defiance for the sake of a nobler purpose, and so elevates the national subject: 'ferocious, mad, and calling hope from desperation, changing torpid misery into active disaffection, and rising by one bound of instinct, rather than reason, from a state of abandonment and contempt, into resistance, into vindictive insurrection, into dangerous deliverance, from its *very* danger agitating the strong, but inert mind, fit only for robust vices, and now roused into a sense of enjoyment, a feeling of pleasurable elevation, by having it placed in his power to die IN BATTLE.' *A Letter to the Right Honourable William Pitt* (Dublin: James Moore, 1799), 26.
32 John Thelwall, 'Stanzas on Hearing for Certainty that We Were to be Tried for High Treason,' in *Romanticism: An Anthology*, ed. Duncan Wu, 2nd ed. (Oxford: Blackwell, 1998), ll. 1–8.
33 Victor Brombert, 'The Happy Prison: A Recurring Romantic Metaphor,' *Romanticism: Vistas, Instances, Continuities*, ed. David Thorburn and Geoffrey Hartman (Ithaca: Cornell University Press, 1973), 68–9; see also Ioan Davies, *Writers in Prison* (Oxford: Basil Blackwell; Toronto: Between the Lines, 1990), 22–4. On the ways in which this is complicated for female prisoners in the era, see Judith Scheffler, 'Romantic Women Writing on Imprisonment and Prison Reform,' *Wordsworth Circle* 19 (1988): 99–103.
34 This remainder, however, is somewhat different from the 'inner life' discussed by Christopher Castiglia because it ties the subject's defiance not to a psychic interiority but to set of external relations organized around dissent. See Christopher Castiglia and Julia Stern, introduction to *Interiority in Early American Literature*, ed. Christopher Castiglia and Julia Stern, a special issue of *Early American Literature* 37 (2002): 1–7. One of the ironies, of course, is

that the incarceration of those involved in radical and nationalist groups deemed criminal by the state meant that members could regroup within the prison and, moreover, communicate with unincarcerated sympathizers through visitors: thus, 'Mid-1790s Newgate became an epicenter of British Jacobin cultural resistance' with such notable visitors as William Godwin (McCalman, 'Newgate in Revolution,' 98).

35 Percy Bysshe Shelley, *Prometheus Unbound*, in *Shelley's Poetry and Prose*, ed. Donald H. Reiman and Sharon B. Powers (New York: Norton, 1977), 1.20, 1.429–31.

36 Discussing the *Sequel*, Elliott suggests that 'Teeling still felt obliged to explain in detail their reasons for seeking foreign assistance, outlining the repressive legislation of the period and showing how the offer of French help came just at the moment when the worst effects were being felt' (*Partners in Revolution*, 33).

37 Janet Todd, *Sensibility: An Introduction* (New York: Methuen, 1986), 5.

38 Adam Smith, *Theory of Moral Sentiments*, 3.

39 In *The Rights of Man*, Thomas Paine argues that the symbols of power are arbitrary and, by implication, deceptive (Paine depends heavily on the notion of an originary, natural state which precedes and is superior to contemporary political organization). For example, the figure of 'the sword assum[ing] the name of sceptre' emblematizes the rise to power and subsequent legitimization of 'a race of conquerors,' *Rights of Man* (1791–2), ed. Henry Collins (Markham, Ont.: Penguin, 1983), 92. Later, Paine asks, 'after all, what is this metaphor called a crown, or rather what is monarchy? Is it a thing, or is it a name, or is it a fraud? ... Doth the virtue consist in the metaphor, or in the man? Doth the goldsmith that makes the crown, make the virtue also? Doth it operate like Fortunatus's wishing-cap, or Harlequin's wooden sword? Doth it make a man a conjuror?' (146).

40 See Ernest Renan, 'What Is a Nation?' (1882), trans. Martin Thom, in *Nation and Narration*, ed. Homi K. Bhabha (New York: Routledge, 1991), 19.

41 See John Jones, *An Impartial Narrative of the Most Important Engagements Which Took Place Between His Majesty's Forces and the Rebels, During the Irish Rebellion, 1798* (Dublin, 1799); a second, significantly revised, edition was published in 1834.

42 This is consistent with Davies' description of prison writing as a genre: 'Books were written in order to break through official barriers of definition and interpretation and to forge a means of communication where others had been denied' (*Writers in Prison*, 5).

43 Alicia Lefanu, *Tales of a Tourist, Containing The Outlaw and Fashionable Connexions*, 4 vols. (London: A.K. Newman and Co., 1823), 1:117.

44 John Philpot Curran, 'Speech of John Philpot Curran, Esq. in Behalf of Archibald Hamilton Rowan, Esq. for a Libel, in the Court of King's-Bench Ireland' (29 January 1794), in *Speeches of the Right Honorable John Philpot Curran, Master of the Rolls in Ireland, on the Late Very Interesting State Trials*, 3rd ed. (Dublin: J. Stockdale, 1811), 197.
45 Hume, *Inquiry Concerning the Principles of Morals*, 18, 34.
46 Morgan uses this phrase in the preface to her novel about the 1798 Uprising, published the year before Teeling's first *Personal Narrative*; see Sydney Morgan, *The O'Briens and the O'Flahertys* (1827; London: Pandora Press, 1988), xv.

Captivating Otherness

CHAPTER 7

A Nation in Chains: Barbary Captives and American Identity

Jennifer Costello Brezina

In the late eighteenth and early nineteenth centuries, there were many American texts that were produced out of what Mary Louise Pratt would term 'contact zones, social spaces where disparate cultures meet, clash and grapple with each other.'[1] Most frequently, when scholars refer to these 'contact zones' of the early literature of the United States, they are referring to North American contacts and conflicts, not those with Africa and Asia. Even in his highly influential work *Orientalism*, which details the ways in which the West has described and dominated what it termed the 'Orient,' Edward Said focuses his attention primarily on the French and British in the seventeenth through nineteenth centuries, arguing that the Americans 'will not feel quite the same about the Orient.'[2] This statement, while somewhat flippant, is also very true, although not necessarily for the reasons that Said suggests. The wars against the Barbary pirates and the events surrounding them were highly significant to United States military and cultural history and deserve closer attention. Leaving a lasting impression on the American psyche, this conflict served as the United States Navy's first international effort after the Revolution, and also sparked the United States' first hint of internal strife with the Whiskey Rebellion of 1794. The Barbary conflict was an important event of the United States' early history and produced a series of texts that attempt to narrate a national identity for the men and women who were learning what it was to be 'American.'

But rather than being voices of domination and colonization, these narratives channel the anxiety and doubt that the United States faced at its genesis. Of particular importance are the issues of slavery and freedom, of nationalism and difference as the United States struggled to position itself as an independent nation within the international community, shaking off its former role as a British colony. Yet, at the same time, these texts display many of the characteristics that Said calls 'Orientalist' when they appear in French and British works. Internally complex and still resonant today, the Barbary Captivity narratives show the United States grappling with its identity, both on the global stage and the domestic one. This situation leads to highly interesting texts, inflected with nationalism and fear, Orientalism and outrage.

The Barbary Conflict

The so-called Barbary States were located in northern Africa and included the nations of Morocco, Algeria, Tunis, and Tripoli. Pirates from these countries had been capturing European ships and sailors for centuries, and many European countries worked out treaties with the Barbary powers that usually included large amounts of money paid in ransom and tribute to these nations in exchange for safe passage for European ships. When the United States was negotiating its independence from England, the Americans wanted to continue to be protected from the Barbary pirates under English treaties, but the English did not agree and a compromise was struck. The treaty stated, 'The King "will employ his good offices and interposition with [the Barbary States] for the benefit, conveniency, and safety of the said United States ... against all violence, insult, attacks, or depredations."'[3] This vague provision was not effective, and within a few years the pirates of North Africa had captured thirteen United States ships and taken over 150 United States citizens as slaves. The United States was outraged and began to debate whether it would be better to pay the ransoms demanded by the pirates or use force to rescue the enslaved citizens. While both methods were ultimately used, neither one was entirely satisfactory to the United States public.

One of the first priorities for the new American nation was to secure treaties with the Barbary States, since English protection had to all intents and purposes been withdrawn. The Continental Navy had been dissolved after the Revolutionary War was over and there was a huge war debt outstanding, so following the European course and paying tribute initially seemed to be the best solution. However, this proved to be a problem very early on. The tributes were expensive, and the dollar amounts kept growing greater and greater. When Algerian pirates captured a United States ship in 1785, Jefferson authorized a ransom of

$200 a man, or $4200, but the Algerians demanded $59,496.[4] Jefferson considered war, but many Americans were still convinced that giving in to the demands would be cheaper. By the time an agreement was reached in 1794, the cost of the treaty had risen to almost $1 million when the entire United States budget for 1796 was only $5.7 million.[5] Because of the money needed to pay for the treaty with Morocco, Congress enacted the 1791 Whiskey Tax, which eventually led to the Whiskey Rebellion, one of the most significant internal conflicts of the nation's history. Tripoli, unhappy with the terms of its treaty after seeing what was paid to Algeria and Morocco, began to agitate for increased tribute. In 1803, in order to demonstrate its power over America, Tripoli paraded American slaves in chains down the main street of the capital. Finally, a national navy was commissioned and war was declared against Tripoli, but the United States still did not have the upper hand. An American ship, the *Philadelphia*, was captured and eventually had to be destroyed because the United States was not able to successfully retake it. The war ended in a draw with the United States paying $66,000 in exchange for the freedom of the American captives and a promise of no further demands or hostilities. Although the war was over and there was a measure of success, the United States was in no way able to 'dominate, restructure, [or] have authority over the Orient' politically or militarily.[6] Instead, the United States' attention turned to the imaginative arena.

As the slaves were ransomed or escaped, they began to write captivity narratives, recounting their experiences in the Orient. As these grew popular, several authors composed fictional accounts of Arab captivity or used the condition of Arab slavery as a backdrop for their tales. These writings share the same qualities of European Orientalism described by Said in spite of the fact that in this situation the power was clearly in the hands of the Eastern captors rather than the Americans. But while it is true that the United States had no imperial power over the Orient during this period, it is important to mention the imperialistic tendencies the United States was already displaying with regard to North America. When the first settlers arrived on the continent it was already inhabited by a large indigenous population. This, however, did not dissuade the colonists from claiming the land for themselves and the king of England. They used force to remove the Indians, pushing them farther and farther west. In time, they would claim the entire North American continent for themselves and create the philosophy of Manifest Destiny to justify and encourage it. Another significant fact to note is that the practice and philosophy of slavery was written into the United States Constitution, showing the ease with which the American mind accepted the idea that African people were less than human. This domestic imperialism that the United States displayed from the very beginning of its history must be considered as part of the context for American Orientalism.

The literature and letters of this period readily acknowledge a lack of power over the Orient. One measure of the effect this conflict had on the American mind is the very proliferation of captivity narratives and other texts about slavery in northern Africa. For there to have been so many of them, it was necessary for there to have been a market in the reading public that was both familiar with and concerned about this situation. The possibility of being captured preyed on the minds of travellers so much that even Thomas Jefferson refused to allow his daughter to travel across the Atlantic on an American ship. In a 1785 letter of instruction to a friend he wrote:

> I do not think that the insurance on our vessels coming to France will be worth one-half per cent, but who can estimate the value of half a per cent on the fate of a child? My mind revolts at the possibility of a capture, so that unless you hear from myself – not trusting the information of any other person on earth – that peace is made with the Algerians, do not send her but in a vessel of French or English property; and these vessels alone are safe from prize from the barbarians.[7]

The difference in protection between United States and English citizenship was an oft-acknowledged fact. James Riley reports in his 1817 narrative that he falsely told his captors that he was an English citizen because he knew the United States did not even have a consul in Morocco and he would receive better treatment if he were thought to be English. Similarly, Tyler writes in *The Algerine Captive* (1797),

> By his side was a man of lighter complexion who, by the captain's command, inquired of me, in good English, if I was an Englishman. I replied I was an American, a citizen of the United States. This was no sooner interpreted to the captain than, at a disdainful nod of his head, I was again seized, handcuffed, and thrust into a dirty hole in the forecastle where I lay twenty-four hours without straw to sleep on or anything to eat or drink.[8]

This very question of national identity is key to these texts. Newly minted Americans would have been proud of their struggle and desired recognition on the international stage. However, this recognition could also entail a significant cost, giving many motive to embrace an English identity. To further explore this problematic construction, it is necessary to take a closer look at how American Orientalism of the late eighteenth and early nineteenth centuries worked to define a shifting national identity.

The Narratives

The exact number of Barbary captivity narratives is unknown, but they range from Joshua Gee's fragmented manuscript, originally penned in 1680 but not printed until 1943, to James Riley's *An Authentic Narrative of the Loss of the American Brig Commerce ... with an Account of the Sufferings of her Surviving Crew*, published in 1817.[9] Most of the narratives follow a similar structure to the better-known Indian captivity narratives: capture, enslavement, and then redemption. Riley's narrative is one of the longest and most detailed, going through twenty-four printings, a sequel, and even a children's book. For the purpose of this section, I will largely limit my discussion of the dynamics of American Orientalism to Riley's narrative, but it is important to note that the other texts also contain similar tendencies. Riley's narrative is especially interesting because pirates did not capture Riley; instead, he and his crew were shipwrecked and then enslaved by Arabs who happened upon them. While this difference seemingly would take the nationalist fervour out of his tale, it instead serves to highlight the struggle of the individual. While Riley is not singled out for his American nationality, he must grapple with his choice as an individual to submit or resist, to claim American citizenship or to remain European in identity. This struggle mirrors the choice faced by every new American at the dawn of the nineteenth century.

Consistent with Said's definition of Orientalism, these Arab captivity narratives often had encyclopedia-like sections, adding to the United States' knowledge base about the Orient. Riley's narrative devotes the last one hundred pages of the book to an academic catalogue of the land, the character of the Arabs, and other 'exotic' items (such as the camel). Riley also strives for the 'authentic,' using Arab words and phrases whenever possible. He claims to have learned to speak Arabic so easily because it was similar to Spanish, which he already knew. An appendix follows the narrative with a chart of Arab characters and words. Riley in this way was contributing to a body of knowledge about the Orient, making it 'knowable' and less threatening at the same time as it emphasized the 'foreign' qualities that set North Africa apart from the United States. Interestingly, though, Riley's observations were often not factually correct, a point belaboured by the reviewer for the British periodical the *Quarterly Review*:

> The addition which Mr. Riley has afforded to our information, respecting the geography and natural history of the Great Desert of Africa, amounts to very little, and that little, not very accurate. We ought not to be surprised, as Riley observes, that one weighted down with weariness and despair, suffering under the most excruciating bodily pains and the most cruel privations, should sometimes mistake one route for another or have erred in the computation of distances in traveling over a vast, smooth and trackless desert: – but we can not avoid wondering that a 'seaman,' and as his American friends call him, 'a man of intelligence,' should uniformly, throughout the whole of his book, mistake the west for east, and the south for the north; or, in other words, that, in his whole journey towards Mogadore, he should carry us, in his book, towards Abyssinia. In his dates, too, he is equally careless, traveling the same day twice over, and mistaking the month, and traveling, and remaining still, on the same day and in the same page, – what is perhaps still more extraordinary, we have dates in abundance while naked and deprived of all means of keeping a journal, but not a single one from the time the travelers reach the 'habitations of men,' where materials could so easily be had to enable them to register events.[10]

But this reviewer is missing the point; for the American reading audience, accuracy was only relevant as it affected the overall perceived veracity of the experience. Indeed, the fabrications and exaggerations only add to the exotic and Orientalist appeal of the text. Riley and, by extension, the United States' reading public, needed an Other to define themselves against – the more foreign the better. At the same time, there was a need to show mastery, to be certain of one's knowledge and interpretations of the world. While Riley often erred in factual matters, it was important that he maintain a sense of control in the narrative. To admit that he did not know the direction of his travels would have been devastating, so he pretends certainty to preserve the appearance of an American in control of his surroundings.

This complex and contradictory relationship is shown again when he tries to describe the character of the Arab in his 'encyclopedia' section: 'The Arab is high-spirited, brave, avaricious, rapacious, revengeful; and, strange as it may appear, is at the same time hospitable and compassionate.'[11] But Riley also describes how his captors stripped him naked to humiliate him and then, after he was sunburned and in great pain, laughed at him and his discomfort. His association of the Arabs' dark skin with cruelty is further shown when he meets a lighter-skinned Arab: 'Hamet was of a much lighter colour than the other Arabs we were with, and I thought he was less cruel, but in this respect I found I was mistaken' (71). At first Riley tries to view Hamet through the familiar trope of skin colour, but finds that his schema breaks down; the notion of the Oriental as cruel remains fixed regardless of skin tone. But just as there were tensions when Riley attempted to display mastery of his environment, there are times when he must confront the limits of his ideas of Arab cruelty. When there was a shortage of food, the Arabs shared equally with their prisoners rather than letting them starve (as Riley expected). At this he begrudgingly remarks, 'Feelings of humanity were not totally extinguished in their bosoms' (57). Arabs in this narrative do not fit neatly into Riley's schema, neither white nor black, neither heartless nor solicitous.

Skin colour is an important marker of identity in the narrative, but, at the same time, it ultimately undermines Riley's white/black dichotomy. The white skin of Riley and his crew becomes a visual marker of their difference from their Arab captors. While once a source of superiority, it also becomes a source of pain as the desert sun burns and blisters them until they are 'nearly skinless' (63). At the same time, though, they are highly conscious of others' skin colour, most notably that of the other slaves. When the crew is first captured, Riley and the ship's African-American cook, Dick, are enslaved together, implying equality in their conditions. However, their master assigns Dick a greater share of the work to be done, creating a distinction in their status. But then Dick is permitted to sleep in a corner of the tent and is given a better diet. Riley is clearly conscious of this as he describes his own sleeping conditions scarcely a page later:

> He made myself and Hogan lie on the ground in a place he chose, where the stones were very thick and baked into the ground so tight that we could not pull them out with our fingers, and we were forced to lie on their sharp points, though at a small distance ... was a spot of sand. This I made him understand (pointing at the same time at my skinless flesh) but he signified to me that if we did not remain where he had ordered, we should get no milk. (71)

Here, again, he describes himself as 'skinless,' describing the literal manifestation of his loss of white privilege. Yet despite his own 'skinless' condition, he continues to make distinctions based on the skin colour of others. Later in the narrative, a fellow slave mocks Riley's group, 'pointing at [them] and making comparisons: then sneeringly addressing [Riley] by the name of Rais, or chief ... show[ing] the Arabs what miserable beings [they] were, who could not even bear the rays of the sun ... to shine upon [them]' (77). One of Riley's companions takes special exception to this ridicule, exclaiming, 'It was bad enough to be reduced to slavery by the savage Arabs; to be stripped and skinned alive and mangled, without being obliged to bear the scoffs and derision of a d——d Negro slave' (77). But his protest is useless. With the power of his whiteness and its associated European privilege erased, he must submit to anything his master permits. This loss mimics the loss of international clout that the United States faced once separated from Great Britain. Once part of the most powerful nation in the world, the United States for a time became one of the most vulnerable, even as it sought to become a colonial power itself.

As the narrative continues, skin colour recedes in importance; nationality and religion emerge as significant instead. Several times Riley is asked about his background. He first replies that he is English, later remarking as he tells the same to his second master, 'I found he had heard of that country' (85). Later, he writes a plea for help, calling for his letter to be delivered to 'the English, French, Spanish, or American consuls, or any Christian merchants in Mogadore or Swerah' (172). In Riley's desperation, any European is an ally. Ironically, it is an Englishman who forwards the ransom money for Riley and his crew, proclaiming, 'How truly I commiserate and enter into all your misfortunes' (183). He also gently chides Riley for masking his nationality in the letter – leaving the reader to deduce it for himself from newspaper reports of the ship docking in Gibraltar. Here, the shared colonial past is enough of a connection for the Englishman to feel 'sincere pity' (182) in spite of Riley's distrust. Once Riley sees an American flag, however, he distances himself from this pan-European position, proclaiming, 'At this blessed and transporting sight, the little blood remaining in my veins, gushed through my glowing heart with wild impetuosity, and seemed to pour a flood of new life through every part of my exhausted frame' (246). This display of sentimental feeling is in direct contrast to the resigned, almost detached, attitude Riley displays earlier in the narrative.

Throughout the majority of the narrative, Riley calls on God to save him and his companions rather than trusting to his own agency. He only writes the ransom letter at the insistence of his Arab master, who would rather ransom Riley than keep him. Faith in a Christian God becomes paramount to Riley's identity, setting him and the other slaves apart from their Muslim captors. The Arabs themselves reinforce this distinction, rationalizing, 'We ... owe these Christian dogs nothing; we have an undoubted right to make merchandise of them, and oblige them to carry our burdens like camels' (185). The association between skin, religion, and slavery is embodied by Clark, one of Riley's companions, who has a tattoo of the cross on his arm. As Riley points out, Clark's cross tattoo remains even as layer after layer of his skin burns, peels away, and is replaced; so, too, Christianity remains a crucial point of identity for the captives. But, as will be discussed later in this essay, Christianity is also paired with the new national identity and Riley's constant belief in both divine Providence and his ultimate redemption.

A National Appeal

The question still remains: How were the American authors able to maintain these patterns of thought in the face of the continued military defeats the United States faced in this time period? And why were these narratives so appealing to American readers? One easy answer is the United States' shared cultural tradition with England. Many of the colonists that formed the American colonies came from England and shared the cultural background that ultimately produced English Orientalism. Also, English books were routinely transported and often reprinted in the United States, giving the two nations a shared literary tradition as well. The problem with this explanation is that at this time the United States was trying to separate itself from England and all it represented; it was struggling to form a national identity and culture distinct from England. Also, most of the citizens of the United States were several generations removed from England, and their identity was as Americans. More importantly, early America was itself a 'contact zone,' a place where people from many nations lived. While, certainly, the British voice was a strong one, many other cultures – Spanish, Native American, French, and German, just to name a few – contributed to the United States' ideas and self-image.

While this theory of shared culture may be only partly true, a further, more interesting possibility is that the Americans were attempting to take their place on the international stage by borrowing the cultural superiority that Europe pretended to. Rather than having their literature mirror their inferior political and military position, Americans used literature to create an 'imagined community' (as Benedict Anderson puts it) of cultural power. As G.A. Starr notices more generally in a 1968 essay on seventeenth-century English captivity narratives: 'However forlorn their plight, the heroes of escape narratives cannot be brought to think of themselves as slaves; this gives them a kind of self-containment that is far from contemptible and enables them to cope with circumstances that might otherwise cripple them with despair.'[12]

Likewise, this optimism of the Barbary captivity narratives appealed to the United States' reading public as it mirrored that public's optimism about the nation's uncertain future. From the beginning, Puritan colonists imagined themselves as divinely selected to inhabit North America. They positioned themselves as the 'city upon a hill,' a model of Christian piety and community. This sense of the United States as a Christian nation persists to this day, in spite of repeated reminders that the two terms are not necessarily synonymous. But this, too, is more internally complex. The United States' position as a recent 'settler colony' of Great Britain placed the new nation in a unique position with regard to imperialism. Although the colonists were a vital part of the imperialist project of 'settling' North America, they also were victims of British imperialism in the form of taxes and military occupation. The United States often figured the relationship between itself and Great Britain as that of slave and master. In his article 'Beyond Freedom and Slavery: Autonomy, Virtue, and Resistance in Early American Political Discourse,' François Furstenberg details the ways in which American colonists used the metaphor of slavery to describe their relationship with Great Britain. The idea of slavery itself became politically and morally charged when patriots such as Thomas Paine argued, 'When republican virtue fails, slavery ensues.'[13] Furstenberg writes, 'If "freedom" was opposed to "slavery," "resistance" to "submission," so was "virtuous" to "abject," a word frequently paired with slavery'; thus, 'If people proved their virtue by maintaining their freedom, they proved their lack of virtue by submitting to slavery. ... A virtuous person would resist slavery, even at the cost of life itself. An abject person, by contrast, would submit and would "justly deserve" the slavery that ensued.'[14] Many Barbary captives agreed with this philosophy. James Cathcart, captured at sea in 1785 and enslaved for eleven years, wrote, 'I never could have endured the anxiety and degradation under which I labored for any length of time had I not placed the greatest confidence in the generosity of my country. I thought it impossible that a nation just emerged from slavery herself would abandon the men who had fought for her independence to an ignominious captivity in Barbary, when they could be immediately redeemed for less than $50,000.'[15]

But Riley, enslaved thirty years later, complicates this national metaphor, working for individual survival rather than national pride. Just as he claims kinship with Europeans to further his chances of ransom, he peacefully submits to slavery when he sees it as the alternative to starvation in the desert. Riley and his crew escape from their first captors, but soon find themselves dying of thirst and starvation, baking in the desert sun. Riley then explains his decision to the readers: 'I had determined, as soon as daylight appeared, to show ourselves to the natives, and submit either to death or life from their hands. I had no doubt of their being Arabs who would take and hold us as slaves ... and that it was a degree of Providence which had set this alternative before us' (51–2). Not only does Riley choose slavery over death, he also thanks God for giving him that opportunity. This statement is in stark contrast to Patrick Henry's famous exhortation, 'Give me liberty, or give me death.' Once enslaved, Riley did not struggle or try to escape. He claims he did 'the utmost to obey and please those whom fortune, fate, or an overruling Providence had placed over me, and to persuade, both by precept and practice, my unhappy comrades to do the same' (61–2). Rather than leading his crew to revolt, he urges them to quietly submit to slavery. This seems to fly in the face of the ideals of the Revolution, but is not surprising given Riley's desire to remain in control of his narrative and his life. By submitting to slavery, he is actively choosing his fate instead of having it decided for him. While he submits to the authority of his Christian God, he does not acknowledge fully his powerless state with regard to the Arabs. He maintains the fiction that he voluntarily chose slavery in order to prevent having to admit total defeat.

As would be expected, the slave experience is a significant motif running throughout the Barbary captivity narratives. The very proliferation of captivity narratives with this emphasis enabled many American authors to write fictitious accounts, using white slavery in northern Africa as a foil for African slavery in the United States. Susana Rowson, author of *Charlotte Temple* and one of the country's early best-selling authors, made this very connection in her 1794 drama *Slaves in Algiers*.[16] She uses the setting of this play as a platform to speak effectively against slavery in the United States. Here, escape from slavery is seen as desirable and even admirable, in stark contrast to the attitude towards escaping African slaves in the United States. Over and over, the injustices done to white American slaves in Barbary are both implicitly and explicitly compared to the situation of African slaves in the United States. Similarly, David Everett's *Slaves in Barbary* (1817) takes an abolitionist tone while telling a story about slavery in Algeria. This play also demonstrates the hypocrisy of many Americans; the Algerian officers laugh while recalling what the American slave said while talking in his sleep: 'He ordered six dozen of port, gave Liberty and Independence for a toast, sung an Ode to Freedom ... gave orders ... to have fifty of his slaves whipped thirty stripes each for singing a liberty song in echo to his own; and six more to be hung up by the heels for petitioning him for a draught of milk and water.'[17]

The same American reading public that provided an outraged market for tales of Barbary captivity also supported the enslavement and brutalization of Africans in the United States. As Paul Baepler aptly notes, there are significant differences between the chattel slavery of Africans in the United States and the enslavement of Americans in North Africa: 'Barbary slaves were not born into captivity or stolen from their homeland; they ventured into danger as travelers engaged in mercantile or military enterprises. Similarly, many white captives, like Joshua Gee, were eventually ransomed and liberated from their slavery. They could return to the intact family and social structures into which they were born.'[18] Nevertheless, the Barbary tales speak to the growing American identity crisis over the domestic slavery debate. How could a nation that prided itself on the freedom it provided its citizens rely on slave labour for much of its economy? How can the ideals of the Constitution be reconciled with the lives of African slaves in the South? But rather than state their cases directly, both authors use the perceived injustice of white American slavery in the Middle East to bolster their abolitionist intent. In this way, they capture the imagination of American readers through a story that seems to reinforce 'American' ideals while implicitly questioning them all the while.

The parallels between Americans enslaved in North Africa and Africans enslaved in the United States become devastatingly clear with Ben Franklin's tongue-in-cheek 1790 letter to the editor of the *Federal Gazette*. Styling himself as 'Historicus,' Franklin places the contemporary debate in Congress on the possibility of ending slavery in the United States in direct contrast to the outrage over American enslavement in the Barbary States. Quoting a (fictitious) letter from Sidi Mehemet Ibrahim, a member of the Divan of Algiers, he writes,

> If we cease our Cruises against the Christians, how shall we be furnished with the Commodities their Countries produce, and which are so necessary for us? If we forbear to make Slaves of their People, who in this hot Climate are to cultivate our Lands? Who are to perform the common Labours of our City, and in our Families? Must we not then be our own Slaves? ... But who is to indemnify their Masters for the Loss? Will the State do it? Is our Treasury sufficient? Will the *Erika* do it? Can they do it? Or would they, to do what they think Justice to the Slaves, do a greater Injustice to the Owners? And if we set our Slaves free, what is to be done with them? Few of them will return to their Countries; they know too well the great Hardships they must there be subject to; they will not embrace our holy Religion; they will not adopt our Manners; our People will not pollute themselves by intermarrying with them. Must we maintain them as Beggars in our Streets, or suffer our Properties to be the Prey of their Pillage? For men long accustom'd to Slavery will not work for a Livelihood when not compell'd. And what is there so pitiable in their present Condition? Were they not Slaves in their own Countries? ... While serving us, we take care to provide them with every thing, and they are treated with Humanity. The Labourers in their own Country are, as I am well informed, worse fed, lodged, and cloathed. The Condition of most of them is therefore already mended, and requires no further Improvement. Here their Lives are in Safety.[19]

While it was simple to spot these arguments as specious when mouthed by African captors, many Americans were deaf to them when voiced by members of their own Congress, ultimately leading to the United States' Civil War. In fact, Abraham Lincoln cited James Riley's narrative as one of the deciding forces in the formation of his views on slavery, once again invoking the image of white slavery in order to end black slavery.[20]

But these narratives also served another function, that of providing hope for the nation; these texts were created by those who had escaped, giving rise to the possibility of future international power. Pratt makes a similar point regarding European literature:

> Throughout the history of early Eurocolonialism and the slave trade, survival literature furnished a 'safe' context for staging alternate, relativizing, and taboo configurations of intercultural contact: Europeans enslaved by non-Europeans, Europeans assimilating to non-European societies, and Europeans confounding new transracial social orders. The context of survival literature was 'safe' for transgressive plots, since the very existence of a text presupposed the imperially correct outcome: the survivor survived,

and sought reintegration into the home society. The tale was always told from the viewpoint of the European who returned.[21]

Likewise, these American tales of surviving Arab captivity reassured the reading public and reasserted the power of the United States. As Joe Snader notes in his article 'The Oriental Captivity Narrative and Early English Fiction,'

> The epistemological framework of Orientalism provides one of several means by which these narratives assert the captives' potential mastery over the captive-taking cultures. In so far as a captivity narrative records a Briton's subjugation at the hands of a supposedly inferior culture, it creates a sense of cultural imbalance, a violation of the imagined national hierarchy that placed Western culture over Eastern cultures. In the very fact of its publication, a captivity narrative marks the restoration of this imbalance by implying both the happy ending of the captive's release and the possibility of knowing and recording the captive-taking culture.[22]

Through writing, Americans could assert power and control in a world where they were largely powerless. Further, the reading of these narratives provided a vicarious sense of strength and identity to citizens who were struggling with the notion of what it meant to be an American. American captives in these narratives clung strongly to their identities, refusing conversion to Islam, which would have signified a shift in national allegiance as well. Further, the very acknowledgment, by both captors and captives, of 'American-ness' as something separate from simple whiteness helped to solidify a national identity for the United States' reading public. Finally, the portrayal of 'American-ness' as an active choice reifies the position taken during the American Revolution that Americans are made, not necessarily born.

According to Ernest Renan's essay 'What Is a Nation?' there are two vital strategies involved in nation building. The first is the establishment of a shared tradition. He uses the example of the conquering Germanic peoples who converted to Christianity and began speaking the language of the Greeks and Romans in order to more firmly establish a bond that would result in nationhood. He further writes, 'More valuable by far than common customs posts and frontiers conforming to strategic ideas is the fact of sharing, in the past, a glorious heritage and regrets, and of having, in the future, [a shared] programme to put into effect, or the fact of having suffered, enjoyed and hoped together. ... [A]nd, indeed, suffering in common unifies more than joy does. Where national memories are concerned, griefs are of more value than triumphs, for they impose duties, and require a common effort.'[23] When seen from this perspective, the Arab captivity narratives serve a clear purpose in the construction of America as a nation. The United States was a country that had no shared past other than the Revolutionary War. As these narratives circulate, a shared suffering is created whereby Americans begin to cling together against a common foe. Although this was also true during the Revolution, it was more difficult because there were large numbers of Loyalists present in the population. These internal conflicts (often present within individual families) undermined the strategy of shared suffering. The North African pirates provided a less complicated 'other' for Americans to define themselves against. There had been a long history of both Barbary captivity and the associated narratives, but it was only at the turn of the nineteenth century that these narratives became so popular.[24] This timing is no coincidence. As abolitionist rhetoric increased and the integrity of nation itself became threatened, narratives such as those written by the Barbary captives carried the cultural capital needed to sustain a wide reading audience.

While the writings of the former Barbary captives share much with Indian captivity narratives, and have a similar relationship to national identity, there are also important differences; in Barbary narratives the nation-building project is at the same time both foregrounded and erased as Americans try to position themselves as apart from Britain yet still a player on the world stage. Rather than being limited to domestic conflicts, Barbary narratives highlight the role of the United States in the larger arena of international politics. In addition, Indian captivity narratives were usually penned by women, often centring on restoration to family and community. On the other hand, Barbary captives were almost exclusively male, owing to the setting of the abduction (merchant vessels sailing the Mediterranean), and, while religion may have had a highly visible role, it was a marker of nationality as much as an individual spiritual contract. While both types of narratives are preoccupied with themes of freedom and justice, cruelty and enslavement, Barbary narratives involve a more active, individual embrace of Christianity. Because the possibility of freedom through conversion to Islam is ever present, a captive's persistent Christianity means choosing to maintain his identity in slavery over receiving freedom.

Furthermore, Barbary captivity narratives had more power for early American readers precisely because they were so limited, paradoxically giving the readers perhaps more access to the captivity experience than their popular Indian counterparts. While Baepler argues that the narratives' popularity derived from the sailors' East Coast roots, leading the Eastern reading public to identify with them,[25] the opposite may be true. The physical distance between the United States and the Barbary nations – the 'foreignness' of the experience – allowed for critical distance as well. In essence, the Barbary narratives replace direct experience with textual experience, essentializing and taming the threatening encounter. By conjuring distant foes rather than focusing on domestic strife, Barbary narratives are more able to lay the imaginative groundwork of nation-building by envisioning the United States as a nation among other nations. For example, the reviewer of Riley's narrative for the *North American Review* was very concerned about the descriptions of the United States consulate in Morocco, scolding,

> We confess it was not very gratifying to our national feelings, to find our consular establishment here [Tangier] so much inferior to that of any other of the European powers, and we sincerely hope our government will not be slow in giving it a respectability, which shall put it on an equality with them. In a country like Morocco, with which our intercourse is very limited, our character as a nation will be in no small degree estimated by the dignity and importance we attach to the offices established there, as channels of communication between the two governments.[26]

By positioning the United States as an international entity, similar to yet separate from 'other of the European powers,' these narratives begin the difficult cultural work involved in the transformation of a colony into a nation.

But the other component of Renan's conception of nationhood involves forgetting the violence and difference upon which the nation was founded. Barbary narratives also serve this purpose. By identifying a new foe, these narratives allowed the new nation to forget the violence and pain involved in its founding and focus its energies on something else. Also, by uniting all Americans against Arabs, these texts allowed the internal tensions that were present during the Revolutionary War to be subsumed into a new nation. An interesting twist to this situation, though, is that after the conflict with the North African nations was settled, it, also, was largely erased. In contrast to the central place that the Native American conflicts occupy in classic American historical narratives, the Barbary Wars are rarely if ever taught as part of the 'canon' of

United States history. Likewise, Barbary captivity narratives have been mostly forgotten when early American literature is discussed and are largely marginalized. This is, perhaps, to be expected, given the aforementioned physical and experiential distance between the Middle East and the early United States. However, the trace of this experience still remains and, as technology made the world more directly 'knowable,' American Orientalism is intensified, as Said notices, in the post–Second World War era.

In its early decades, the United States had a complex and changing position with regard to the other nations with which it came in contact. While it was Western in the sense that it shared a cultural history with the countries of Europe, it also had been exploited by British imperialism and was not militarily powerful. At the same time, the United States itself colonized North America, held African slaves, and engaged in conflicts with the nations of North Africa. In the midst of all this, Americans produced texts that include the same characteristics displayed by French and English texts that are readily identified as Orientalist. While Said maintains that American Orientalism played no significant role in America before the Second World War, it is clear that when Barbary captivity narratives are viewed through its prism, the United States' nation-formation was in many ways dependent on the new nation's ability to define itself through conflicts with an Orientalized Other. Experiences of captivity and insurrection resonate with the ethos of the American Revolution, at the same time that a foreign Other allows the United States to distance itself from the experience of colonization. Often ignored, the narratives (and fiction) written surrounding the Barbary conflicts played an important role in the formation of national identity in the United States.

Postscript

With the events of September 11, 2001, the issue of American identity as seen through its relation to the Arab world has come full circle. Once again reminded that the balance of power is not always static (and not always tilted towards the United States), Americans struggle for national identity in an increasingly globalized age. A new nationalism has taken hold, as Americans define themselves against the Arab world yet again. Instead of 'pirates,' 'terrorists' have become the target of American outrage. But 'terrorist' has quickly become conflated with 'Arab,' leading to an attack on the civil liberties of many American citizens and legal residents.

And rather than having a clear, foreign target, Americans are taking a closer look at those living among them. Most threatening of all is the idea that these 'terrorists' have lived largely 'American' lives, remaining undetected, destroying the myth that the Other is visibly marked and can be easily seen. While racial profiling and discrimination serve as an attempt to redefine the notion of 'American' as something that can be racialized and 'seen,' they also resonate with the narratives of the Barbary captives and the resurgence of Orientalism. Renan's notion of nation-building through shared suffering has, likewise, tragically been proven true.

This essay is dedicated to all of those affected by the events of September 11, 2001.

NOTES

1 Mary Louise Pratt, *Imperial Eyes: Travel Writing and Transculturation* (New York: Routledge, 1992), 4.
2 Edward Said, *Orientalism* (New York: Vintage Books, 1979), 1.
3 Gardner W. Allen, *Our Navy and the Barbary Corsairs* (Hamden, CT: Archon Books, 1965), 25.
4 Michael L.S. Kitzen, *Tripoli and the United States at War: A History of American Relations with the Barbary States, 1785–1805* (Jefferson, NC: McFarland and Co., 1993), 11.
5 Ibid., 20.
6 Said, *Orientalism*, 3.
7 Qtd. in Kitzen, *Tripoli and the United States at War,* 12.
8 Royall Tyler, *The Algerine Captive* (1797; New Haven: College and University Press, 1970), 117.
9 See Paul Baepler, *White Slaves, African Masters: An Anthology of American Barbary Captivity Narratives* (Chicago: University of Chicago Press, 1999) for a bibliography.
10 Rev. of *An Authentic Narrative of the Loss of the American Brig Commerce ... with an Account of the Sufferings of her Surviving Crew,* The Quarterly Review 16 (1817): 307.
11 James Riley, *An Authentic Narrative of the Loss of the American Brig Commerce ... with an Account of the Sufferings of her Surviving Crew* (1817; reprint, New York: Clarkson N. Potter, 1965), 308; hereafter cited parenthetically in the text.

12 G.A. Starr, 'Escape from Barbary: A Seventeenth-Century Genre,' *Huntington Library Quarterly* 29 (1968): 37.
13 Qtd. in François Furstenberg, 'Beyond Freedom and Slavery: Autonomy, Virtue, and Resistance in Early American Political Discourse,' *Journal of American History* 89 (2003) http://www.historycooperative.org/journals/jah/89.4/furstenberg.html (2 September 2003): par. 15.
14 Ibid., pars. 17, 16.
15 James Cathcart, *The Captives: Eleven Years a Prisoner in Algiers*, in Baepler, *White Slaves, African Masters*, 118.
16 Susana H. Rowson, *Slaves in Algiers* (Philadelphia: Wrigley and Berriman, 1794).
17 David Everett, *Slaves in Barbary* (Boston, 1817), 111–12.
18 Paul Baepler, 'The Barbary Captivity Narrative in Early America,' *Early American Literature* 30 (1995): 108.
19 Benjamin Franklin (Historicus), 'On the Slave Trade,' *Federal Gazette* (23 March 1790).
20 R. Gerald McMurty, 'The Influence of *Riley's Narrative* upon Abraham Lincoln,' *Indiana Magazine of History* 30 (1934): 137.
21 Pratt, *Imperial Eyes*, 87.
22 Joe Snader, 'The Oriental Captivity Narrative and Early English Fiction,' *Eighteenth-Century Fiction* 9.3 (April 1997): 276.
23 Ernest Renan, 'What Is a Nation?,' trans. Martin Thom, in *Nation and Narration*, ed. Homi K. Bhabha (New York: Routledge, 1990), 19.
24 Baepler, *White Slaves, African Masters*, 24.
25 Ibid., 25.
26 Rev. of *An Authentic Narrative of the Loss of the American Brig Commerce ... with an Account of the Sufferings of her Surviving Crew*, in *North American Review* 5 (1817): 408.

CHAPTER 8

A Prison Officer and a Gentleman: The Prison Inspector as Imperialist Hero in the Writings of Major Arthur Griffiths (1838–1908)

Christine Marlin

Prisons do not generally receive a favourable treatment in the Victorian novel. Of course, prisons were never meant to be pleasant places; but the British novel of the nineteenth century presents the British prison as harsher than it has to be, and rife with abuses. A host of examples of Victorian novels advocating prison reform readily spring to mind. Charles Reade's *It Is Never Too Late to Mend* (1856) castigates the brutality of the system of solitary confinement. In *Little Dorrit* (1855–7), Charles Dickens satirizes a system of prison administration in which 'somebody came from some Office, to go through some form of overlooking something, which neither he nor anybody else knew anything about ... while this somebody pretended to do his something; and made a reality of walking out again as soon as he hadn't done it – neatly epitomising the administration of most of the public affairs in our right little, tight little, island.'[1] Henry James's *Princess Casamassima* (1886) presents a gloomy picture of Millbank Penitentiary as Miss Pynsent takes young Hyacinth to visit his dying mother there:

> They knew it, in fact, soon enough, when they saw it lift its dusky mass from the bank of the Thames, lying there and sprawling over the whole neighbourhood, with brown, bare, windowless walls, ugly, truncated pinnacles, and a character unspeakably sad and stern. It looked very sinister and wicked, to Miss Pynsent's eyes, and she wondered why a prison should have such an evil face if it was erected in the interest of justice and order – an expression of the righteous forces of society.[2]

This stark portrayal, and the later description of the unsanitary conditions within, are no doubt justified, given that the prison had been considered fit to be abolished in 1884 – though the fact that James spent just one morning in 1884 inspecting it in preparation for this scene makes him seem something of an armchair critic.[3]

Against this dominant trend, however, another literary practice emerges in the late Victorian period. Its chief practitioner is the prolific Major Arthur Griffiths (1838–1908), prison inspector and novelist. His tendency is to present the British prison system as ideal and superior to all other prison systems. Although Griffiths is, to my knowledge, the only Victorian *novelist* consistently to create a positive portrayal of British prisons, his approach fits into a larger and important phenomenon of the late Victorian period – namely, that of viewing the prison system as one aspect of the smoothly running machinery of British society that makes it better than all other societies and that therefore morally justifies the project of imperialism. This phenomenon continues what Michel Foucault has described as the movement of modern society from spectacle to surveillance in the discipline of its subjects – as the rise of an all-seeing power that exerts itself with maximum efficiency and militaristic rigour.[4] If the panopticon is a system of power relations that 'dispens[es] with the need for a prince,'[5] then, in the context of late nineteenth-century Britain, the centralized prison system supplants the imperial monarch by projecting the power of the imperial state in institutional form. This imperial function of the new British prison system, and the ways in which it is constructed and advanced by Arthur Griffiths, will be the focus of this chapter.

To understand this phenomenon, and Griffiths's contribution to it, we must look at some of the changes that were taking place with regard to prison administration in the last three decades of the nineteenth century; then examine Griffiths's role in applying these changes; and finally analyse his non-fictional and fictional works to see how they work to create a positive identification between the prison system and empire in a way that bolsters both. I aim to show that Griffiths, as a representative of the new system in his role of prison inspector, deploys a number of strategies to accomplish this ideological work. While both his non-fiction and his fiction present contemporary British prisons as superior to those of any other time and place, his fiction uses the additional strategy of enlisting the genre of romance to give poignancy and emotive power to his claims for the unparalleled excellence of the British system and its enforcers. The figure of the prison inspector appears in several of Griffiths's works as a chivalric hero who personally tends to the captives in his domain, thus demonstrating the magnanimous nature of the prison administrator and by extension of the imperialist structure of which he forms a representative part.

Underpinning the analysis below is Said's argument in *Orientalism* that writing about the East by the West is inextricably shaped and informed by the unequal power relations between the two in the modern era. Griffiths's works about prisons uphold 'the idea of European identity as a superior one in comparison with all the non-European peoples and cultures,'[6] in a way that is inseparable from his status as promoter of empire. Indeed, so energetic is his imperialist stance that he takes the further step of debasing other European powers, particularly if they are England's imperial rivals. Only those countries that have received the blessing of Britain's colonizing influence escape the full force of the invective in his works.

Historically, the end of transportation as a form of punishment in Britain in 1867 marked a turning point in the administration of British prisons.[7] To accommodate the increase in the prison population at home, there was a need for a shift from a motley collection of county jails to a more controlled, centralized system. The harbinger of a purportedly streamlined and more rational system was Sir Edmund Du Cane, a former military man known for his stern discipline.[8] He favoured a militaristic approach to prison work – that is, nationalist fervour combined with bureaucratic efficiency and practicality. Du Cane's efforts helped to bring about the creation of national inspectors of prisons with the Prisons Act of 1877, which brought local jails under the control of central government. Whereas previously individual counties were allowed to run their prisons independently of one another, the new administration set national standards and rules and made each county accountable to the Home Secretary.

According to the *Public Record Office: Current Guide*, before 1877 the courts of law were largely responsible for the administration and maintenance of prisons, with the central courts overseeing the main prisons, and the local justices supervising the county and borough jails.[9] Gradually, however, the home secretary gained greater powers of supervision. In 1835, he was granted the right to appoint officers at convict prisons and inspectors for the local jails; in 1846 he could name a surveyor general of prisons; in 1849 he could select five general inspectors of prisons; and in 1850 he could choose a board of directors of convict prisons to replace the earlier separate boards of commissioners. In 1877, the movement towards centralization reached a watershed with the passing of the Prisons Act, which brought local jails under government management with the establishment of a new Prison Commission, whose job was to 'administer and inspect prisons in England and Wales in accordance with the general or special directions of the secretary of state.'[10] By this time, the government had fully installed a 'para-military staff structure ... involving the frequent employment of ex-servicemen, and perhaps epitomized in the person of Du Cane himself, who retained his army commission long after his appointment to the prison service.'[11] Though support for these changes was not unanimous, as we shall see later, most high-level prison officers sympathized with Du Cane's ambitions and cooperated in creating a national system of prison administration in Britain. The revitalized state of Britain's prisons became a point of national pride. As Du Cane himself writes, 'The condition of prisons in former times is of interest and importance now as showing what our present laws and system have redeemed us from.'[12] The superiority of the British prison system thus became a celebrated point among imperialists.

Among the most fervent supporters of the Du Cane régime was Major Arthur Griffiths. As one who, like Du Cane, embarked first on a military career and subsequently a career in prison administration, Griffiths felt fully at home with Du Cane's military style of prison administration and, in turn, Du Cane rewarded him with increasing power and speedy advancement up the ranks. Military imperialism had in fact shaped Griffiths's identity from the beginning: he was born at Poona, India, on 9 December 1838, the son of Lieutenant-Colonel John Griffiths of the Sixth Royal Warwickshire Regiment. When Griffiths's family returned to England and settled at Douglas, Isle of Man, young Arthur was surrounded by ex-military men who fascinated him with stories of their heroic service. At King William's College, his teachers celebrated military traditions and accomplishments; his first master, a former lieutenant, hung his sabre and sash in his study, and 'descanted by the hour upon marches and skirmishes on the Llobregat and the Ebro.'[13] Griffiths himself embarked on a military career in 1855, and his army experiences would stretch from active service in the Crimea to training in Nova Scotia and administration at Gibraltar, before his partial retirement in favour of prison administration in 1870, and then full retirement from the army in 1875.

Griffiths's prison career was equally varied, encompassing positions at Gibraltar, Chatham, Millbank, and Wormwood Scrubs. His first experience of managing prisons, however, took place in a colonial setting, when in 1869, during his military post at Gibraltar, he was asked to intervene to quell a threatened rebellion at the convict prison there – foregrounding the notion of the prison as a tool for 'silencing rebellion' in the colonies.[14] Griffiths did such an efficient job at Gibraltar that he established himself as a highly skilled prison administrator from that day forward. In 1878, when he was deputy-governor of Wormwood Scrubs, he was appointed as one of the seven new inspectors of prisons created by the 1877 Prisons Act. The choice of Griffiths was due, he says, to 'the goodwill of Mr. Cross [the Home Secretary], on the kindly recommendation of my old chief, Sir Edmund du Cane.'[15] Griffiths's mandate was to assist Du Cane in ensuring that standards and practices did not vary significantly across the country. One of his first tasks was to unify the books and printed forms used in the prisons. He was also in charge of the 'codification and simplification of prison rules.'[16]

A firm believer in the centralized system, Griffiths writes that, before the centralized system, there was a 'marked difference in the methods of government in the various gaols. The discipline in one was much more severe than in another. In one county the offended was let off easily, pampered and overfed; he did little or no work, and laughed at the penalties imposed. In the neighbouring county the very reverse obtained.'[17] In addition, the financial waste in the local system was considerable, he argues, since in one county prisons might be overcrowded and in another they might be empty, but there was no organized way of redistributing the inmates. 'The need for reorganisation, concentration, and unification,' he concludes, 'was obvious.'[18] Griffiths was active in bringing about these changes in his capacity as prison inspector until he retired in 1899 to devote all his time to his first love, writing.

But Griffiths already had three decades of success in the literary realm under his belt when he took up writing full time. A highly prolific author, he concentrated much of his writing, both fictional and non-fictional, on prisons and their administration.[19] As has been mentioned, what is striking about these works is the extent to which they hail the British prison system as, while not exactly flawless, a benevolent and enlightened system, displaying the superiority of the British as administrators in general. Griffiths's non-fictional writings about the prison include numerous hefty tomes. *Records of York Castle*, coauthored with Anthony Twyford, *The Chronicles of Newgate*, *Secrets of the Prison-House*, *Memorials of Millbank*, and the Grolier Society Series of histories of prisons in various countries all attempt to give a comprehensive account of prison life, covering such aspects as diet, architecture, punishment, work within prison, sleeping arrangements, types of criminals confined, and escapes from prison.[20]

In *Chronicles of Newgate* (1884), which delves into the annals of this prison and tells of some of the famous criminals incarcerated therein, Griffiths invokes the tremendous progress that has been made in Britain in the movement towards a more humanitarian prison system. In the preface, for example, he states that the history of Newgate is the story of the transition from the days of 'pitiless ferocity' to the time when 'thanks to the incessant protests of humanitarian and philanthropist, a milder system of punishment became the rule.'[21] Griffiths traces a steady march, since the publication of John Howard's *State of Prisons* in 1777, towards a more enlightened system of law and punishment in Britain, featuring such developments as the reduction in the number of offences punishable by death, the standardization and modification of prison discipline, and the curtailment of the system of free association in which prisoners of different categories are allowed to mingle.

A decade later, Griffiths is even more bold in his assertion of the superiority of Britain's prisons, and more elaborate in his condemnation of other systems. In *Secrets of the Prison-House* (1893), a two-volume historical survey of prisons in England and around the world, he once again makes the case that while no prison system in the past has been perfect, and while Britain has made its share of embarrassing and even shameful mistakes, the current system in Britain is now, on the whole, the model for all future systems. He points to the fact that there have been no serious disturbances in British prisons since the rebellion at Chatham in 1861 as evidence of the good discipline of these prisons, arising from the balance of appropriate supervision with 'an amount of freedom that is the greatest compliment to the system' (*Secrets*, 1:146). He summarizes his views neatly when he says, 'It will, I think, be seen in the end, that however imperfect our methods may be, judged by the highest and most exacting standard, they do, generally, things worse elsewhere' (*Secrets*, 1:160). Subsequent chapters serve to illustrate this point. In volume 2, part 7 ('General Conclusions'), the first chapter is devoted to 'British Prisons of To-Day,' and it is essentially a panegyric on the glories of the British prison system in Griffiths's time. Noting that, since 1877, every prisoner 'from Land's End to the Orkney Isles' is given the same treatment, according to his category, Griffiths goes on to describe in detail what that treatment comprises. The prisoner begins in solitary confinement, in a cell 'the dimensions of which assure him a minimum air-content of 800 cubic feet, and which has been duly certified by one of her Majesty's Prison Inspectors as fit for his occupation, being lighted, heated, ventilated, and provided with bell (in some new prisons of electric) communications' (*Secrets*, 2:449). The system is thus shown to be consistent across Britain; to be organized humanely and rationally, down to the number of cubic feet of air; and to be closely monitored by the state, each cell being individually certified by Her Majesty's watchdogs.

Further, Griffiths demonstrates the activity of the convict within the prison to be similarly logically planned and controlled:

> His day's task is fixed; if he is able-bodied he must do six hours on the tread-wheel, half in the fore-noon, half in the after-noon, with five minutes' rest after fifteen minutes' spell; and executing everywhere the same total ascent of 8640 feet, at 32 feet per second. This, the most severe phase of his prison-life, continues for one month, or more exactly, until he has earned 224 marks in the first of a series of 'progressive stages,' which have been ingeniously devised to secure industry and good conduct. (*Secrets*, 2:449)

The plethora of precise numerical figures in this passage gives the impression of a supremely rational system, until one realizes that what is actually being measured is precisely nothing: the prisoner is neither going anywhere nor accomplishing anything. Griffiths himself would later criticize the use of the treadwheel in *Fifty Years of Public Service*, but only *after* it was abolished in 1898, as William Forsythe has pointed out.[22] Moreover, Griffiths upholds the fact that the regime in 1893 allows the prisoner to 'earn privileges and improve his position' (*Secrets*, 2:450) through exemplary behaviour, whereas American penologists of the same period saw that system as encouraging 'servility' and aimed for the reverse system in which prisoners were accorded rights which would be lost upon bad behaviour, as a recent history has noted.[23] The system Griffiths is describing is in fact less than ideal, then, but his laudatory portrayal makes it seem so.

Conversely, when he turns to foreign prisons, Griffiths's whitewashing becomes defamatory. In a chapter entitled 'Secondary Punishment at Home and Abroad,' he focuses his attention on 'Japanese, Chinese, and Moorish prisons.' Moroccan prisons, he claims, are 'the foulest and most detestable in the world' (*Secrets*, 1:394). The atrocities he describes are indeed horrific, but the loaded language with which he depicts them makes them seem doubly vile. One can never forget, he says, 'the horrid, awful aspect of [the] half-starved, heavily-chained, continuously-tortured inmates' (*Secrets*, 1:394–5) of the prison at Tangiers, a site which he visited himself. The emotive adjectives and double-barrelled epithets create a sensational effect, which continues in the next sentence: 'These dark, gruesome dungeons, reek with filth and noxious effluvia; there is absolutely no drainage, and this in a southern climate where the temperature is high' (*Secrets*, 1:395). Moreover, on the same page Griffiths compares the inmates of the prison to 'wild beasts' who 'fight ... for the food that is given them,' a simile that invokes Darwinian theories of atavism, thus presenting these people as throwbacks to an earlier stage of evolution.[24] While Griffiths depicts the British prison inspector as the epitome of all that is right about England, he performs the inverse operation here by describing the Moroccan warden as the embodiment of corruption: 'Everything rests with the cruel and extortionate gaoler, whose heart is only softened by backsheesh' (*Secrets*, 1:395). And in case the political import of this sketch has been lost on Griffiths's readers, he drives the point home at the conclusion of the chapter: 'The sufferings endured by the Sultan's prisoners is only one of many causes that have produced the recent insurrections in Morocco' (*Secrets*, 1:395). Griffiths's portrayal of the prisons of Morocco – and of a host of other foreign countries, in this work and others – serves the political end of showing the superiority (and stability) of Britain as a nation and race, and therefore also its entitlement to the status of imperial power.

Griffiths repeats the strategy of showing the superiority of British to non-British prisons as an implicit justification of imperialism in his twelve-volume series on prisons for the Grolier Society. In *Oriental Prisons*, for example, he characterizes Asian prison history as 'one long record of savage punishments culminating in the death penalty, aggravated by abominable tortures.'[25] To convey an impression of horrendous barbarity, Griffiths catalogues, in repetitive, encyclopedic fashion, the gruesome methods used in various 'Oriental' countries throughout the ages. His descriptions always contain macabre details of physical suffering, often combined with suggestions of excruciating psychological torment. These accounts are 'educational,' but have a sensational effect. One punishment purportedly invented by a Chinese emperor, for example, consisted of a long hollow column of brass with openings for fuel, into which the authorities placed the criminals, and 'lighted a great fire in the inside; and thus roasted them until they were reduced to ashes.'[26] Relating prison practices in China to the feudal political system in place there, and presenting the Chinese as a race of slaves controlled by a minority of tyrants, Griffiths proceeds to paint a harrowing picture of prison methods exerted by the powerful over the oppressed in that 'unenlightened' country. He reviles the Chinese system in no uncertain terms: 'The penal code is ferocious, the punishments inflicted are fiendishly cruel, and the prisons pig-stys [*sic*] in which torture is hardly more deadly than the diseases engendered by the most abominable neglect.'[27]

At the end of the chapter, Griffiths drives the point home that this rotten system is the fruit of a poisonous national character: 'Cruelty, which is one of the strongest characteristics of the Chinese nature, manifests itself not only in the application of criminal law, but with a peculiar callousness they delight to torture dumb animals and enjoy witnessing the sufferings of children and adults of their own race.'[28] He concludes, 'It is but natural to expect that in a country where such occurrences are common, the punishments inflicted on the really guilty should exceed anything known in the practices of the enlightened nations of today.'[29] In this chapter and others, such as those on Burma and Turkey, primitive prison methods are presented as a reflection of primitive cultures, and the British system, in every way more advanced and humane than those devised by Asian cultures, becomes the standard against which Asian systems fall short, and a symbol of the superiority of British civilization. In the case of China the background of the Opium Wars between Britain and China of 1839–42 and 1856–60 serves as a particular incentive to stress British superiority over the Chinese.

The exceptions to this pattern of describing Oriental prison systems damningly are not really exceptions at all. India under the Raj; Japan, a British ally; and Egypt under the British receive more sympathetic treatment than the countries discussed above. In *Secrets of the Prison-House*, for example, when Griffiths gives an account of Japanese prisons, some of the practices he describes could have been presented as outrageous, but instead he describes them in gentle terms; and Japan itself is characterized as an 'enlightened and progressive country' (*Secrets*, 1:376). Punishment in Japanese prisons may include isolation in a dark cell, a diet of salt and water only for up to seven days, and 'the obligation to drag a four-pound shot attached to the leg by a chain ... for terms varying from one to five, and even ten years' (*Secrets*, 1:378). How different are these conditions from those of the 'half-starved, heavily-chained' Moroccan inmate? And yet Griffiths hurries on without condemning them, remarking merely, 'But the general good conduct of Japanese prisoners is remarkable' (*Secrets*, 1:378). The difference in tone and import of the description of Japanese prisons in comparison with those of most other nations is no doubt related to the fact that Japan was a political ally and thus the need to establish this country's inferiority to Britain is diminished.

In his assessment of European prisons Griffiths is not as biting in his criticism as he is on the subject of Asian prisons, but the impression of British superiority is still strongly conveyed. Although he recognizes some of the positive features of modern French prisons, such as the division of prisoners into cell blocks according to category of prisoner at Fresnes, for example, he manages nevertheless to suggest the ultimate inferiority of the French system and by extension of the French character. A case in point is his description of the system of cellular confinement at La Santé prison, which involved a division between first offenders and recidivists: 'There were the same radiating wings, extending like the spokes of a wheel round a central nave, the *rond point*; in which was [a] glass house, or observatory with an altar on top, towards which all the cell doors, as to their Mecca, religiously turned for the Mass.'[30] The comparison of Catholicism to Islam, for Griffiths's readers, would have made the former seem outlandish and primitive. This trope serves to underscore the imperialist message of Griffiths's non-fictional writings on European prisons by connecting them with the even more backward histories of those Oriental prisons that have not had the benefit of British influence. The message is further reinforced by occasional references to the positive impact of English-language culture on European prison systems, such as the following description of a French prison library: 'The only novels permitted however at La Santé, – and the choice implies a high compliment to English literature, – were translations of Dickens, Fenimore Cooper, Bulwer-Lytton, Marryat and Scott, which were admitted confessedly on account of their morality and purity of tone. These, it was said, were the books in most constant demand.'[31] Griffiths's presentation of the French prison system is thus not purely penological but becomes a commentary on the very character of the French, who are seen to be morally and culturally inferior to the British. Griffiths is deliberately thumbing his nose at Britain's old imperial rival, who, according to Said, was striving to 'catch up with and emulate the British' in matters relating to empire after the French defeat by the Prussians in 1870–1.[32] The purported moral superiority of the British is an implicit justification of the continued political supremacy of the British *vis-à-vis* the French, a message which Griffiths drives home more directly elsewhere.[33]

Turning now to Griffiths's fiction, we see that the strategy described above of berating foreign prisons to underscore the excellence of Britain's own, and thus also the fitness of Britain for imperial rule, is carried over to his novels and stories as well, albeit more implicitly and seemingly incidentally. Though there are many examples, one – *Thrice Captive* (1908), a historical novel set largely in prisons – will suffice. The three captures of the protagonist and narrator, James ('Jem') Stuart Austen, are first by the English, who construe him as a Jacobite and traitor to King William, despite his protestations of innocence; second by French Jacobite spies; and third by spies of the King of Spain. Because the tale is set in the seventeenth century, the abuses of the old régime are very much a reality and Griffiths does not fail to reproduce them, even with regard to the English scene. He still manages, however, to show that however bad English prisons were, foreign prisons were worse, thus preserving the imperialist import of the treatment of prisons that characterizes his oeuvre as a whole.

When Jem is consigned to Newgate after his first capture, the prison is described as 'a horrid abode of misery,'[34] and much is made of the fact that there is no system of classification, so that unconvicted, genteel persons are forced to cohabit with the worst sorts of ruffians imaginable, from habitual thieves to callous murderers. Several chapters later, however, when Jem is taken captive on board a French ship and then thrown into a French jail, we are told that, in comparison with this jail, 'Newgate was quite a paradise.'[35] Jem is then sentenced to serve fourteen years at the galleys as a traitor to France, an experience that gives him direct insight into the particular atrocities of the French system. Of his five chain companions, 'one was a murderer, a second a thief, a third a highway robber, the fourth a burglar and the fifth a Turk from Constantinople, who had voluntarily sold himself into bondage.'[36] From this description it can be seen that no attempt at classification is made – that the mildest of criminals associate closely with the worst. Moreover, the anti-Catholic sentiment that appeared in Griffiths's non-fictional writings about France appears here again as he refers to the 'cruel penalties' that were inflicted upon the Huguenots, who were sent into 'villainous durance, as the associates of the most brutal, and degraded criminals' by the 'savage King' in his 'merciless fanaticism.'[37] And when Jem is deposited at the Castle of Tournelle in Paris, a prison for galley-slaves, the abuses therein are unfathomable. Along with the other inmates, Jem is reduced to an object in the hands of his captors and subjected to humiliating treatment: 'We were now ordered to lie down full length on the floor, twenty men in a row, and one by one the iron collar was fitted round our necks, and rivetted with hammer and anvil. We were thus debarred from all movement, and forbidden to lift our heads or rise even to a sitting posture.'[38] For food they are forced to eat 'black bread from the floor,' and for drink to lap up 'mouthfuls of water like brute beasts.'[39] The sense of France as a benighted Catholic nation and the notion that her prison system was cruel and irrational are thus fused into one harsh castigation of the way she has administered punishment for convicts, highlighting the relative innocuousness of the British system even during this dark period. The impressions of Spanish prisons are equally shocking. All of these descriptions have an air of truth because they are conveyed by a subject whom Griffiths has constructed as having experienced the prison systems in question from the inside. Through this fictional character, Griffiths strengthens the claims of British superiority communicated in his non-fiction, by giving them enhanced emotional force and vividness.

What is more, the fiction deploys a new technique for enhancing the reader's estimation of the British prison system, that of incorporating the romance genre. In several cases, the inspector of prisons is presented as a noble gentleman who comes to the rescue of a poor criminal with personal troubles, thus emerging as a chivalric hero in the manner of the knights of British lore – a hero who may be seen as a representative of the British empire itself. The most striking example of this phenomenon is Griffiths's *A Prison Princess: A Romance of Millbank Penitentiary* (1893). In this novel the prison inspector is an educated and kindly military man whose interaction with prisoners is both well intentioned and beneficial to them. It contrasts tellingly with one of the earlier reformist novels mentioned above, namely Charles Reade's *It Is Never Too Late to Mend* (discussed by Monika Fludernik in chapter 5 of the present volume), in which the solitary system, gaining prominence in England but the target of criticism by humanitarians such as Dickens, is depicted as insupportably cruel.[40]

In Reade's narrative, the visiting justices are completely out of touch with the day-to-day life of the prison. When the chaplain of the prison, the Reverend Mr Eden, urges the 'Inspector of Prisons' to investigate the abuses that occur at the prison, after a suicide has taken place, the cool response is disheartening. One of the justices replies that he is 'instructed to examine into charges made against the governor of —— Gaol; but that he had no instructions to make an irregular visit for that purpose,' and that his next scheduled visit is in six weeks' time. The narrator describes the man with deliberate irony as 'a salaried officer of the Crown enlightened by a large comparison of many prisons,' who, 'residing at a distance, was not open to the corrupting influences of association and personal sympathy with the governor, as were the county magistrates.'[41] From this ironic remark it is clear that Reade is opposed to the very thing that Griffiths upholds as progress – the centralized system. For Reade, the detached perspective of the civil servant prevents him from having the emotional involvement that is necessary for him to be sufficiently dedicated to the welfare of the inmates. Furthermore, the civil servant's lack of regular personal involvement at the prison presents a barrier to his proper assessment of crisis situations because of his unfamiliarity with the people and events that led up to it.

Griffiths finds Reade's novel to be 'a little over-coloured,' as he gently puts it.[42] His own presentation of the prison inspector contrasts sharply with Reade's; instead of being the embodiment of a harsh, merciless régime, Griffiths's prison inspector is the incarnation of the new British system that is both rational and militaristic, and humane and caring. In the opening pages of *A Prison Princess*, a committee visits Millbank Penitentiary for inspection. The committee is chaired by one Sir Alfred Audley, 'a veteran magistrate, well versed in prison administration and the vagaries of prisoners.'[43] He is accompanied by several others, including General Macintire (the military designation is notable), also an experienced and talented prison inspector. The abilities of these officials are called into play when the group is introduced to one odd jailbird, Nada, the prison princess of the title, of whom the prison matron says, 'She's so strange, so different from the rest. I don't know what to do with her; she seems half-dazed and in a sort of stupor.'[44] Nada's origins are obscure; she speaks four languages, refers to herself in full as 'Marie Nadaievna Sergheitch Pahlovsky,' but is occasionally identified as Mary Walgate. General Macintire approaches this curiosity delicately and makes the effort to talk to Nada in Spanish, showing both intelligence and an interest in the particular needs of the prisoner – completely unlike Reade's ignorant and insensitive inspectors. He speaks to her with 'chivalrous candour' and treats her with exceptional reverence, 'as though she were a duchess in her drawing room and he her guest.'[45]

The General allows Nada to tell her story: she was wooed and won by the honey-tongued Hugh Walgate, who after their marriage took her from hotel to hotel but without the money to pay for these escapades, unbeknownst to her. When he was finally caught for hotel swindling, he deserted her and let her take the fall for his criminal behaviour. Macintire's reaction to Nada's plight is one of compassion; he believes that 'It was all so real, so circumstantial, that its truth was self-evident, and not to be denied – not, at least, by a kindly, sympathetic soul who still could trust in his fellow-creatures.'[46] He resolves to help Nada in whatever way he can.

Unfortunately, the General is ill for a while and so disappears temporarily from the narrative. Meanwhile, Nada falls into bad company in the prison; she meets the habitual criminal Sappy Sal, who lures her into a plot to recover stolen jewels left in the prison by a former convict.[47] Feigning hysteria, Nada gets herself transferred to the cell in which the jewels are hidden, and emerges with them on her release. Nada and Sal begin to pawn their loot, only to meet face to face with one of the original owners of the jewels, who was devastated by the theft, and who asks that the jewels be returned to him. They deny him his property, and continue to pawn until the original jeweller sets his nephew on their trail, forcing them to flee to a resort at Lake Como. There they are joined by a Mr Vansittart, a gallant American of whom Nada has become enamoured. Their liaison is interrupted, however, by a visit from Nada's husband, who attempts to steal the jewels during the night. Hugh shoots at Sal when she catches him, and Hugh is stabbed in return; whether by Nada or by Sal is never known. Both Hugh and Sal die, and Nada sinks into permanent imbecility, forcing Vansittart to exchange dreams of romance for the fatherly role of caregiver.

While very much in the background after the opening chapters, General Macintire does, however, reappear at a significant moment. Nada's conscience never ceases to prick her over the fact that the jewels rightfully belong to the jeweller, and while she is at Lake Como she finally decides to relinquish them. The General, who has been following Nada out of concern, emerges just in time to accept the mission of taking the jewels back to England to restore them to their owner (so that Hugh's attempt to steal them is pointless in any case). Whatever the truth surrounding Hugh's death, we know that Nada is finally cleared of the guilt surrounding the theft of the jewels. Thus the General has, like a true knight, appeared in time to save the Princess's moral character. In Griffiths's fiction, then, the British prison system – and its representative, the prison inspector, embodied here in Griffiths's alter-ego, General Macintire – far from damaging the lives of individual prisoners, improves them by providing officials who have sufficient knowledge and ability to attend to the particular needs of prisoners of varied backgrounds and circumstances, and whose characters have been informed by British notions of chivalry and justice. Symbolically, the General's unobtrusive but crucial presence in Nada's life represents the kind of benevolent control that the new prison administration, and by extension the imperial monarch in whose service it is run, exercise in the eyes of Griffiths and others of his mind-set. Moreover, the use of the romance genre encourages an attitude not merely of acceptance of this control but of gratefully embracing it.

A similar type of characterization is at work in Griffiths's short-story collection, *Tales of a Government Official* (1902). We know from the outset of the work that the narrator (who is also closely modelled on Griffiths himself) is not only an advocate of but also a former member of the centralized prison system, and that he takes pride in the élite status that has been bestowed upon him. He tells us, for example, that he is accustomed to being stopped by people on the street who claim to be former inmates and who are proud of their association with him. He even claims that one night as he was leaving the theatre a man called a cab for him, 'using as his recommendation the mystic words, "Pentagon Three Sir!"' On another occasion, a man walked up to him 'claiming fellowship because "he had served along o' me" at Wormwood Scrubs, his service having been "penal" and enforced through me.'[48] In the eyes of the prisoners on the inside, he was 'a cynosure, an object of general interest, the symbol of authority, the embodiment of power, the god from the machine.'[49] One can hardly think of more glowing terms in which Griffiths could have glorified his former position as a high-ranking official within the centralized system.

The narrator of these stories takes pains to show that the high esteem in which he is held as a prison official results from his showing a direct and personal concern for the inmates under his inspection. Chapter 16, entitled 'A Traitor's Fate,' recounts a story that conveys a sense of the tender compassion he shows towards the prisoners with whom he comes into contact. On his way to visit the prison at Portland, the narrator offers a ride to a woman heading for the prison with two children; when she asks whether he has any friends at the prison, he replies, 'About eleven hundred ... At least, I like them to think me their friend. I desire to befriend them. That is the object of my visit: to hear their complaints and grievances, and, if it is in my power, to remedy them.'[50] When she realizes that he is 'her Majesty's Inspector,' the woman wants to descend from the carriage, since she is only a convict's wife, but the narrator gallantly insists that she stay, and offers to hear her husband's story in case he can help him. The woman innocently claims that her husband, Gregory Tarrant, has been framed, though the narrator remembers him and knows better. Still, he arranges for husband and wife to be permitted a meeting, and kindly offers to get the woman some lunch afterwards. The consequence of this generosity is that the woman foolishly agrees to meet an old 'friend' of her husband after talking with him, and this man attempts to blackmail the wife; he is caught, put in jail, and later murdered by the woman's husband for his treachery.

The conclusion one might reach on reading the story is that too much kindness on the part of officials is bound to be abused, but Griffiths does not drive that point home. The narrator simply tells the reader of his magnanimous conduct, and the story convinces us that the government official does all he can to ensure the well-being of the prisoners he meets. The prison inspector thus emerges again as gentlemanly and chivalric. Not only does Griffiths's fiction uphold the superiority of the British prison system in the manner of the non-fiction, then, but it also bolsters this view through the weaving into his narratives of the genre of romance, with the prison inspector as chivalric hero. Griffiths's use of this trope in his fiction about prisons gives increased narrative energy to the myth that is present throughout his works – the idea that the excellence of the British prison system is but one aspect of the overall superiority of British practices and manners, making imperialism not only a right but a duty.

Needless to say, this is only one side of the story – the side of those in power. Not everyone had the same cheerful view of the changes taking place in the British penal system, or indeed of the system as a whole. Historian Seán McConville has suggested that the move towards a centralized system was a terrible mistake, and that its facilitation was due almost entirely to the dictatorial personality of its enforcer, Du Cane, rather than to any inherent merits.[51] In McConville's opinion, centralization merely led to the more intolerant and less personal administration of prisons which he claims still characterizes British prisons today. Oscar Wilde's letter to the editor of the *Daily Chronicle* of 28 May 1887 indicates that some of Griffiths's contemporaries were less than happy with the centralized system. Wilde, who also had intimate knowledge of prison life by this time, is convinced that 'Wherever there is centralization there is stupidity. What is inhuman in modern life is officialism.

Authority is as destructive to those who exercise it as to those on whom it is exercised. It is the Prison Board, and the system that carries it out, that is the primary source of the cruelty that is exercised on a child in prisons.'[52]

Indeed, many people thought the Du Cane régime was too harsh. The Irish radical Michael Davitt, imprisoned in England for political crimes, criticized Du Cane's system in his *Leaves from a Prison Diary* (1885) for its failure to effect reform, owing to 'its obvious essential tendency to deal with erring human beings – who are still men despite their crimes – in a manner which mechanically reduces them to a uniform level of disciplined brutes.'[53] In addition, the *Daily Chronicle* in 1894 ran a series on the condition of Britain's prisons called 'Our Dark Places.' As John Stokes has written, the point of this series was 'to bear human witness to statistics which already demonstrated that Sir Edmund's régime, with its military discipline and its reliance upon solitary confinement, had led not only to an increase in recidivism but to a growing number of cases of madness and suicide.'[54]

Griffiths continued to defend Britain's prison system, declaring in an interview with Raymond Blathwayt in 1898, 'I cannot sufficiently emphasize the truth of the remark, our prison system is the best in the world. There is more systematic treatment as to punishment and more genuine attempt at moral reformation, so far as it can possibly be accomplished, than could be found anywhere else in the world.'[55] But the fact that British socialist Edward Carpenter could remark in 1905 that 'Penology, though made much of as a science on the Continent and in the United States, is little studied in Britain; and there is little doubt that in some respects even Russian and Siberian prisons are more humanely conducted than ours'[56] shows that Griffiths's romantic attitude towards the modern British prison system was not a view universally endorsed. There is a clear division on this issue between those who both have and endorse power, of whom Griffiths is a representative, and those (for example, the Irish and political radicals) who are critical of the powers that be – in the prison system, and beyond it to the imperialist state. The prison in the late Victorian period, then, emerges as a contested site in which ideological battles are being fought concerning not only penology but also imperialism and the very question of British identity. Indeed, an interesting phenomenon is the way in which, in Griffiths's writings, the British prison inmate becomes 'foreignized,' a type of the 'other within' (Nada herself is a good example of this), as if to demonstrate that to be British is by definition to be superior and on the side of those in control. But that, as they say, is another story – or rather, in this case, another version of the same story.

NOTES

1 Charles Dickens, *Little Dorrit*, ed. Harvey Peter Sucksmith (Oxford: Clarendon Press, 1979), 58, 59.
2 Henry James, *The Princess Casamassima*, ed. Patricia Crick (London: Penguin Books, 1987), 79–80.
3 See Crick, in ibid., 594.
4 See Michel Foucault, *Discipline and Punish: The Birth of the Prison*, trans. Alan Sheridan (London: Penguin Books, 1977), 195–228.
5 Ibid., 208.
6 Edward Said, *Orientalism* (1978; New York: Vintage Books, 1979), 7.
7 On the topic of transportation, it is possible to speculate that since, as Jason Haslam and Julia Wright note in the introduction to this volume, transportation was hardly an economical way of dispensing with prisoners unless the benefits of colonial expansion are taken into account, Britain abandoned transportation when it found a more economical way of extending its borders – namely, fully annexing countries and getting natives to do the work.
8 Sir Edmund Du Cane (1830–1903) was variously Chairman of Commissioners of Prisons, Chairman of Directors of Prisons, Inspector-General of Military Prisons, and Surveyor-General of Prisons.
9 *Public Record Office: Current Guide*, 3 vols. (London: Public Record Office, 1994), vol. 2, section 406/1/1.
10 Ibid., 406/1/2.
11 Christopher Harding, Bill Hines, Richard Ireland, and Philip Rawlings, *Imprisonment in England and Wales: A Concise History* (London: Croom Helm, 1985), 200.
12 Sir Edmund F. Du Cane, *The Punishment and Prevention of Crime* (London: Macmillan, 1885), 33.
13 Major Arthur Griffiths, *Fifty Years of Public Service* (1898; London: Cassell and Company, 1904), 2.
14 See the introduction to this volume.
15 Griffiths, *Fifty*, 251.
16 Ibid., 265–7.
17 Ibid., 251.
18 Ibid., 252.

19 By the time of his death in 1908, he had produced twenty-nine novels, five short-story collections, one play, nearly thirty volumes of historical works, and countless articles for a wide range of periodicals.
20 Arthur Griffiths and Anthony Twyford, *Records of York Castle: Fortress, Court House, and Prison* (London: Griffiths and Farran, 1880); Arthur Griffiths, *The Chronicles of Newgate*, 2 vols. (London: Chapman and Hall, 1884); Arthur Griffiths, *Secrets of the Prison-House; or, Gaol Studies and Sketches*, 2 vols. (1893; London: Chapman and Hall, 1894), hereafter *Secrets* and cited parenthetically in the text; Arthur Griffiths, *Memorials of Millbank, and Chapters in Prison History*, 2 vols. (London: Henry S. King and Company, 1875); and Arthur Griffiths, *The History and Romance of Crime: From the Earliest Times to the Present Day*, 12 vols. (London: Grolier Society, c. 1900).
21 Griffiths, *Chronicles*, 1:vi–vii.
22 William Forsythe, *The Reform of Prisoners, 1830–1900* (London: Croom Helm, 1987), 201.
23 Harding et al., *Imprisonment in England and Wales*, 209.
24 Griffiths, who served as British representative at the Fourth Congress of Criminal Anthropology at Geneva (1896), was highly knowledgeable about the new science of criminal anthropology developed by Cesare Lombroso and others, which used Darwinian theory to defend the idea of a 'born criminal.' Griffiths's writings as a whole show that he was ultimately unconvinced of the scientific truth of this notion, but that he was willing to use it for rhetorical effect.
25 Arthur Griffiths, *Oriental Prisons: Prisons and Crime in India – the Andaman Islands – Burmah – China – Japan – Egypt – Turkey* (London: Grolier Society, c. 1900), vi.
26 Ibid.
27 Ibid., 205.
28 Ibid., 225.
29 Ibid., 226.
30 Arthur Griffiths, *Modern French Prisons: Bicêtre – St. Pélagie – St. Lazare – La Force – the Concièrgerie – La Grande et la Petite Roquettes – Mazas – La Santé* (London: Grolier Society, c. 1900), 189.
31 Griffiths, *Modern French Prisons*, 194–5.
32 Said, *Orientalism*, 218.
33 See, for example, Arthur Griffiths, *The Great Adventurer: A Life of Napoleon* (London: Anthony Traherne and Co., 1902). Griffiths displays his staunch support for British imperialism in general in numerous works, including 'The Conquest of the Soudan,' *Fortnightly Review* 66 (November 1896), 680–92; *The Wellington Memorial: Wellington, His Comrades and Contemporaries* (Lon-

don: George Allen, 1897); *The English Army: Its Past History, Present Condition, and Future Prospects* (London: Cassel, Petter and Galpin, 1878); and *Famous British Regiments* (London: T. Fisher Unwin, 1900).
34 Arthur Griffiths, *Thrice Captive* (London: F.V. White and Company, 1908), 86.
35 Ibid., 140.
36 Ibid., 144–5.
37 Ibid., 151.
38 Ibid., 153.
39 Ibid.
40 See Philip Collins, *Dickens and Crime* (1962; 3rd ed., New York: St Martin's Press, 1994), ix. The debate between advocates of the solitary system, in which prisoners have almost no contact with other people, and the associated system, in which criminals work and even lodge together but are expected to keep a strict rule of silence, was gradually being resolved in Griffiths's time in favour of a solitary existence tempered by periods of controlled association. Griffiths was enthusiastic about the prospects for the management of criminals under this new system.
41 Charles Reade, *It Is Never Too Late to Mend* (1856; London: Walter Scott, n.d.), 202.
42 Griffiths, *Memorials of Millbank*, 1:189.
43 Griffiths, *A Prison Princess: A Romance of Millbank Penitentiary* (London: Cassell and Company, 1893), 4.
44 Ibid., 5.
45 Ibid., 21, 13.
46 Ibid., 27.
47 The implicit criticism of the system of free association in prison, later abandoned, should be noted.
48 Griffiths, *Tales of a Government Official* (London: F.V. White and Company, 1902), 3.
49 Ibid., 2.
50 Ibid., 208.
51 Seán McConville, 'Chapter Five: The Victorian Prison, England, 1865–1965,' in *The Oxford History of the Prison: The Practice of Punishment in Western Society*, ed. Norval Morris and David J. Rothman (Oxford: Oxford University Press, 1995), 131–67.
52 Oscar Wilde, letter to the editor of the *Daily Chronicle*, 28 May 1887, in *Complete Works of Oscar Wilde* (Glasgow: HarperCollins, 1994), 1060.
53 Michael Davitt, *Leaves from a Prison Diary; or, Lectures to a 'Solitary' Audience* (1885; Shannon: Irish University Press, 1994), 1.249.

54 John Stokes, *In the Nineties* (London: Harvester Wheatsheaf, 1989), 96.
55 Raymond Blathwayt, 'Prison Discipline: A Talk with Major Arthur Griffiths,' *Great Thoughts from Master Minds*, August 1898, 296–8.
56 Edward Carpenter, *Prisons, Police and Punishment: An Inquiry into the Causes and Treatment of Crime and Criminals* (London: Arthur C. Fifield, 1905), 5.

Bibliography

Allen, Gardner W. *Our Navy and the Barbary Corsairs.* Hamden, CT: Archon Books, 1965.

Althusser, Louis. 'Ideology and Ideological State Apparatuses (Notes towards an Investigation).' In *Lenin and Philosophy,* trans. Ben Brewster, 121–73. London: New Left, 1971.

Anderson, Benedict. *Imagined Communities: Reflections on the Origin and Spread of Nationalism.* 1983. Rev. ed. London and New York: Verso, 1991.

Andrews, William L. *To Tell a Free Story: The First Century of Afro-American Autobiography, 1760–1865.* Urbana: University of Illinois Press, 1986.

Austin, J.L. *How to Do Things with Words.* Cambridge: Harvard University Press, 1962.

Babington, Anthony. *The Power to Silence: A History of Punishment in Britain.* London: Robert Maxwell, 1968.

Baepler, Paul. 'The Barbary Captivity Narrative in Early America.' *Early American Literature* 30 (1995): 95–120.

Baepler, Paul, ed. *White Slaves, African Masters: An Anthology of American Barbary Captivity Narratives.* Chicago: University of Chicago Press, 1999.

Baker, Houston A., Jr. *Blues, Ideology, and Afro-American Literature: A Vernacular Theory.* Chicago: University of Chicago Press, 1984.

Bakhtin, Mikhail. *The Dialogic Imagination.* Ed. Michael Holquist, trans. Caryl Emerson and Michael Holquist. Austin: University of Texas Press, 1981.

Baldry, W. Burton. *From Hampstead to Holloway: Depicting the Suffragette in Her Happiest Moods.* London: John Ouseley, 1909.

Balfour, Jabez Spencer. *My Prison Life.* London: Chapman and Hall, 1907.

Barker-Benfield, G.J. *The Culture of Sensibility: Sex and Society in Eighteenth-Century Britain.* Chicago: University of Chicago Press, 1992.

Beaumont, Gustave, and Alexis de Tocqueville. *On the Penitentiary System in the United States and Its Application in France.* 1833. Trans. Francis Lieber. Carbondale: Southern Illinois University Press, 1964.

Bell, Michael. *Sentimentalism, Ethics and the Culture of Feeling.* London: Palgrave, 2000.

Bender, John. *Imagining the Penitentiary: Fiction and the Architecture of Mind in Eighteenth-Century England.* Chicago: University of Chicago Press, 1987.

Bentham, Jeremy. *The Works of Jeremy Bentham, Now First Collected.* Ed. John Bowring. Vol. 3. Edinburgh: William Tait, 1838.

Bhabha, Homi K. 'Introduction: Narrating the Nation.' In *Nation and Narration*, ed. Homi K. Bhabha, 1–7. New York: Routledge, 1990.

Bibb, Henry. *Narrative of the Life and Adventures of Henry Bibb, an American Slave, Written by Himself.* In *Slave Narratives*, ed. William L. Andrews and Henry Louis Gates, Jr, 425–566. New York: Library of America, 2000.

Blathwayt, Raymond. 'Prison Discipline: A Talk with Major Arthur Griffiths.' *Great Thoughts from Master Minds* (August 1898): 296–98.

Boethius. *Tractates: The Consolation of Philosophy.* 523. Trans. H.F. Stewart et al. Loeb Classical Library, 74. Cambridge: Harvard University Press, 1973.

Bolotov, Andrei Timofeevich. *Life and Adventures.* CA. 1816.

Brocklehurst, F. *I Was in Prison.* London: Unwin, 1898.

Brombert, Victor. *La prison romantique: Essai sur l'imaginaire.* Paris: José Corti, 1975.

– 'The Happy Prison: A Recurring Romantic Metaphor.' In *Romanticism: Vistas, Instances, Continuities*, ed. David Thorburn and Geoffrey Hartman, 62–79. Ithaca: Cornell University Press, 1973.

– *The Romantic Prison: The French Tradition.* Princeton: Princeton University Press, 1978.

Burgett, Bruce. *Sentimental Bodies: Sex, Gender, and Citizenship in the Early Republic.* Princeton: Princeton University Press, 1998.

Burke, Kenneth. *A Rhetoric of Motives.* Berkeley: University of California Press, 1969.

Butler, Judith. *Excitable Speech: A Politics of the Performative.* New York: Routledge, 1997.

– 'Imitation and Gender Insubordination.' In *Inside/Out*, ed. Diana Fuss, 13–31. New York: Routledge, 1991.

Caldwell, Tanya. '"Talking Too Much English": Languages of Economy and Politics in Equiano's *The Interesting Narrative.*' *Early American Literature* 34 (1999): 263–80.

Carlyle, Thomas. *Thomas Carlyle's Collected Works.* Vol. 19: *Latter-Day Pamphlets.* London: Chapman and Hall, 1870.

Carnochan, W.B. 'The Literature of Confinement.' In *The Oxford History of the Prison: The Practice of Punishment in Western Society,* ed. Norval Morris and David J. Rothman, 426–55. New York: Oxford University Press, 1995.

Carpenter, Edward. *Prisons, Police and Punishment: An Inquiry into the Causes and Treatment of Crime and Criminals.* London: Arthur C. Fifield, 1905.

Carretta, Vincent. 'Defining a Gentleman: The Status of Olaudah Equiano or Gustavus Vassa.' *Language Sciences* 22.3 (2000): 385–99.

Castiglia, Christopher. *Bound and Determined: Captivity, Culture-Crossing, and White Womanhood from Mary Rowlandson to Patty Hearst.* Chicago: University of Chicago Press, 1996.

Castiglia, Christopher, and Julia Stern. Introduction to *Interiority in Early American Literature,* ed. Christopher Castiglia and Julia Stern, a special issue of *Early American Literature* 37 (2002): 1–7.

Charles d'Orléans. *The English Poems of Charles d'Orléans.* Ed. Robert Steele. EETS o.s. 215. Oxford: Oxford University Press, 1941.

Chesterton, George Laval. *Revelations of Prison Life: With an Enquiry into Prison Discipline and Secondary Punishments.* Rev. ed. Vol. 1. London: Hurst and Blackett, 1856.

Coleman, Deirdre. Introduction to *Maiden Voyages and Infant Colonies: Two Women's Travel Narratives of the 1790s,* 1–42. London: Leicester University Press, 1999.

Collins, Philip. *Dickens and Crime.* 1962. 3rd ed. New York: St Martin's Press, 1994.

Colmore, Gertrude. *Suffragettes: A Story of Three Women.* London: Pandora, 1984. Rpt. of *Suffragette Sally,* 1911.

'A Convict's Views of Penal Discipline.' *Cornhill Magazine* 10.6 (December 1864): 722–33.

Corbett, Mary Jean. *Representing Femininity: Middle-Class Subjectivity in Victorian and Edwardian Women's Autobiographies.* Oxford: Oxford University Press, 1992.

Cox, Stephen. 'Sensibility as Argument.' In *Sensibility in Transformation: Creative Resistance to Sentiment from the Augustans to the Romantics,* ed. Syndy McMillen Conger, 63–82. Toronto: Associated University Presses, 1990.

Crosby, Christina. 'Reading the Gothic Revival: "History" and *Hints on Household Taste.*' In *Rewriting the Victorians: Theory, History, and the Politics of Gender,* ed. Linda M. Shires, 101–15. New York: Routledge, 1992.

Cullen, Louis M. 'The Internal Politics of the United Irishmen.' In *The United Irishmen: Republicanism, Radicalism and Rebellion,* ed. David Dickson, Dáire Keough, and Kevin Whelan, 176–96. Dublin: Lilliput Press, 1993.

Curran, John Philpot. *Speeches of the Right Honorable John Philpot Curran, Master of the Rolls in Ireland, on the Late Very Interesting State Trials.* 3rd ed. Dublin: J. Stockdale, 1811.
Curtin, Nancy J. *The United Irishmen: Popular Politics in Ulster and Dublin, 1791–1798.* Oxford: Clarendon Press, 1994.
D'Auberteuil, Michel René Hilliard. *Miss McCrea: A Novel of the American Revolution.* 1784. In *American Captivity Narratives*, ed. and intro. Gordon M. Sayre, 352–76. Boston: Houghton Mifflin, 2000.
Davies, Ioan. *Writers in Prison.* Oxford: Basil Blackwell, 1990; Toronto: Between the Lines, 1990.
Davis, Angela Y. 'Race, Gender, and Prison History: From the Convict Lease System to the Supermax Prison.' In *Prison Masculinities*, ed. Don Sabo, Terry A. Kupers, and Willie London, 35–45. Philadelphia: Temple University Press, 2001.
– 'Racialized Punishment and Prison Abolition.' In *The Angela Y. Davis Reader*, ed. Joy James, 96–107. Oxford: Blackwell, 1998.
Davis, Philip. 'Victorian Realist Prose and Sentimentality.' In *Rereading Victorian Fiction*, ed. Alice Jenkins and Juliet John, 13–28. London: Palgrave, 2002.
Davitt, Michael. *Leaves from a Prison Diary; or, Lectures to a 'Solitary' Audience.* 1885. Intro. T.W. Moody. Shannon: Irish University Press, 1994.
Deane, Seamus. 'The Production of Cultural Space in Irish Writing.' *boundary 2* 21.3 (1994): 117–44.
De Beaumont, Gustave, and Alexis de Tocqueville. *On the Penitentiary System in the United States and its Application in France.* Trans. Francis Lieber. 1833. Carbondale: Southern Illinois University Press, 1964.
Dedmond, Francis B. '"Many Things to Many People": Thoreau in His Time and Ours.' *Forum* 30 (1989): 60–9.
Delany, Samuel R. *Longer Views: Extended Essays.* Hanover: Wesleyan University Press, 1996.
de Man, Paul. *The Rhetoric of Romanticism.* New York: Columbia University Press, 1984.
Derrida, Jacques. *Limited Inc.* Evanston: Northwestern University Press, 1988.
Dickens, Charles. *American Notes and Pictures from Italy.* London: Oxford University Press, 1957.
– *David Copperfield.* 1849–50. Ed. Jeremy Tambling. London: Penguin, 1997.
– 'In and Out of Jail.' *Household Words* 7.164 (Saturday, 14 May 1853): 241–5.
– 'The Italian Prisoner.' Chapter 17 of *The Uncommercial Traveller and Reprinted Pieces* (1860), ed. Leslie C. Staples, 169–78. London: Oxford University Press, 1968.
– *Little Dorrit.* 1855–7. Ed. Harvey Peter Sucksmith. Oxford: Clarendon Press, 1979.

- *Martin Chuzzlewit*. 1843–4. Ed. Margaret Cardwell. Oxford: Clarendon Press, 1982.
- *Sketches by Boz; Illustrative of Every-Day Life and Every-Day People*. 1833–6. Illus. George Cruikshank and 'Phiz.' London: Oxford University Press, 1957.

Dixon, [William] Hepworth. *The London Prisons: With an Account of the More Distinguished Persons Who Have Been Confined in Them: To Which Is Added a Description of the Chief Provincial Prisons*. London: Jackson and Walford, 1850.

d'Orléans, Charles. *The English Poems of Charles d'Orléans*. Ed. Robert Steele. EETS o.s. 215. Oxford: Oxford University Press, 1941.

Douglass, Frederick. *Narrative of the Life of Frederick Douglass, an American Slave, Written by Himself*. In *Slave Narratives*, ed. William L. Andrews and Henry Louis Gates, Jr, 267–368. New York: Library of America, 2000.

Drennan, William. *Letter to the Right Honourable William Pitt*. Dublin: James Moore, 1799.
- 'Protest against an Union with Great Britain.' In *Fugitive Pieces in Verse and Prose*, 210–16. Belfast: F.D. Finlay, 1815.

DuBois, W.E.B. *The Souls of Black Folk*. 1903. New York: Fawcett, 1961.

Du Cane, Sir Edmund F. *The Punishment and Prevention of Crime*. London: Macmillan, 1885.

Edwards, Paul. 'Three West African Writers of the 1780s.' In *The Slave's Narrative*, ed. Charles T. Davis and Henry Louis Gates, Jr, 175–98. Oxford: Oxford University Press, 1983.

Elliott, Marianne. 'Defenders in Ulster.' In *The United Irishmen: Republicanism, Radicalism and Rebellion*, ed. David Dickson, Dáire Keough, and Kevin Whelan, 222–33. Dublin: Lilliput Press, 1993.
- *Partners in Revolution: The United Irishmen and France*. New Haven: Yale University Press, 1982.
- *Wolfe Tone: Prophet of Irish Independence*. New Haven: Yale University Press, 1989.

Ellmann, Maud. *The Hunger Artists: Starving, Writing, and Imprisonment*. Cambridge: Harvard University Press, 1993.

Equiano, Olaudah. *The Interesting Narrative and Other Writings*, ed. and intro. Vincent Carretta. New York: Penguin, 1995.

Eriksson, Torsten. *The Reformers: An Historical Survey of Pioneer Experiments in the Treatment of Criminals*. Trans. Catherine Djurklou. New York: Elsevier, 1976.

Ernest, John. *Resistance and Reformation in Nineteenth-Century African-American Literature: Brown, Wilson, Jacobs, Delany, Douglass, and Harper*. Jackson: University Press of Mississippi, 1995.

Eustance, Claire. 'Meanings of Militancy: The Ideas and Practice of Political Resistance in the Women's Freedom League, 1907–14.' In *The Women's Suffrage Movement: New Feminist Perspectives*, ed. Maroula Joannou and June Purvis, 51–64. Manchester: Manchester University Press, 1998.

Evans, Robin. *The Fabrication of Virtue: English Prison Architecture, 1750–1840.* Cambridge: Cambridge University Press, 1982.
Everett, David. *Slaves in Barbary.* Boston, 1817.
Faith, Karlene. *Unruly Women: The Politics of Confinement and Resistance.* Vancouver: Press Gang, 1993.
Felman, Shoshana. *What Does a Woman Want? Reading and Sexual Difference.* Baltimore: Johns Hopkins University Press, 1993.
Felski, Rita. *Beyond Feminist Aesthetics: Feminist Literature and Social Change.* Cambridge: Harvard University Press, 1989.
– *The Gender of Modernity.* Cambridge: Harvard University Press, 1995.
Ferris, Ina. 'From Trope to Code: The Novel and the Rhetoric of Gender in Nineteenth-Century Critical Discourse.' In *Rewriting the Victorians: Theory, History, and the Politics of Gender,* ed. Linda M. Shires, 18–30. New York: Routledge, 1992.
Fichtelberg, Joseph. *Critical Fictions: Sentiment and the American Market, 1780–1870.* Atlanta: University of Georgia Press, 2003.
Field, Daniel. *Rebels in the Name of the Tsar.* Boston: Unwin Hyman, 1989.
Five Years' Penal Servitude: By One Who Has Endured It. 1877. New York: Garland, 1984.
Fludernik, Monika. 'Carceral Topography: Spatiality, Liminality and Corporality in the Literary Prison.' *Textual Practice* 13.1 (Spring 1999): 43–77.
Forsythe, William. *The Reform of Prisoners, 1830–1900.* London: Croom Helm, 1987.
Foster, R.F. *Modern Ireland, 1600–1972.* Markham, Ont.: Penguin, 1989.
Foucault, Michel. *Discipline and Punish: The Birth of the Prison.* Trans. Alan Sheridan. New York: Vintage, 1979. Trans. of *Surveiller et punir: Naissance de la prison.* Paris: Gallimard, 1975.
– 'The Politics of Health in the Eighteenth Century.' In *Power/Knowledge: Selected Interviews and Other Writings 1972–1977,* ed. Colin Gordon, trans. by Colin Gordon, Leo Marshall, John Mepham, and Kate Soper, 66–82. New York: Pantheon, 1980.
– 'Technologies of the Self.' In *Technologies of the Self: A Seminar with Michel Foucault,* ed. Luther H. Martin, Huck Gutman, and Patrick H. Hutton, 16–49. Amherst: University of Massachusetts Press, 1988.
Franklin, Benjamin (Historicus). 'On the Slave Trade.' *Federal Gazette* (23 March 1790).
Franklin, H. Bruce. 'The American Prison in the Culture Wars.' *The Prison Issue.* Feature issue of *Workplace: A Journal for Academic Labor* 3.2 (December 2000). Ed. and intro. Bruce Simon. 14 March 2001. http://www.louisville.edu/journal/workplace/issue61.

- *Prison Literature in America: The Victim as Criminal and Artist.* Expanded ed. of *The Victim as Criminal and Artist: Literature from the American Prison.* 1978. Oxford: Oxford University Press, 1989.
Freedman, Estelle B. *Their Sisters' Keepers: Women's Prison Reform in America, 1830–1930.* Ann Arbor: University of Michigan Press, 1981.
Friedman, Susan Stanford. 'Women's Autobiographical Selves: Theory and Practice.' In *The Private Self: Theory and Practice of Women's Autobiographical Writings,* ed. Shari Benstock, 34–62. Chapel Hill: University of North Carolina Press, 1988.
A Full Report of the Trial at Bar in the Court of King's Bench, of William Drennan, MD Upon an Indictment Charging Him with Having Written and Published a Seditious Libel with the Speeches of Counsel, and the Opinions of the Court at Large. Dublin: Rea and Johnson, 1794. Rpt. in *The Trial of William Drennan,* ed. John Francis Larkin, 35–120. Dublin: Irish Academic Press, 1991.
Furstenberg, François. 'Beyond Freedom and Slavery: Autonomy, Virtue, and Resistance in Early American Political Discourse.' *Journal of American History* 89 (2003). http://www.historycooperative.org/journals/jah/89.4/furstenberg.html.
Gagnier, Regenia. *Subjectivities: A History of Self-Representation in Britain, 1832–1920.* Oxford: Oxford University Press, 1991.
Gardiner, Gordon. *Notes of a Prison Visitor.* London: Oxford University Press, 1938.
Gardiner, Judith Kegan, ed. and intro. *Provoking Agents: Gender and Agency in Theory and Practice.* Urbana: University of Illinois Press, 1995.
Garland, David. *Punishment and Modern Society: A Study in Social Theory.* Chicago: University of Chicago Press; Oxford: Clarendon Press, 1990.
- *Punishment and Welfare: A History of Penal Strategies.* Aldershot: Gower, 1985.
Gates, Henry Louis, Jr. *The Signifying Monkey: A Theory of African-American Literary Criticism.* New York: Oxford University Press, 1988.
- Introduction to *The Classic Slave Narratives,* ed. Henry Louis Gates, Jr, ix–xviii. New York: Penguin, 1987.
Gelfland, Elissa D. *Imagination and Confinement: Women's Writings from French Prisons.* Ithaca: Cornell University Press, 1983.
Gellner, Ernest. *Nations and Nationalism.* Ithaca: Cornell University Press, 1983.
Gerzina, Gretchen Holbrook. 'Mobility in Chains: Freedom of Movement in the Early Black Atlantic.' *South Atlantic Quarterly* 100.1 (2001): 41–59.
Gilman, Charlotte Perkins. 'The Yellow Wallpaper.' In *Daughters of Decadence: Women Writers of the 'Fin de Siècle,'* ed. Elaine Showalter, 98–117. New Brunswick, NJ: Rutgers University Press, 1993.
Gilmartin, Kevin. 'Radical Print Culture in Periodical Form.' In *Romanticism,*

History, and the Possibilities of Genre: Re-Forming Literature, 1789–1837, ed. Tilottama Rajan and Julia M. Wright, 39–63. Cambridge: Cambridge University Press, 1998.
Gilroy, Paul. *The Black Atlantic: Modernity and Double Consciousness.* Cambridge: Harvard University Press, 1993.
Godwin, William. *Caleb Williams.* 1794. Ed. David McCracken. Oxford: Oxford University Press, 1991.
Goffman, Erving. *Stigma: Notes on the Management of Spoiled Identity.* Englewood Cliffs, NJ: Prentice-Hall, 1963.
Göller, Karl Heinz. 'The Metaphorical Prison as an Exceptional Image of Man.' *Fifteenth-Century Studies* 17 (1990): 121–45.
Green, Barbara. *Spectacular Confessions: Autobiography, Performative Activism, and the Sites of Suffrage 1905–1938.* New York: St Martin's Press, 1997.
Griffiths, Arthur. *The Chronicles of Newgate.* 2 vols. London: Chapman and Hall, 1884.
- 'The Conquest of the Soudan.' *Fortnightly Review* 66 (November 1896), 680–92.
- *The English Army: Its Past History, Present Condition, and Future Prospects.* London: Cassel, Petter and Galpin, 1878.
- *Famous British Regiments.* London: T. Fisher Unwin, 1900.
- *Fifty Years of Public Service.* 1898. London: Cassell and Company, 1904.
- *The Great Adventurer: A Life of Napoleon.* London: Anthony Traherne and Company, 1902.
- *The History and Romance of Crime: From the Earliest Times to the Present Day.* 12 vols. London: Grolier Society, n.d. (c. 1900).
- *Memorials of Millbank, and Chapters in Prison History.* 2 vols. London: Henry S. King and Company, 1875.
- *Modern French Prisons: Bicêtre – St. Pélagie – St. Lazare – La Force – the Concièrgerie – La Grande et la Petite Roquettes – Mazas – La Santé.* Vol. 7 of *The History and Romance of Crime.* London: Grolier Society, n.d. (c. 1900).
- *Oriental Prisons: Prisons and Crime in India – the Andaman Islands, Burmah – China – Japan – Egypt –Turkey.* Vol. 12 of *The History and Romance of Crime.* London: Grolier Society, n.d. (c. 1900).
- 'The Practical Treatment of Habitual Crime.' In *Report to the Secretary of State for the Home Department on the Proceedings of the Fourth Congress of Criminal Anthropology, Held at Geneva in 1896*, 29–37. London: Eyre and Spottiswoode, 1896.
- *A Prison Princess: A Romance of Millbank Penitentiary.* London: Cassell and Company, 1893.
- *Secrets of the Prison-House: or, Gaol Studies and Sketches.* 1893. 2 vols. London: Chapman and Hall, 1894.

- *Tales of a Government Official.* London: F.V. White and Company, 1902.
- *Thrice Captive.* London: F.V. White and Company, 1908.
- *The Wellington Memorial: Wellington, His Comrades and Contemporaries.* London: George Allen, 1897.

Griffiths, Arthur, and Anthony Twyford. *Records of York Castle: Fortress, Court House, and Prison.* London: Griffiths and Farran, 1880.

Gronniosaw, James Albert Ukawsaw. *A Narrative of the Most Remarkable Particulars in the Life of James Albert Ukawsaw Gronniosaw, an African Prince, as Related by Himself.* In *Slave Narratives*, ed. William L. Andrews and Henry Louis Gates, Jr, 1–34. New York: Library of America, 2000.

Habermas, Jürgen. *Strukturwandel der Öffentlichkeit: Untersuchungen zu einer Kategorie der bürgerlichen Gesellschaft.* 1961. New ed. Frankfurt am Main: Suhrkamp, 1990. *The Structural Transformation of the Public Sphere: An Inquiry into a Category of Bourgeois Society.* Cambridge, MA: MIT Press, 1989.

Hall, Stuart. 'Cultural Identity and Diaspora.' In *Identity, Community, Culture, Difference*, ed. Jonathan Rutherford, 222–37. London: Lawrence and Wishart, 1990.

Hansen, Olaf. *Aesthetic Individualism and Practical Intellect: American Allegory in Emerson, Thoreau, Adams, and James.* Princeton: Princeton University Press, 1990.

Harding, Christopher, Bill Hines, Richard Ireland, and Philip Rawlings. *Imprisonment in England and Wales: A Concise History.* London: Croom Helm, 1985.

Harding, Christopher, and Richard W. Ireland. *Punishment: Rhetoric, Rule, and Practice.* New York: Routledge, 1989.

Harlow, Barbara. *Barred: Women, Writing, and Political Detention.* Hanover: Wesleyan University Press, 1992.

- *Resistance Literature.* New York: Methuen, 1987.

Haslam, Jason. '"They locked the door on my meditations": Thoreau and the Prison House of Identity.' *Genre: Forms of Discourse and Culture* 35.2 (2002): 449–78.

- 'Discovering Identity in James Tyman's *Inside Out: An Autobiography of a Native Canadian.*' *English Studies in Canada* 26.4 (2000): 473–92.

Hathaway, Heather. '"Maybe Freedom Lies in Hating": Miscegenation and the Oedipal Conflict.' In *Refiguring the Father: New Feminist Readings of the Patriarchy*, ed. Patricia Yaeger and Beth Kowaleski-Wallace, 153–67. Carbondale: Southern Illinois University Press, 1989.

Hekman, Susan. 'Subjects and Agents: The Question for Feminism.' In *Provoking Agents: Gender and Agency in Theory and Practice*, ed. Judith Kegan Gardiner, 194–207. Urbana: University of Illinois Press, 1995.

Henriques, U.R.Q. 'The Rise and Decline of the Separate System of Prison Discipline.' *Past and Present* 54 (February 1972): 61–93.

Herrlinger, Wolfgang. *Sentimentalismus und Postsentimentalismus: Studien zum englischen Roman bis zur Mitte des 19. Jahrhunderts*. Tübingen: Niemeyer, 1987.

Hibbert, Christopher. *The Roots of Evil: A Social History of Crime and Punishment*. London: Weidenfeld and Nicolson, 1963.

Hinds, Elizabeth Jane Wall. 'The Spirit of Trade: Olaudah Equiano's Conversion, Legalism, and the Merchant's Life.' *African American Review* 32.4 (1998), 635–47.

Hirsch, Adam J. *The Rise of the Penitentiary: Prisons and Punishment in Early America*. New Haven: Yale University Press, 1992.

Hirst, P.Q. 'The Concept of Punishment.' In *A Reader on Punishment*, ed. R.A. Duff and David Garland, 264–80. Oxford: Oxford University Press, 1994.

History of the Press-Yard: or, a Brief Account of the Customs and Ocurrences that are Put in Practice, and to be met with in that Antient Repository of Living Bodies, called His Majesty's Gaol of NEWGATE in London. London, 1717.

Hobsbawm, E.J. *Nations and Nationalism since 1780: Programme, Myth, Reality*. Cambridge: Cambridge University Press, 1990.

Hogan, James Francis, ed. *The Convict King: Being the Life and Adventures of Jorgen Jorgenson, Monarch of Iceland, Naval Captain, Revolutionist, British Diplomatic Agent, Author, Dramatist, Preacher, Political Prisoner, Gambler, Hospital Dispenser, Continental Traveller, Explorer, Editor, Expatriated Exile, and Colonial Constable*. London: Ward and Downey, 1891.

Holton, Sandra Stanley. *Suffrage Days: Stories from the Women's Suffrage Movement*. New York: Routledge, 1996.

Home, Henry (Lord Kames). *Sketches of the History of Man*. 1774. 4 vols. Hildesheim: Georg Olms Verlagsbuchhandlung, 1968.

Horkheimer, Max, and Theodor W. Adorno. *Dialektik der Aufklärung: Philosophische Fragmente*. 1944. Frankfurt am Main: S. Fischer, 1969.

Horsman, Reginald. *Race and Manifest Destiny: The Origins of American Racial Anglo-Saxonism*. Cambridge: Harvard University Press, 1981.

Howlett, Caroline J. 'Writing on the Body? Representation and Resistance in British Suffragette Accounts of Forcible Feeding.' In *Bodies of Writing, Bodies in Performance*, ed. Thomas Foster, Carol Siegel, and Ellen E. Berry, 3–41. New York: New York University Press, 1996.

Hume, David. *An Inquiry Concerning the Principles of Morals*. 1751. Ed. Charles W. Hendel. New York: Bobbs-Merrill, 1957.

– 'Of National Characters.' 1742. In *Essays: Moral, Political, and Literary*, ed. Eugene F. Miller, 197–215. Indianapolis: LibertyClassics, 1985.

Ignatieff, Michael. *A Just Measure of Pain: The Penitentiary in the Industrial Revolu-

tion, 1750–1850. New York: Columbia University Press, 1978; New York: Pantheon, 1978.

Ingram, Angela, and Daphne Patai, ed. and intro. *Rediscovering Forgotten Radicals: British Women Writers, 1889–1939.* Chapel Hill: University of North Carolina Press, 1993.

James, Henry. *The Princess Casamassima.* 1886. Ed. Patricia Crick. London: Penguin Books, 1987.

James, Joy. *Resisting State Violence: Radicalism, Gender and Race in US Culture.* Minneapolis: University of Minnesota, 1996.

Jameson, Fredric. *The Political Unconscious: Narrative as a Socially Symbolic Act.* Ithaca: Cornell University Press, 1981.

[Jeffrey, Mark.] *A Burglar's Life: Or, The Stirring Adventures of the Great English Burglar, Mark Jeffrey: A Thrilling History of the Dark Days of Convictism in Australia.* 1893. Ed. W. Hiener and J.E. Hiener. Sydney: Angus and Robertson, 1968.

Joannou, Maroula. 'Suffragette Fiction and the Fictions of Suffrage.' In *The Women's Suffrage Movement: New Feminist Perspectives,* ed. Maroula Joannou and June Purvis, 101–16. Manchester: Manchester University Press, 1998.

Johnson, Barbara. 'Is Female to Male As Ground Is to Figure?' In *Feminism and Psychoanalysis,* ed. Richard Feldstein and Judith Roof, 255–68. Ithaca: Cornell University Press, 1989.

Jones, John. *An Impartial Narrative of the Most Important Engagements Which Took Place Between His Majesty's Forces and the Rebels, During the Irish Rebellion, 1798.* Dublin, 1799.

Kaplan, Caren. 'Resisting Autobiography: Out-Law Genres and Transnational Feminist Subjects.' In *De/Colonizing the Subject: The Politics of Gender in Women's Autobiography,* ed. Sidonie Smith and Julia Watson, 115–38. Minneapolis: University of Minnesota Press, 1992.

Kaplan, Fred. *Sacred Tears: Sentimentality in Victorian Literature.* Princeton: Princeton University Press, 1987.

Karpenstein-Eßbach, Christa. *Einschluß und Imagination: Über den literarischen Umgang mit Gefangenen.* Tübingen: Edition Diskord, 1985.

Kenney, Annie. *A Militant.* Ed. Marie Mulvey Roberts and Tamae Mizuta. London: Routledge/Thoemmes, 1994. Rpt. of *Memories of a Militant,* 1924.

Kent, Susan Kingsley. *Gender and Power in Britain, 1640–1990.* New York: Rowtledge, 1999.

– *Sex and Suffrage in Britain, 1860–1914.* Princeton: Princeton University Press, 1987.

Kingsmill, Joseph. *Chapters on Prisons and Prisoners, and the Prevention of Crime.* 3rd ed. London: Longman, Brown, Green, and Longmans, 1854.

Kitzen, Michael L.S. *Tripoli and the United States at War: A History of American Rela-*

tions with the Barbary States, 1785–1805. Jefferson, NC: McFarland and Co., 1993.

Kolchin, Peter. *Unfree Labor: American Slavery and Russian Serfdom.* Cambridge, Mass.: Belknap Press of Harvard University Press, 1987.

Kristeva, Julia. *Etrangers à nous-mêmes.* Paris: Fayard, 1988.

– *Powers of Horror: An Essay on Abjection.* Trans. Leon Roudiez. New York: Columbia University Press, 1982.

Kucich, Greg. '"The Wit in the Dungeon": Leigh Hunt and the Insolent Politics of Cockney Coteries.' *European Romantic Review* 10 (1999): 242–53.

Kurmacheva, M.D. *Krepostnaia Intelligentsia Rossii: Vtoraia polovina XVII-nachalo XIX veka.* Moscow: Nauka, 1983.

Lauterbach, Frank. 'Textual Errands into the Carceral Wilderness: Fictions of Imprisonment as Narratives of Social Alterity.' In *In the Grip of the Law: Prisons, Trials, and the Space Between*, ed. Monika Fludernik and Greta Olson. Frankfurt am Main: Peter Lang, 2004.

Lefanu, Alicia. *Tales of a Tourist, Containing The Outlaw and Fashionable Connexions.* 4 vols. London: A.K. Newman and Company, 1823.

Leighton, Marie C., and Robert Leighton. *Convict 99: A True Story of Penal Servitude.* London: Grant Richards, 1898.

'A Letter from a Convict in Australia to a Brother in England.' *Cornhill Magazine* 13.5 (May 1866): 489–512.

Levinas, Emmanuel. *Totalité et infini: Essai sur l'exteriorité.* Phaenomenologica 8. La Haye: M. Nijhoff, 1961.

Lewis, Jane, ed. *Before the Vote Was Won: Arguments for and against Women's Suffrage.* New York: Routledge and Kegan Paul, 1987.

Lewis, Orlando F. *The Development of American Prisons and Prison Customs, 1776–1845: With Special Reference to Early Institutions in the State of New York.* Albany: Prison Association of New York, 1922; Montclair: Patterson Smith, 1967.

Liddington, Jill. *The Long Road to Greenham: Feminism and Anti-Militarism in Britain since 1820.* London: Virago, 1989.

Lillo, George. *The London Merchant; or, The History of George Barnwell.* 1731. In *The Beggar's Opera and Other Eighteenth-Century Plays*, ed. David W. Lindsay, 259–326. London: Dent, 1993.

Lilly, W.S. 'Griffiths' Secrets of the Prison House.' *Nineteenth Century* (February 1894): 234.

Lloyd, David, and Paul Thomas. *Culture and the State.* New York: Routledge, 1998.

Lovelace, Sir Richard. 'To Althea, from Prison.' In *The Collected Works of Sir Richard Lovelace*, 78–9. Oxford: Oxford University Press, 1963.

Lukács, Georg. *The Historical Novel*, trans. Hannah and Stanley Mitchell, intro. Fredric Jameson. Lincoln: University of Nebraska Press, 1983.

Lytton, Constance. Letter to Mr Broadbent, 10 January 1908. Folded into British Library's copy of *Marah*, by Owen Meredith (Robert Bulwer-Lytton). 3rd ed. London: Longmans, 1893.
- *'No Votes for Women': A Reply to Some Recent Anti-Suffrage Publications.* London: A.C. Fifield, 1909.
- *Prisons and Prisoners: Some Personal Experiences.* London: William Heinemann, 1914.

MacKay, John. '"And Hold the Bondman Still": Biogeography and Utopia in Slave and Serf Narratives.' *Biography* 25.1 (Winter 2002): 110–29.

Mackenzie, Peter. *The Life of Thomas Muir ... Who was Tried for Sedition before the High Court of Justiciary in Scotland, and Sentenced to Transportation for Fourteen Years, with a Full Report of his Trial.* Glasgow: W.R. M'Phun, Trongate, 1831.

Markley, Robert. 'Sentimentality as Performance: Shaftesbury, Sterne, and the Theatrics of Virtue.' In *The New Eighteenth Century: Theory, Politics, English Literature,* ed. Felicity Nussbaum and Laura Brown, 210–30. London: Methuen, 1987.

Marlow, Joyce, ed. *Votes for Women: The Virago Book of Suffragettes.* London: Virago, 2000.

Marrant, John. *A Narrative of the Lord's Wonderful Dealings with John Marrant.* 1785. In *American Captivity Narratives,* ed. and intro. Gordon M. Sayre, 203–24. Boston: Houghton Mifflin, 2000.

Mason, Mary G. 'The Other Voice: Autobiographies of Women Writers.' In *Life/Lines: Theorizing Women's Autobiographies,* ed. Bella Brodzki and Celeste Schenk, 19–44. Ithaca: Cornell University Press, 1988.

The Matron of Erin: A National Tale. London: Simpkin and Marshall, 1816.

Mayhew, Henry, and John Binny. *The Criminal Prisons of London and Scenes of Prison Life.* London: Griffin, Bohn, 1862; London: Frank Cass, 1971.

McBride, Dwight. *Impossible Witnesses: Truth, Abolitionism, and Slave Testimony.* New York: New York University Press, 2001.

McCalman, Iain. 'Newgate in Revolution: Radical Enthusiasm and Romantic Counterculture.' *Eighteenth-Century Life* 22 (1998): 95–110.

McConville, Seán. 'Chapter Five: The Victorian Prison, England, 1865–1965.' In *The Oxford History of the Prison: The Practice of Punishment in Western Society,* ed. Norval Morris and David J. Rothman, 131–67. Oxford: Oxford University Press, 1995.

McDonald, Peter D. *British Literary Culture and Publishing Practice, 1880–1914.* Cambridge: Cambridge University Press, 1997.

McMurty, R. Gerald. 'The Influence of *Riley's Narrative* upon Abraham Lincoln.' *Indiana Magazine of History* 30 (June 1934): 133–8.

Melossi, Dario, and Massimo Pavarini. *Carcere e fabbrica: Alle origini del sistema penitenziario (XVI–XIX secolo)*. Quaderni della rivista *La questione criminale* 1. Bologna: Società editrice il Mulino, 1977.

Memoirs of Jane Cameron, Female Convict. By a Prison Matron, Author of 'Female Life in Prison.' 2 vols. London: Hurst and Blackett, 1864.

Meyer, Michael. *Several More Lives to Live: Thoreau's Political Reputation in America*. Contributions in American Studies 29. Westport, CT: Greenwood, 1977.

Miller, D.A. *The Novel and the Police*. Berkeley: University of California Press, 1988.

'Miscegenation: The Theory of the Blending of the Races Applied to the American White Man and Negro.' New York: H. Dexter, Hamilton, and Company, 1864.

More, Sir Thomas. *A Dialogue of Comfort against Tribulation*. 1534. Vol. 12 of *The Yale Edition of the Complete Works of St. Thomas More*, ed. Louis L. Martz and Frank Manley. New Haven: Yale University Press, 1976.

Mullan, John. *Sentiment and Sociability: The Language of Feeling in the Eighteenth Century*. Oxford: Clarendon Press, 1988.

Mulvey-Roberts, Marie. 'Militancy, Masochism, or Martyrdom? The Public and Private Prisons of Constance Lytton.' In *Votes for Women*, ed. June Purvis and Sandra Stanley Holton, 159–80. London: Routledge, 2000.

Myall, Michelle. '"No Surrender!": The Militancy of Mary Leigh, a Working-Class Suffragette.' In *The Women's Suffrage Movement: New Feminist Perspectives*, ed. Maroula Joannou and June Purvis, 173–87. Manchester: Manchester University Press, 1998.

Nairn, Tom. *Faces of Nationalism: Janus Revisited*. New York: Verso, 1997.

Neale, Erskine. 'The Gaol Chaplain.' *Bentley's Miscellany* 13 (1843)–19 (1846).

News about Russia. Vesti o Rossii: Povest' v stikhakh krepostnogo kres'ianina. Ed. T.G. Snytko. Iaroslavl': Iaroslavskoe knizhnoe izdatel'stvo, 1961. MS in the State Archive of the Russian Federation (GARF), archive 109, file 100, 1850.

Newton, Judith. 'Engendering History for the Middle Class: Sex and Political Economy in the *Edinburgh Review*.' In *Rewriting the Victorians: Theory, History, and the Politics of Gender*, ed. Linda M. Shires, 1–17. New York: Routledge, 1992.

'Nineteenth-Century Reformism: A Discussion.' In *Humanitarianism or Control? A Symposium on Aspects of Nineteenth-Century Social Reform in Britain and America*, ed. Martin J. Wiener. Special issue of *Rice University Studies* 67.1 (Winter 1981): 75–84.

[No. 7]. *Twenty-Five Years in Seventeen Prisons: The Life-Story of an Ex-Convict: With His Impressions of Our Prison System: By 'No. 7.'* London: F.E. Robinson, 1903.

Norquay, Glenda, ed. *Voices and Votes: A Literary Anthology of the Women's Suffrage Campaign*. Manchester: Manchester University Press, 1995.

Norris, Anna. *L'écriture du Défi: Textes Carcéreaux Feminins du XIXe et du XXe Siècles.* Birmingham, Ala.: Summa Publications, 2003.
'Of a National Character in Literature.' *Blackwood's Edinburgh Magazine* 3 (September 1818): 707–9.
Ogude, S.E. 'Facts into Fiction: Equiano's *Narrative* Reconsidered.' *Research in African Literatures* 13 (1982): 31–43.
Olney, James. '"I Was Born:" Slave Narratives, Their Status as Autobiography, and as Literature.' In *The Slave's Narrative*, ed. Charles T. Davis and Henry Louis Gates, Jr, 148–62. New York: Oxford University Press, 1985.
[One Who Has Endured It]. *Five Years' Penal Servitude: By One Who Has Endured It.* London: Richard Bentley and Son, 1877.
[One Who Has Tried Them]. *Her Majesty's Prisons: Their Effects and Defects: By One Who Has Tried Them.* Vol. 1. London: Sampson Low, Marston, Searle, and Rivington, 1881.
[One Who Has Suffered It]. 'Concerning Imprisonment.' *Hibbert Journal* 8.3 (April 1910): 582–602.
Owenson, Sydney (Lady Morgan). *Woman; Or, Ida of Athens.* 4 vols. London: Longman, Hurst, Rees, and Orme, 1809.
– *The O'Briens and the O'Flahertys.* 1827. London: Pandora Press, 1988.
Paine, Thomas. *Rights of Man.* 1791–2. Ed. Henry Collins. Markham, ON: Penguin, 1983.
Parker, Andrew, and Eve Kosofsky Sedgwick, eds. *Performativity and Performance.* New York: Routledge, 1995.
Patterson, Orlando. *Slavery and Social Death: A Comparative Study.* Cambridge: Harvard University Press, 1982.
Pellico, Silvio. *My Prisons.* 1868. Boston: Roberts Brothers, 1970.
Pethick-Lawrence, Emmeline. *My Part in a Changing World.* London: Victor Gollancz, 1938.
Potkay, Adam. 'History, Oratory, and God in Equiano's *Interesting Narrative.*' *Eighteenth-Century Studies* 34.4 (2001): 601–14.
Pratt, Mary Louise. *Imperial Eyes: Travel Writing and Transculturation.* New York: Routledge, 1992.
Priestley, Philip. *Victorian Prison Lives: English Prison Biography, 1830–1914.* 1985. New ed. London: Pimlico, 1999.
Public Record Office: Current Guide. 3 vols. London: Public Record Office, 1994.
Purvis, June. 'The Prison Experiences of the Suffragettes in Edwardian Britain.' *Women's History Review* 4.1 (1995): 103–33.
Raboteau, Albert J. *Slave Religion: The 'Invisible Institution' in the Antebellum South.* Oxford: Oxford University Press, 1978.
Radzinowicz, Leon. *A History of English Criminal Law and Its Administration from*

1750. Vol. 1: *The Movement for Reform*. Foreword Lord Macmillan. London: Stevens and Sons, 1948.

Rafter, Nicole Hahn. *Partial Justice: Women, Prisons, and Social Control*. 2nd ed. New Brunswick, NJ: Transaction, 1990.

Rajan, Tilottama. 'Autonarration and Genotext in Mary Hays' *Memoirs of Emma Courtney*.' *Studies in Romanticism* 32.2 (Summer 1993): 149–76.

Reade, Charles. *It Is Never Too Late To Mend*. London: Collins, 1856.

'Reminiscences of Prison Life.' *Blackwood's Edinburgh Magazine* 130.1 [=789] (July 1881): 21–35.

Renan, Ernest. 'What is a Nation?' Trans. Martin Thom. In *Nation and Narration*, ed. Homi K. Bhabha, 8–22. New York: Routledge, 1990.

Review of *An Authentic Narrative of the Loss of the American Brig Commerce ... with an Account of the Sufferings of her Surviving Crew ...* In *North American Review* 5 (1817): 389–409.

Review of *An Authentic Narrative of the Loss of the American Brig Commerce ... with an Account of the Sufferings of her Surviving Crew ...* In *Quarterly Review* 16 (1817): 287–321.

Review of Griffiths's *Chronicles*. In *Spectator* (23 February 1884): 257–8.

Review of Griffiths's *Chronicles*. In *The Times* (28 December 1883): 5b.

Review of Griffiths's *Secrets*. In *Athenaeum* (January 1894): 41.

Review of Griffiths's *Secrets*. In *Blackwood's Magazine* (January 1894): 123.

Review of Griffiths's *Secrets*. In *Daily Chronicle* (27 November 1893): 3c.

Review of Griffiths's *Secrets*. In *The Times* (17 November 1893): 3a.

Riley, James. *An Authentic Narrative of the Loss of the American Brig Commerce ... with an Account of the Sufferings of her Surviving Crew ...* New York: T. and W. Mercein, 1817. Rpt. New York: Clarkson N. Potter, 1965.

Rosen, Andrew. *Rise Up, Women! The Militant Campaign of the Women's Social and Political Union 1903–1914*. London: Routledge and Kegan Paul, 1974.

Rousseau, Jean-Jacques. *Confessions*, trans. Angela Scholar, ed. and intro. Patrick Coleman. Oxford: Oxford University Press, 2000.

Rowson, Susana H. *Slaves in Algiers*. Philadelphia: Wrigley and Berriman, 1794.

Rusche, Georg, and Otto Kirchheimer. *Punishment and Social Structure*. Foreword Thorsten Sellin. New York: Columbia University Press, 1939.

Rust, Marion. 'Speaking of Olaudah Equiano.' In *Passing and the Fictions of Identity*, ed. Elaine K. Ginsberg, 21–36. Durham, NC: Duke University Press, 1996.

Rychkov, Petr Ivanovich. 'Zapiski' ['Notes']. CA. 1774.

Sahlins, Marshall. *Culture and Practical Reason*. Chicago: University of Chicago Press, 1976.

Said, Edward W. *Orientalism*. 1978. New York: Vintage Books, 1979.

Samuels, Shirley. 'Miscegenated America: The Civil War.' *American Literary History* 9 (1997): 482–501.
Samuels, Wilfred D. 'Disguised Voice in *The Interesting Narrative of Olaudah Equiano or Gustavus Vassa, the African.*' *Black American Literature Forum* 19.2 (1985): 64–9.
Sartre, Jean-Paul. *Search for a Method.* Trans. and intro. Hazel E. Barnes. New York: Knopf, 1963.
Sayre, Gordon M. Introduction to *Olaudah Equiano, Mary Rowlandson, and Others: American Captivity Narratives,* ed. Gordon M. Sayre. Boston: Houghton Mifflin, 2000.
Scheffler, Judith. 'Romantic Women Writing on Imprisonment and Prison Reform.' *Wordsworth Circle* 19 (1988): 99–103.
Schmücker, Alois. 'Anfänge und erste Entwicklung der Autobiographie in Russland (1760–1830).' In *Die Autobiographie: Zu Form und Geschichte einer literarischen Gattung,* ed. Günter Niggl, Darmstadt: Wissenschaftliche Buchgesellschaft, 1998. 414–58.
Scougal, Francis. *Scenes from a Silent World: Or, Prisons and Their Inmates.* Edinburgh: William Blackwood and Sons, 1889; New York: Garland, 1984.
Sellin, J. Thorsten. *Slavery and the Penal System.* New York: Elsevier, 1976.
S[haw], D[onald]. *Eighteen Months' Imprisonment.* London: Routledge and Sons, 1883.
Shelley, Percy Bysshe. *Shelley's Poetry and Prose,* ed. Donald H. Reiman and Sharon B. Powers. New York: Norton, 1977.
Shipov, Nikolai. 'Istoriia moei zhizni: Razskaz byshago krepostnago krest'ianina N.N. Shipova.' *Russkaia Starina* 30 (1881).
Simon, Bruce. 'Introduction: The Prison Issue.' *Workplace: A Journal for Academic Labor* 3.2 (December 2000). http://www.louisville.edu/journal/workplace/issue6/prisonintro.html.
Simon, Jonathan. 'Discipline and Punish: The Birth of a Postmodern Middle-Range.' In *Required Reading: Sociology's Most Influential Books,* ed. Dan Clawson, 47–54. Amherst: University of Massachusetts Press, 1998.
Sloop, John M. *The Cultural Prison: Discourse, Prisoners, and Punishment.* Tuscaloosa: University of Alabama Press, 1996.
Smirnov, Nikolai. 'Avtobiografiia krespostnogo intelligenta kontsa 18-ogo veka.' *Istoricheskii arkhiv* 5. Ed. K.V. Sivkov, 288–99. Leningrad: Izdatel'stvo Akademii Nauk SSSR, 1950.
Smith, Adam. *The Theory of Moral Sentiments.* 1759. London: Bohn, 1853; rpt. New York: Kelley, 1966.
Smith, Anthony D. *National Identity.* Rpt. Reno: University of Nevada Press, 1991.
– 'Neo-Classicist and Romantic Elements in the Emergence of Nationalist Con-

ceptions.' In *Nationalist Movements*, ed. Anthony D. Smith, 74–87. London: Macmillan, 1976.
– *Theories of Nationalism*. 1971. 2nd ed. London Duckworth, 1983.
Smith, Paul. *Discerning the Subject*. Intro. John Mowitt. Minneapolis: University of Minnesota Press, 1988.
Smith, Sidonie. 'Performativity, Autobiographical Practice, Resistance.' In *Women, Autobiography, Theory: A Reader*, ed. Sidonie Smith and Julia Watson, 108–15. Madison: University of Wisconsin Press, 1998.
– 'Resisting the Gaze of Embodiment: Women's Autobiography in the Nineteenth Century.' In *American Women's Autobiography: Fea(s)ts of Memory*, ed. Margo Culley. Madison: University of Wisconsin Press, 1992.
– *Subjectivity, Identity, and the Body: Women's Autobiographical Practices in the Twentieth Century*. Bloomington: Indiana University Press, 1993.
Smith-Rosenberg, Carroll. 'Captured Subjects/Savage Others: Violently Engendering the New American.' *Gender and History* 5 (1993): 177–95.
Smyth, Jim, ed. *Revolution, Counter-Revolution, and Union: Ireland in the 1790s*. Cambridge: Cambridge University Press, 2001.
Snader, Joe. 'The Oriental Captivity Narrative and Early English Fiction.' *Eighteenth-Century Fiction* 9.3 (April 1997): 267–98.
Sollors, Werner. 'Ethnicity.' In *Critical Terms for Literary Study*. 1990. Ed. Frank Lentricchia and Thomas McLaughlin, 288–305. 2nd ed. Chicago: University of Chicago Press, 1995.
Spillers, Hortense. 'Mama's Baby, Papa's Maybe: An American Grammar Book.' In *An Anthology of African American Criticism from the Harlem Renaissance to the Present*, ed. Angelyn Mitchell, 454–81. Durham, NC: Duke University Press, 1994.
Starr, G.A. 'Escape from Barbary: A Seventeenth-Century Genre.' *Huntington Library Quarterly* 29 (1968): 35–52.
Stendhal, Henri [Beyle]. *The Charterhouse of Parma*. 1839. Trans. Margaret R.B. Shaw. London: Penguin, 1958.
Sterne, Laurence. *A Sentimental Journey through France and Italy by Mr. Yorick*. 1768. Ed. Ian Jack. Oxford: Oxford University Press, 1984.
Stirling, Edward. *Margaret Catchpole, the Heroine of Suffolk: or, The Vicissitudes of Gaol Life*. 1855. London, 1885.
Stokes, John. *In the Nineties*. London: Harvester Wheatsheaf, 1989.
'The Story of the Liberator Crash: With Some Account of the Career and Character of Jabez Spencer Balfour.' Special issue of *'Westminster Gazette' Popular* 5 (November 1893).
Stowe, Harriet Beecher. *Uncle Tom's Cabin*. 1851–2. New York: Bantam, 1981.
'Suffragist or Suffragette?' *Suffragette*, 1 May 1914: 55–6.

Teeling, Charles Hamilton. '*History of the Irish Rebellion of 1798*' and '*Sequel to the History of the Irish Rebellion of 1798.*' Intro. Richard Grenfell Morton. Shannon: Irish University Press, 1972.
- *Observations on the History and Consequences of the 'Battle of the Diamond.'* Belfast: John Hodgson, 1838.
- *Personal Narrative of the Irish Rebellion of 1798.* London: Henry Colburn, 1828.
- *Sequel to Personal Narrative of the Irish Rebellion of 1798.* Belfast: John Hodgson, 1832.

Thelwall, John. 'Stanzas on Hearing for Certainty that We Were to be Tried for High Treason.' In *Romanticism: An Anthology*, ed. Duncan Wu, 161. 2nd ed. Oxford: Blackwell, 1998.

Therborn, Göran. *The Ideology of Power and the Power of Ideology.* London: Verso, 1980.

Thomas, Sue. 'Scenes in the Writing of "Constance Lytton and Jane Warton, Spinster": Contextualising a Cross-Class Dresser.' *Women's History Review* 12.1 (2003): 51–71.

Thoreau, Henry David. 'Resistance to Civil Government' ('Civil Disobedience'). In *Reform Papers*, ed. Wendell Glick, 63–90. Princeton: Princeton University Press, 1973.

Thuente, Mary Helen. *The Harp Re-Strung: The United Irishmen and the Rise of Irish Literary Nationalism.* Syracuse: Syracuse University Press, 1994.

[Ticket-of-Leave Man]. *Convict Life: Or, Revelations concerning Convicts and Convict Prisons: By a Ticket-of-Leave Man.* 2nd ed. London: Wyman and Sons, 1879.

Tickner, Lisa. *The Spectacle of Women: Imagery and the Suffrage Campaign 1907–14.* Chicago: University of Chicago Press, 1988.

Todd, Janet. *Sensibility: An Introduction.* New York: Methuen, 1986.

Trotter, David. *Cooking with Mud: The Idea of Mess in Nineteenth-Century Art and Fiction.* Oxford: Oxford University Press, 2000.

Trumpener, Katie. *Bardic Nationalism: The Romantic Novel and the British Empire.* Princeton: Princeton University Press, 1997.

Turk, Horst. 'Alienität und Alterität als Schlüsselbegriffe einer Kultursemantik.' *Jahrbuch für Internationale Germanistik* 22.1 (1990): 8–31.

Twelve Months Imprisonment of a Manchester Merchant in a Kirkdale Gaol: His Experience of Prison and Prisoners. With Suggestions of Improvement in Prison Discipline. Manchester: Abel Heywood, 1880.

'Twenty Years' Penal Servitude.' *Chambers's Journal of Popular Literature, Science, and Art.* 4th series 200 (26 October 1867): 673–8.

Tyler, Royall. *The Algerine Captive.* 1797. New Haven: College and University Press, 1970.

United Kingdom. Departments of States and Official Bodies, Home Office. 'Suf-

fragist Women Prisoners.' 18 December 1909. *Home Office Papers and Memoranda*, 1889–1910.
VanDerBeets, Richard. 'A Surfeit of Style: The Indian Captivity Narrative as Penny Dreadful.' *Research Studies* 39 (1971): 297–306.
van Sant, Ann Jessie. *Eighteenth-Century Sensibility and the Novel: The Senses in Social Context.* Cambridge: Cambridge University Press, 1993.
Vasilieva, M.E. 'Zapiski krepostnoi.' *Russkaia Starina* 145 (1911): 140–51. 'Notes of a Serf Woman by M.E. Vasilieva.' Ed. and trans. John MacKay. *Slavery and Abolition* 21.1 (April 2000): 146–68.
'Views and Comments.' *Egoist: An Individualist Review* 10.1 (15 May 1914): 182–5.
Wall, Charles. 'The Condemned Cells.' *Fraser's Magazine* 22 (1840)–24 (1841).
Walvin, James. *Black and White: The Negro and English Society 1555–1945.* London: Penguin, 1973.
Ward, Julia K. 'The Master's Tools: Abolitionist Arguments of Equiano and Cugoano.' In *Subjugation and Bondage: Critical Essays on Slavery and Social Philosophy*, ed. Tommy L. Lott, 79–98. New York: Rowman and Littlefield, 1998.
Waters, Chris. *British Socialists and the Politics of Popular Culture, 1884–1914.* Manchester: Manchester University Press, 1990.
Webb, Sidney, and Beatrice Webb. *English Prisons under Local Government.* Pref. Bernard Shaw. English Local Government 6. London: Longmans, Green and Co., 1922.
Weigel, Sigrid. *Und selbst im Kerker frei! Schreiben im Gefängnis.* Marburg/Lahn: Guttandin und Hoppe, 1982.
Weitling, Wilhelm. *Gerechtigkeit. Ein Studium in 500 Tagen.* Kiel: Mühlan, 1929.
Whelan, Kevin. 'The United Irishmen, the Enlightenment and Popular Culture.' In *The United Irishmen: Republicanism, Radicalism and Rebellion*, ed. David Dickson, Dáire Keough, and Kevin Whelan, 269–96. Dublin: Lilliput Press, 1993.
Wiener, Martin J. *Reconstructing the Criminal: Culture, Law, and Policy in England, 1830–1914.* Cambridge: Cambridge University Press, 1990.
Wilde, Oscar. Letter to the editor of *Daily Chronicle.* 28 May 1897. In *Complete Works of Oscar Wilde.* Glasgow: HarperCollins, 1994.
Williams, Carolyn D. 'Another Self in the Case: Gender, Marriage and the Individual in Augustan Literature.' In *Rewriting the Self: Histories from the Renaissance to the Present*, ed. Roy Porter, 97–118. London: Routledge, 1997.
Witt, Mary Ann Frese. *Existential Prisons: Captivity in Mid-Twentieth-Century French Literature.* Durham, NC: Duke University Press, 1985.
Wollstonecraft, Mary. Rev. of *The Interesting Narrative.* Rpt. in *The Interesting Narrative of the Life of Olaudah Equiano*, ed. Angelo Costanzo, 262–3. Peterborough, ON: Broadview Press, 2001.

Wright, Julia M. 'Courting Public Opinion: Handling Informers in the 1790s.' *Éire-Ireland* 33 (1997–8): 144–69.
- '"The Nation Begins to Form": Competing Nationalisms in Morgan's *The O'Briens and the O'Flahertys*.' *ELH* 66 (1999): 939–63.

Yonge, Charlotte M. *The Trial; or, More Links of the Daisy Chain*. 1864. London: Macmillan, 1902.

Contributors

Jennifer Costello Brezina received her Ph.D. from the University of California at Riverside and is currently an Associate Professor of English at College of the Canyons. Her previous work examines how women use public space in American urban novels at the turn of the twentieth century, challenging the traditional paradigm of gendered space.

Tess Chakkalakal is Assistant Professor of African American Literature in the English Department at Williams College. She is currently completing a book entitled *The Uncle Tom Trade: Fictions of the Black Home in 19th-Century America*.

Monika Fludernik is Professor of English Literature at the University of Freiburg, Germany. She is the author of *The Fictions of Language and the Language of Fiction* (Routledge, 1993), *Towards a 'Natural' Narratology* (Routledge, 1996), which was awarded the Perkins Prize by the Society for the Study of Narrative Literature, and *Echoes and Mirrorings: Gabriel Josipovici's Creative Oeuvre* (Peter Lang, 2000). Fludernik has edited several collections of essays, among these *Hybridity and Postcolonialism: Twentieth-Century Indian Literature* (Stauffenberg, 1998) and *Diaspora and Multiculturalism* (Rodopi, 2003).

Jason Haslam is Assistant Professor of English at Dalhousie University. He has written widely on US culture and prison writing, and is the author of several articles that appear or are forthcoming in such journals as *English Studies in Canada*, *Genre*, *Gothic Studies*, and *Modern Language Studies*. He is the author of *Fitting Sentences: Identity in Nineteenth- and Twentieth-Century Prison Narratives* (University of

Toronto Press, forthcoming) and is completing an edition of Constance Lytton's *Prisons and Prisoners* for Broadview Press.

Frank Lauterbach is lecturer for English, Spanish, and Comparative Literature at Georg-August-University, Göttingen, Germany. His research focuses on prison writing, urban literature, the British novel of the eighteenth and nineteenth centuries, nation-building and cultural identity in the United States and Spanish America, and Chicano literature. He has coedited a collection of essays on the formation of cultural identities in Europe and the Americas, and has published articles on early US- and Spanish-American prose and poetry, nineteenth-century British travel writing, Charles Dickens, Raymond Williams, Juan Boscán, and Andrés Bello.

John MacKay is Assistant Professor of Slavic Languages and Literatures at Yale University. He received his Ph.D. from Yale's Comparative Literature department, and has published essays on serf and slave narratives, on representations of the Holocaust, and on silent cinema. Currently he is working on a comparative study of the literatures of US slavery and Russian serfdom, and on a critical biography of the Soviet documentary filmmaker Dziga Vertov.

Christine Marlin is Chair in Literature at Our Lady Seat of Wisdom Academy in Barry's Bay, Ontario. She has taught at the University of the United Arab Emirates, Carleton University, and Bullingdon Prison, Oxford. Her publications include 'A Passing Enchantment: George Eliot's Response to Catholicism' (*Allen Review*, 1997) and a book for children, *Pamela Walks the Dog* (Bethlehem Books, 2001).

Julia M. Wright is Canada Research Chair in European Studies at Dalhousie University, and specializes in nineteenth-century British and Irish literature. She is the author of *Blake, Nationalism, and the Politics of Alienation* (Ohio University Press, 2003) and over twenty essays in various journals and essay collections, the editor of *The Missionary: An Indian Tale* by Sydney Owenson, Lady Morgan (Broadview, 2002), and the coeditor of *Romanticism, History, and the Possibilities of Genre* (Cambridge University Press, 1998) and *Nervous Reactions: Victorian Recollections of Romanticism* (SUNY Press, 2004).

Index

Adorno, Theodor W., 115
Althusser, Louis, 11
Anderson, Benedict, 15, 18n4, 134, 143n93, 195, 210
Andrews, William L., 81–2n14, 83n21
Arnold, Matthew, 9
Auburn system, 7, 140n54
Augustine, 57
Austin, J.L., 94, 109n23

Babington, Anthony, 136n4
Baepler, Paul, 212, 216
Bakhtin, Mikhail, 57–60, 81n12
Baldry, W. Burton, 50n12, 51n21
Balfour, Jabez Spencer, 113–15, 119–20, 136n2, 153, 156–7
Banim, Michael, 176
Barrington, Jonah, 176
Bender, John, 141–2n66, 145, 171n5
Bentham, Jeremy, 6, 134, 143n92, 154, 192
Bhabha, Homi K., 195n17
Billington-Grieg, Teresa, 45–6, 55–6n57

Bibb, Henry, 68, 72, 81
Binny, John, 133
Blathwayt, Raymond, 236
Boethius, 44, 144
Bolotov, Andrei Timofeevich, 82n18
Brocklehurst, F., 156, 172n23
Brombert, Victor, 45, 118, 144–6, 169, 182–3
Bulwer-Lytton, Edward, 28, 229
Bulwer-Lytton, Robert, 52n23
Bulwer-Lytton, Victor, 28
Burgett, Bruce, 10
Burke, Kenneth, 82n15
Butler, Judith, 54n42

Caldwell, Tanya, 89
Carlyle, Thomas, 133
Carnochan, W.B., 118
Carpenter, Edward, 236
Carretta, Vincent, 87, 103–4, 106n1, 108n18, 109nn24, 30
Castiglia, Christopher, 3, 11, 18, 196n34

Index

Castlereagh, Lord (Robert Stewart), 177, 185–6, 188, 194n13
Cathcart, James, 210–11
Catherine the Great, 84n31
Charles d'Orléans, 144
Chesterton, George Laval, 133
Churchill, Winston, 37
Coleman, Deirdre, 20n19
Colmore, Gertrude, 49n10
'A Convict's Views of Penal Discipline,' 122
Corbett, Mary Jean, 32, 43, 45–6
Craft, William, 80
Crawford, William, 140n54
Cullen, Susanna, 103, 105, 109n34
Curran, John Philpot, 191–2, 194n10

Davies, Ioan, 7, 118, 138n28, 197n42
Davis, Angela Y., 5–7, 19nn5–8
Davis, David Brion, 135
Davis, Philip, 171n10
Davitt, Michael, 236
Deane, Seamus, 179
de Beaumont, Gustave, 7, 140n54
Defoe, Daniel, 160
Delany, Samuel R., 18
de Man, Paul, 81n1
Desnitski, Semyon, 64
de Tocqueville, Alexis, 7, 140n54
Dickens, Charles, 149–50, 152, 157–61, 165–6, 169, 220, 229, 231
Dixon, William Hepworth, 133
Douglass, Frederick, 68, 72–3, 80–1
Drennan, William, 179, 181, 194n10, 196n31
DuBois, W.E.B., 92
Du Cane, Sir Edmund F., 133, 222–4, 235–6, 237n8
Dunlop, Mary Wallace, 37

Edwards, Paul, 87
Edgeworth, Maria, 188
Elliott, Marianne, 194n10, 197n36
Ellmann, Maud, 54–5n48
Equiano, Olaudah, 14–15, 72, 86–106, 108nn16, 18, 109nn24, 29, 30, 34
Eriksson, Torsten, 115
Ernest, John, 63
Eustance, Clare, 55n57
Evans, Robin, 137n10
Everett, David, 212

Felman, Shoshana, 42, 46
Felski, Rita, 44, 55n54, 56n63
Fenians, 119, 127–8, 156
Fichtelberg, Joseph, 108n16
Field, Daniel, 83nn24, 28
Fielding, Sarah, 147
Fielding, Henry, 171n5
Fludernik, Monika, 141n59, 142n66, 231
Forsythe, William, 226
Foucault, Michel, 3, 5–7, 25, 35–6, 49n6, 115, 133–4, 145, 171n5, 221
Franklin, Benjamin, 212–13
Franklin, H. Bruce, 3–4, 6–7, 18n2, 124, 138n17
Friedman, Susan Stanford, 48
Fry, Elizabeth, 194n7
Frye, Northrop, 58
Fugitive Slave Act (1850), 68
Furstenberg, François, 210

Gagnier, Regenia, 46
Gardiner, Judith Kegan, 56n57
Gates, Henry Louis, Jr, 88
Gee, Joshua, 205, 212
Gellner, Ernest, 19n4, 195n16
Gilman, Charlotte Perkins, 53n35

Gilmartin, Kevin, 175
Gilroy, Paul, 86
Godwin, William, 155, 197n34
Goldsmith, Oliver, 147
Golitsyn, Andrei Mikhailovich, 64
Gramsci, Antonio, 11
Green, Barbara, 27–8, 35–6, 39, 46, 49n10
Griffiths, Arthur, 16–17, 221–39
Gronniosaw, James Albert Ukawsaw, 84n35

Habermas, Jürgen, 10, 130
Hall, Stuart, 86
Harlow, Barbara, 7–8, 10
Haslam, Jason, 6–7, 140n52, 237n7
Hekman, Susan, 29
Henriques, U.R.Q., 136n4
Hibbert, Christopher, 115
Hinds, Elizabeth Jane Wall, 89
Hirsch, Adam J., 6
Hirst, P.Q., 48n1
Hobsbawm, E.J., 195n16
Hogan, James Francis, 132
Home, Henry (Lord Kames), 180–1, 186
Horkheimer, Max, 115
Horsman, Reginald, 140n51
Howard, John, 225
Howlett, Caroline J., 37–8, 40, 43, 46, 51n22
Hume, David, 180–1, 192
Hunt, Leigh, 175, 182

Ignatieff, Michael, 137n10, 145, 171n5
Insurrection Act (1796), 187–8

Jacobs, Harriet, 80
James, Henry, 220–1

James, Joy, 5–6
Jameson, Fredric, 58
Jefferson, Thomas, 202–4
Jeffrey, Mark, 139n41
Joannou, Maroula, 27, 53n37
Johnson, Barbara, 12
Johnson, Samuel, 100
Jones, John, 188
Jorgenson, Jorgen, 120, 132
Julius, Nicolaus Heinreich, 140n54

Kaplan, Caren, 44
Karpenstein-Eßbach, Christa, 118
Kenney, Annie, 29, 51n17
Kent, Susan Kingsley, 53n35
Kimberley Commission (1879), 129–30
Kingsmill, Joseph, 133
Kirchheimer, Otto, 116
Kolchin, Peter, 83n24
Kristeva, Julia, 8, 126

Lauterbach, Frank, 137–8n16, 146, 149–50
Lefanu, Alicia, 176, 191
Leighton, Marie C., 131, 166
Leighton, Robert, 131, 166
'A Letter from a Convict,' 121–2, 129, 131–2
Levinas, Emmanuel, 126
Lewis, Orlando F., 7, 140n54
Lillo, George, 166
Lincoln, Abraham, 213
Lloyd, David, 9
London Corresponding Society, 175, 182
Long, Edward, 96
Lovelace, Sir Richard, 144
Lukács, Georg, 81n4
Lytton, Constance, 12–14, 25–56

Mackenzie, Henry, 147
Marsden, Dora, 52n31
Mason, Mary G., 43–4
The Matron of Erin, 181
Mayhew, Henry, 123, 133
McBride, Dwight, 87
McCalman, Iain, 175, 197n34
McConville, Seán, 235
Melossi, Dario, 116
Memoirs of Jane Cameron, 165–6
'Miscegenation,' 108n20
Mondelet, Dominique, 140n54
Moore, Thomas, 175–6
More, Sir Thomas, 144
Muir, Thomas, 8
Mulvey-Roberts, Marie, 34–5, 41, 47, 52n26, 54n46, 55n48, 56n70
Myall, Michelle, 53n37

National Union of Women's Suffrage Societies, 49n10
Neale, Erskine, 163–5
Neilson, John, 140n54
Nicholas I, 76, 83n24
'No. 7,' 113, 115, 120, 123–5, 127–9, 135
Norquay, Glenda, 28, 51n15

Ocean's Eleven, 3
Ogude, S.E., 87
Olney, James, 88–9
'One Who Has Endured It,' 119–23, 127–32, 139n43, 139–40n50, 140n52, 141nn56, 62, 63, 142n73, 172n13
'One Who Has Tried Them,' 120, 131
'One Who Has Suffered It,' 131
Opium Wars, 228
Owenson, Sydney (Lady Morgan), 176, 181, 192, 193n6, 198n46

'P' ('Petr O.'), 62, 72–7, 80, 83n24, 85n44
Paine, Thomas, 8, 179, 186, 197n39, 210
Pankhurst family, 45–6, 49n10
Parker, Andrew, 86, 109n23
Patterson, Orlando, 61, 83n20
Pavarini, Massimo, 116
Pellico, Silvio, 171n6
Pethick-Lawrence, Emmeline, 29
Philadelphia system, 7, 140n54, 161
Porter, James, 194n10
Pratt, Mary Louise, 201, 213–14
Priestley, Philip, 136n3
Prisons Act (1877), 222–6
Purvis, June, 49n9, 53n37

Raboteau, Albert J., 64
Radbruch, Gustav, 140n53
Radzinowicz, Leon, 136n4
Rajan, Tilottama, 93–4, 102–4
Reade, Charles, 154, 166, 169, 220, 231–2
'Reminiscences of Prison Life,' 142n78
Renan, Ernest, 186, 214–16, 218
Representation of the People Act, 27
Revolution, American, 16, 201–2, 211, 214–17
Revolution, French, 173, 177–8, 195n16
Riley, James, 204–9, 211, 213, 216
Rousseau, Jean-Jacques, 43–4, 82n15
Rowan, Archibald Hamilton, 176, 191, 193n6
Rowson, Susana H., 211–12
Rusche, Georg, 116
Rychkov, Petr Ivanovich, 61, 82n17

Sahlins, Marshall, 117

Said, Edward, 16, 201–3, 217, 222, 229
Samuels, Wilfred D., 87
Sandel, Michael, 43
Sayre, Gordon M., 90
Scheffler, Judith M., 196n33
Schmücker, Alois, 61
Schreiner, Olive, 46
Scougal, Francis, 131, 170
Sedgwick, Eve Kosofsky, 86, 109n23
Sellin, Thorsten, 20n13, 140n53
Shelley, Percy Bysshe, 183
Shipov, Nikolai, 62, 67–72
Simon, Bruce, 18n2
Simon, Jonathan, 115
Sloop, John M., 25–6
Smirnov, Nikolai, 60, 62, 64–8, 73–4, 80, 83n23, 84nn31, 32, 35
Smith, Adam, 64, 180–1, 185
Smith, Anthony D., 19n4
Smith, Paul, 48n1, 81n11
Smith, Sidonie, 29–30, 44–6, 55n54, 60
Snader, Joe, 214
Sollors, Werner, 139n49
Starr, G.A., 210
Stendhal, Henri Beyle, 144
Stern, Julia, 11
Sterne, Laurence, 147, 160–1, 171n5
Stirling, Edward, 166
Stokes, John, 236
Stowe, Harriet Beecher, 62
The Suffragette, 49–50n10

Teeling, Bartholomew, 177–8
Teeling, Charles Hamilton, 16, 175–92, 193n1, 194n15
Teeling, Luke, 178, 188, 194n15
Teeling, Mary, 185
Thelwall, John, 182–3
Therborn, Göran, 59
Thomas, Paul, 9
Thomas, Sue, 45–6, 52–3n31
Thoreau, Henry David, 30, 52n23
Thuente, Mary Helen, 193n5
'Ticket-of-Leave Man,' 120–2, 131
Tickner, Lisa, 27, 51–2n22
Tobin, James, 94
Trumpener, Katie, 196n31
Turk, Horst, 126, 141n60
Turner, Victor, 141–2n66
Twelve Months Imprisonment, 156
'Twenty Years' Penal Servitude,' 122
Two Acts (1795), 182
Twyford, Anthony, 224
Tyler, Royall, 204

United Irishmen, Society of, 175–9, 181–4, 188, 191–2, 194nn9, 10, 196n31
US Constitution, 5–6, 8, 203–4, 212

Vasilieva, M.E., 62–3, 77–81
von der Trenck, Friedrich, 171n7

Wall, Charles, 161–3, 165
Walvin, James, 96–7
Ward, Julia K., 89
Webb, Beatrice, 137n13
Webb, Sidney, 137n13
Weitling, Wilhelm, 171n6
Whiskey Rebellion, 201, 203
Wiener, Martin J., 33, 129, 138n29
Wilde, Oscar, 169, 235–6
Williams, Carolyn D., 96

Witt, Mary Ann Frese, 118
Wollstonecraft, Mary, 108n21, 155
Women's Freedom League, 27, 55–6n57
Women's Social and Political Union, 26–7, 31, 36, 38, 45, 48, 49–50n10, 55–6n57
Wright, Julia M., 140n52, 194n10, 237n7

Yonge, Charlotte M., 166–9

www.ingramcontent.com/pod-product-compliance
Lightning Source LLC
Chambersburg PA
CBHW020400080526
44584CB00014B/1100